swimming
pools
&spas

Consulting Editor: Don Vandervort

Staff for this Book:

Senior Editors: Jim McRae, Pierre Home-Douglas

Art Director: Odette Sévigny

Assistant Editors: Rob Lutes, Jennifer Ormston

Researcher: Adam Van Sertima

Designers: Jean-Guy Doiron, Robert Labelle

Picture Editor: Jennifer Meltzer

Production Coordinator: Dominique Gagné

Systems Director: Edward Renaud

Scanner Operators: Martin Francoeur, Sara Grynspan

Technical Support: Jean Sirois

Proofreader: Judy Yelon

Indexer: Linda Cardella Cournoyer

Book Consultants:

Alison Osinski

Ron Conner

Swimming Pools & Spas was produced in conjunction with
ST. REMY MULTIMEDIA

Cover:

Design: Vasken Guiragossian

Photography: Philip Harvey

Photo Styling: Joann Masaoka Van Atta

Vice President, Editorial Director, Sunset Books, Bob Doyle

5 6 7 8 9 10 11 12 QPD QPD 05 04 03 02 01 00

ISBN 0-376-01609-4

Library of Congress Catalog Card Number: 97-80058

Printed in the United States

For additional copies of *Swimming Pools & Spas*, or any other
Sunset book, call 1-800-526-5111, or visit our website at
www.sunsetbooks.com

swimming pools & spas

Sunset

Table of Contents

Enjoying
POOLS AND SPAS

*For anyone who has taken a refreshing dip in a
pool on a hot summer's eve, a soothing soak in a hot tub
after a tension-filled day at the office, or a cleansing bath in
the relaxing heat of a sauna, it's not hard to understand why
these facilities—once aristocratic luxuries—have become
common features in the landscape of many backyards today.
The following photo section offers different examples of the
pools and spas available to homeowners. They range
from personalized creations that reflect the taste or interest
of the owner—such as the musical note indoor-outdoor lap
pool shown above—to simple units that fall within
more modest budgetary or space constraints.*

The edge of this pool seems to vanish into the sea beyond, adding dramatic effect to an already stunning vista. A narrow basin below the edge directs water back into the system. Terra-cotta tiling covers the deck around the pool, complementing the natural, rough-hewn look of the overhead.

With landscaping features incorporated into the decking, the modern lines of this pool are softened by nature's touch. Lighting is used to accentuate focal points, and to create an inviting, safe environment for nighttime use. *Design: KJS Designs*

A naturalistic waterfall is the main visual element of this free-form pool, enhancing the view of the placid lake beyond. Lush plantings in the foreground connect the poolscape with the mature trees to the right.

In spite of its small scale, the owners of this unusually shaped pool managed to tuck a spa into one corner. The curved stockade-style fence reflects the curves of the pool and garden.
Design: Art Downing, Sherwood Stockwell

While the in-ground pool is certainly the focal point of this back-yard, the lot is large enough to accommo-date extensive decking, a fair-size pool house, and an elaborate garden. These elements make the pool area an inter-esting place for activities other than swimming.

The bold lines along the bottom of the pool at left contrast vividly with the Southwestern flavor of the wall and cabana. Lush plantings form a friendly border between the two.

Naturalistic pools don't come any closer to mimicking nature than the one shown below. Using an oasis as the theme, designers were exacting in every detail—from the tropical vegetation to the simulated sand finish of the roll-over coping to the pebbled bottom of the pool.

A deck with built-in seating offers a place to relax or entertain beside this above-ground pool; mounting a couple of steps brings bathers to water level. White stones and hardy plantings are strategically placed in the splash area.

Giant ferns and lush foliage turn this poolside spa into a private escape for a relaxing hot soak. The slabs that enclose the spa repeat the flagstone pavement laid around the pool.
Design: Jack Buktenica

Rich foliage borders, and in some cases overhangs, frame this pool, creating a watery hideaway. The serpentine lines along the bottom of the pool lead bathers to a separate water garden at the far end. A watchtower-cum-cabana looks down over the lush scene.

Extending your home to enclose a pool will ensure
year-round swimming enjoyment. The "pool room"
above features a vaulted ceiling with surrounding panel
windows that help to maximize natural light.
In the photo opposite (bottom), the floor-to-ceiling-
length windows are designed to take advantage of a
view to an outside garden. The pool was built first and
enclosed later, when the owners' budget permitted it.
Design: Tom Kessler

A sauna is the perfect complement to a pool or spa. Though spacious in feel, this cedar sauna is small enough to make an electric heater practical. Bench heights and widths were calculated to make a maximum number of people comfortable. For more on saunas, see page 170. *Design: John Kolkka, Finnish American Sauna*

Matching the wood of the hot tub to the siding of the home helps tie this backyard together visually. The wood deck and loungers—ideal for relaxing—continue the motif.
Design: Van Hattum-Simmons

Ideal for lots where space is at a premium, the prefab spa shown at left offers soakers all the pleasures of a spa on a small, but no less enjoyable, scale.

For a varied effect, the landscaping around the spacious kidney-shaped spa at right changes from plantings and stones to wood decking and masonry tiles.

Planning
FOR YOUR
POOL OR SPA

*Careful planning is an essential first step to any building
project, and pools and spas are no exception. Before
a shovel touches the soil, a site must be carefully chosen,
and budgetary and legal restrictions taken into account.
The following chapter will guide you through all the other
important decisions that need to be tackled before your pool
or spa becomes a reality. As you begin to plan the addition of
either of these water features to your own home or backyard,
keep in mind that they are permanent structures and will be
prominent features in or around your home for a long time
to come. This fact alone should encourage you to spend the
time and energy necessary to create a facility that will
still give you pleasure years after completion.*

A Private Pool or Spa for You

Swimming pools and spas are hardly a recent invention. The remains of 5000-year-old pools are still visible in India and Egypt today. Yet never before have so many people enjoyed the benefits and pleasures of these facilities in their own homes and backyards. Today, the United States lays claim to more than 8 million pools and spas. That's not surprising, when you consider the various benefits of owning these facilities. Pools and spas provide the entire family with a great place to relax, exercise, escape the heat, and spend time with friends and family.

WHICH POOL FOR YOU?

As you plan your pool or spa, one of the first things you need to consider is how you will use it. You may want a spot where you can relax and entertain guests. Or you may see a pool as a healthful exercise or therapy center. Each use has certain requirements, and defining the uses now will help you choose the best location for your pool and decide on the style of pool that best meets your needs.

A pool used for relaxation and entertainment should have a large shallow area to splash around in, space around the pool for sunning, and adequate room to set up tables and chairs nearby. If you intend to swim for exercise, your best choice will be a rectangular pool—the longer the better, and deep enough at both ends to negotiate turns safely. See page 40 for a discussion of pool styles, and page 52 for a more detailed discussion of choosing the right spa design for you.

FINANCIAL CONSIDERATIONS

In addition to deciding how you will use your pool, you need to consider the financial aspects of owning a pool or spa: the effect of a pool or spa on your property value, the expenses of maintaining your pool or spa, and the legal responsibilities you'll incur as your new facility attracts friends and kids from the neighborhood.

Property value: When you add a swimming pool or spa to your property, the value of the property usually increases, though not necessarily dollar for dollar. The design of your pool can also affect the ease

Set apart from the home, this pebble-surfaced, gunite pool with flagstone coping and a cascading waterfall evokes images of a clear mountain lake.

This colorful prefabricated acrylic spa converts the corner of a backyard deck into a secluded place of respite for family and friends. The spa is set into the deck but supported from below.

with which you can sell your home. If the pool is attractive and not highly specialized, it will be considered an asset, although perhaps not by families who have small children or who don't want the upkeep of a pool.

Property taxes: Though construction is usually the major cost of a pool or spa, there are other ownership expenses. Because these features generally increase the value of your property, the assessed valuation may go up, resulting in an increase in your property taxes. Assessors don't treat all pools in the same way. In-ground pools are permanent structures and are taxed on the same basis as your home. Above-ground pools are usually taxed as permanent structures, especially if they are framed by decking, although some communities look on them as temporary and not subject to taxes. In areas where a pool can be used only for part of the year, the taxes may be reduced proportionally.

Insurance: The need for insurance protection begins when the first employee of the pool builder sets foot on your property. Though the contractor and his subcontractors should carry liability and property damage insurance, you'll want to check with your insurance agent before work begins to be sure you have adequate protection.

Owning a swimming pool can actually lower your fire insurance cost. If you live in an area where fire hazard is high, or where there is no municipal water supply, your pool will be a valuable source of water for fighting a fire.

Utility costs: You will require water to fill your pool, fuel to heat it, and electricity to operate the filtration system. You'll have to pay for water to fill your pool, unless your community allows pool owners a free fill. Expect a higher water bill for the month when you fill the pool.

Gas, oil, or electricity to heat your pool will be the biggest utility expense. Rates can vary widely, depending on the type of fuel as well as the size, use, and water temperature of your pool. For suggestions on minimizing heating costs, see pages 24-27. The pump in the filtration system requires electricity, but the expense of running the pump will be significantly less than your heating cost. The pool's size and water temperature, the area's climate and electric rates, and the length of time the filtration system needs to be operated will determine the cost. To obtain a rough estimate of your total utility costs, check with your local utility companies, pool builders, and other pool owners in your neighborhood.

Pool maintenance: Routine pool maintenance will include keeping the water chemically balanced and sanitary, maintaining the support equipment, and cleaning the pool surfaces. You can contract a pool service company to perform these chores, or you can do some or all of them yourself.

If you elect to do your own maintenance, your major expense will be for sanitizers and oxidizers to keep the water clean. Their cost will depend on the pool size, the water temperature, the amount of time the pool is used, the number of people using it, and whether or not the pool is covered. Again, pool service companies, aquatic consultants, pool builders, and pool-owning neighbors can help you calculate your maintenance costs. For more information see pages 140-155.

Owner responsibilities: The regulations and laws relating to an owner's responsibilities and liabilities vary from state to state and from community to community. Your best assurance of safe operation is to comply with your community's zoning laws and health, safety, and building codes.

For added protection, surround your pool area with a childproof fence and a pool alarm, or a multiple barrier system. You also should have a phone by the pool at all times. Make sure that young children using your pool are supervised by an adult who has proper lifesaving skills. If you have a pool safety cover, keep it in place when the pool is not in use, and remove it completely whenever anyone is in the pool. Keeping water clear and in proper chemical balance and the pool in good repair will also help to ensure the safety of swimmers.

Connected to a comely wooden deck, an above-ground pool with a vinyl liner takes on a look of permanence. The pool provides plenty of room for recreational activities, while the adjacent deck offers ample space for entertaining.

Choosing a Pool or Spa Site

As well as giving pleasure to its users, a pool or a spa also represents a dramatic physical feature in any backyard. So it makes sense to choose its location with the same type of care you would give to any other important project involving your home.

There are various professionals who can help you decide where to situate your pool or spa. These include architects, landscape architects and designers, soils and structural engineers, aquatic consultants, and pool and landscape contractors. But even if you decide to seek their help, you should do a little homework beforehand—studying the microclimates of your property, familiarizing yourself with building codes and other regulations, sizing up the landscape, and evaluating possible sites, par-

ticularly if your property has some unusual features.

Building a swimming pool or spa—like any other addition or alteration to your property—entails a myriad of legal requirements set forth in deed restrictions, zoning laws, and building, health, electrical, fire, and safety codes. Take the time to look into all of these before you commit yourself to doing the job. When you design landscaping for your installation *(page 104)*, remember that additions such as fences, decks, and gazebos must also conform to these same requirements.

Building codes: Aimed at protecting you from faulty construction methods, these codes set minimum standards for design, construction, and materials used in building. Some communities have specific

codes for pools and spas; others apply the requirements of the regular building code.

Though most local codes are patterned after one of the national codes, communities can modify or add to these standards to satisfy local needs. For example, some communities do not allow vinyl-lined pools, while others ban one-piece fiberglass pools. Check with your building department early in the planning stage—your pool options may be fewer than were first apparent.

Health and safety codes: Your community may have specific laws covering such facets of pool ownership as water quality, lifesaving equipment, and protective fences and gates. Some communities incorporate provisions for pool construction into their health and safety

Connected to the home by a striking wooden pathway, this naturalistic pool provides a stunning setting for swimming and relaxing. Three styles of decking materials lend a fanciful element to the site.

codes, rather than in their building code; you need to consult both your local health and building departments to determine pool requirements and the jurisdiction each department has in pool construction and operation.

Additional regulations: Drought, an energy shortage, a pool accident, or some other crisis often prompts additional government control. Among the different regulations proposed by local and state government agencies are:

• restricting the use of water for filling pools
• banning the use of natural gas for heating pools or spas
• mandating solar heating for all new pools
• requiring that an alarm be

Deed Restrictions and Zoning Laws

Deed restrictions: Somewhere in the deed to your property you may find restrictions that could affect the design and location of your pool, spa, and accompanying structures. These restrictions may bind you to rules set by a homeowners' association or provide for a utility easement or right-of-way under, over, or through your property. Though the rules of a homeowners' association can be changed by a vote of the members, deed restrictions can be altered only by mutual agreement among all parties bound by the restrictions or by court action.

Zoning laws: These city or county laws govern land use—yours included. They can determine where you can place your pool or spa, how close to the property lines you can build, and how large you can make any structures. They may also contain ordinances governing the amount of lighting and noise you can create.

Zoning laws usually have provisions for the granting of variances. If you can show that meeting the precise requirements of the laws would create an "undue hardship," and that you would not be encroaching on the privacy of your neighbors, a hearing officer or zoning board of appeals can grant you a variance. Application must be made through your local building or planning department.

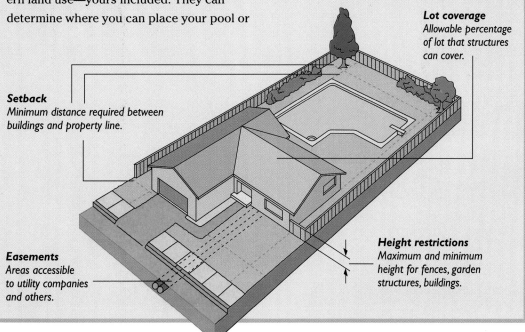

Lot coverage
Allowable percentage of lot that structures can cover.

Setback
Minimum distance required between buildings and property line.

Height restrictions
Maximum and minimum height for fences, garden structures, buildings.

Easements
Areas accessible to utility companies and others.

installed on all new pools or spas
• requiring window alarms or automatic closers on new structures
• banning a specific type of swimming pool or spa
• requiring that covers be sold with new pools or spas
• requiring fencing and self-closing gates around pools or spas.
Utility companies and building and planning departments can tell you about any restrictions currently applicable in your community.

CLIMATE AND WEATHER

Weather records can determine the average length of the swimming season in your area, but it's the day-to-day weather on your property that determines your poolside comfort.

Since the warmth or coolness of any outdoor pool or spa will be decided largely by its orientation, it is a good idea to study the microclimates of your property along with the regional climate and weather patterns. Any buildings, trees, or other obstructions on— or even near—your property can have quite an effect on the amount

Trees, shrubs, and plants that can withstand splashing or serve as windbreaks are ideal for the poolside.
Design: Richard Murray
Pool: Peri-Bilt Pools

TRACKING THE SUN

Observing and recording the daily and seasonal patterns of sunlight and shade created on your property will help you place your pool to make maximum use of the available sunlight during swimming hours. Expect longer shadows (particularly in winter) from the house, fences, and trees on the north side of the house.

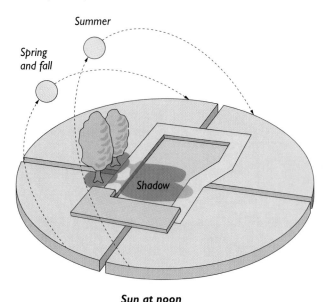

Sun at noon

Sun at 4 p.m.

Shadows
Changing shadows during the day and in different seasons affect the amount of sunlight that will reach the pool area.

of sunlight and wind the property around your pool site receives.

A pool or spa in almost any outdoor location will serve well in midsummer, but wise planning can extend the season by several weeks, or even months. In many locations, if a proper design is adopted, there is no reason to close for winter at all.

If you've lived in your present area for a number of years, you should have a feeling for the general climate in terms of average seasonal air temperatures, rain and/or snowfall patterns, prevailing wind directions, and number of sunny days. If not, you can get climate information from the National Oceanic and Atmospheric Admini-

stration (NOAA), National Climatic Center, Asheville, NC 28801. Request the current annual issue of the Local Climatological Data for your area.

You also may be able to get accurate climate and weather information through U.S. Weather Bureau offices, public power and utility companies, meteorology departments on college and university campuses, and agricultural extension offices.

No matter how much official information you gather, take stock of the local weather as well as you can. Your neighborhood almost certainly will vary somewhat from the recording stations. And by all means talk with the "old-timers" in your neighborhood. They can

extend your knowledge of the local climate by many years.

Sun and shade: Theoretically a pool or spa with a southern exposure (in the Northern Hemisphere) will be warmer than one that faces north. One that is west-facing will be warmer than one with an eastern exposure. And a pool facing south will be warmer than one facing west.

There are exceptions to this rule, though. In desert areas, where noontime temperatures can be extremely high for several months during the year, a north-facing pool can hardly be considered cold. In some coastal areas, on the other hand, a south- or west-facing pool can be cold

A spa set in a deck provides a soothing spot to relax while offering a stunning view of the hillside.
Design: Jerry Smania

because of ocean winds and chilly fogs in summer.

If you're installing a lap pool, orient it on a north-south plane to reduce eye strain from the sun.

Consider the wind: Wind is almost as important a factor in selecting an outdoor pool or spa site as the sun. Too much wind blowing across the area on a temperate day can be unpleasant, as can no breeze at all on a hot summer day. Wind also draws heat from the pool or spa and causes water and chemicals to evaporate, adding to your energy bill and overall operating expenses.

Place the pool where it uses the winds to the best advantage, then control the wind, if necessary, with fences, screens, trees, or plants. A grove of trees clustered around a pool, for example, can divert and disperse the wind, making any additional screening unnecessary. For a spa, there are various options with barriers such as a solid fence and baffles *(opposite)*.

Three wind systems—prevailing, diurnal (daily), and irregular, high-velocity winds—can have an effect on your poolside comfort.

Prevailing winds: In some parts of the world, like the trade wind belt between the equator and 30° latitudes, the prevailing wind blows constantly for weeks or even months without letup. In the United States, prevailing winds are felt only in Hawaii, the Mojave Desert, in the high mountains of the West, and in parts of the Great Plains states. **Diurnal or daily wind:** Fortunately, these winds—important factors to consider in choosing a pool site—are predictable. Some of them are most prevalent during the swimming season.

In coastal areas and on the shores of large lakes, the still air of morning gradually gives way to increasingly strong breezes from the water during the afternoon. These onshore winds die down when the sun sets. By early evening, the air flow has reversed. In some areas, these afternoon sea breezes, approaching gale force, swoop down over the coastal mountains and make most pool activity impossible unless adequate windscreens have been installed.

Inland mountain areas also experience reversible daily winds. Generally, the air flow is upslope during the day and downslope after sunset. Near the entrances to canyons and valleys, the evening breezes can be quite strong and cool.

Irregular, high-velocity winds: Meteorologists call these winds "foehns" (pronounced "ferns"), but residents know them under various local names—chinooks, bores, Santa Anas, or Boulder winds. They flow downslope or out of mountain basins. Though these winds are usually hot and dry, in some areas they feel cool relative to the local air; in the Pacific Northwest, the foehn can be moist.

PROTECTING A SPA FROM THE WIND

To pinpoint wind currents in your yard, try posting small flags where you want wind protection and observe their movements. The illustrations below demonstrate the effects different barriers have on the wind.

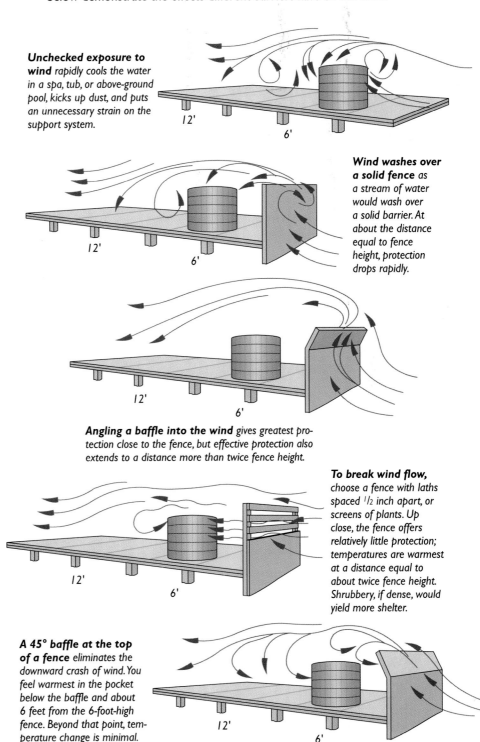

Unchecked exposure to wind rapidly cools the water in a spa, tub, or above-ground pool, kicks up dust, and puts an unnecessary strain on the support system.

Wind washes over a solid fence as a stream of water would wash over a solid barrier. At about the distance equal to fence height, protection drops rapidly.

Angling a baffle into the wind gives greatest protection close to the fence, but effective protection also extends to a distance more than twice fence height.

To break wind flow, choose a fence with laths spaced 1/2 inch apart, or screens of plants. Up close, the fence offers relatively little protection; temperatures are warmest at a distance equal to about twice fence height. Shrubbery, if dense, would yield more shelter.

A 45° baffle at the top of a fence eliminates the downward crash of wind. You feel warmest in the pocket below the baffle and about 6 feet from the 6-foot-high fence. Beyond that point, temperature change is minimal.

Sizing up the Landscape

Before you make any decisions about the location of your pool, take a close look at how it will fit within the overall makeup of your property. A plot plan allows you to do this with ease. You will also need to consider such issues as access to the site by the contractor, landscaping elements, such as trees, your view of and from the pool, the slope of the site, the character of the soil, and any drainage problems.

MAKING A PLOT PLAN

You will find it easier to evaluate the placement of various sizes and shapes of pools in your home-garden environment if you work with a plan showing all the features of your property. Later on, you can use the plan to draw in decks and other structures, as well as landscaping and lighting. Several companies offer excellent, reasonably priced computer software for this purpose. Otherwise, you can make a scale drawing on graph paper with provision for overlay sheets of tracing paper. The tracing paper allows you to sketch various pool ideas without redrawing the base each time.

Surveyor's drawings usually locate your property and show streets, property corners, and distances between corners, plus the locations of any structures on the site when the lot was surveyed. Available through your county recorder or title company, these plans make an excellent starting point for your base map; simply transfer information from the plot plan to your graph paper.

You'll save hours of complicated measuring if you can obtain copies of a surveyor's plot plan, architect's drawings or house plans, and contour maps that illustrate vital statistics of the lot and buildings.

Architect's drawings usually show site plan, floor plan, elevations, and foundation details.

Contour maps show the slope of the land with a series of lines, each separated from the next by a fixed difference in elevation—very helpful if you are building a pool on a hill-

A large, naturalistic pool and spa take full advantage of this wide open backyard. Ample space between the house and pool lends the feeling of pastoral calm and relaxation.

side lot. Ask for contour maps in the city or county engineer's office or in the department of public works.

ACCESS FOR THE CONTRACTOR

Before excavation can begin, you must provide adequate access for heavy equipment. The minimum width for access to the pool site is about 8 feet, though 10 feet is preferable. Sometimes, small equipment can enter through a space only 5 feet wide, but because excavation will take longer, the cost will be higher. If equipment cannot be brought in, the pool must be hand dug at a prohibitive cost. (This technique is still often used in southern California to excavate hillside lots with existing homes and landscaping.) Alternatively, you may be able to bring in the equipment over a neighbor's property, but you, not the pool builder, must make the arrangements. You may have to remove fences and gates. If heavy equipment will cross a sidewalk, patio, or lawn, take measures to prevent damage. Again, this will be your responsibility.

Though you don't want to build your pool over a gas or water main or under a power line, your pool site should have ready access to necessary utilities. Some pool contracts require additional payment for unusually long runs to utility lines. Check that these costs have been included in the builder's bid.

TREES AMD SHRUBS

Generally, it's preferable not to build a pool or spa too close to trees and large shrubs. Leaves, blossoms, and

> ### YOUR PLOT PLAN
> Your plot plan for a pool or spa should show the following:
> • Dimensions of your lot
> • Location of your house on the lot, as well as any doors and windows and the rooms from which they open
> • Location of decks, patios, walks, fences, walls, and other structures
> • Points of the compass—north, east, south, and west
> • Location of easements or any other rights-of-way contained in your deed
> • Utilities (water, gas, and sewers) and underground wires that could affect your spa or tub location. (Units should never be located beneath utility wires.)
> • Sun and wind patterns
> • Potential problems beyond the lot lines that might affect sun, view, or privacy—tall trees or a neighbor's second-story windows—for example, front, side, and backyard setback boundaries
> • Contours of your lot (if you don't have a contour map, mark high and low spots, direction of slopes and natural drainage patterns)
> • Natural features, such as rock outcrops, soil types, or wet spots

SAMPLE PLOT PLAN
The plot plan below indicates three possible locations for an outdoor pool and the considerations that affect their choice.

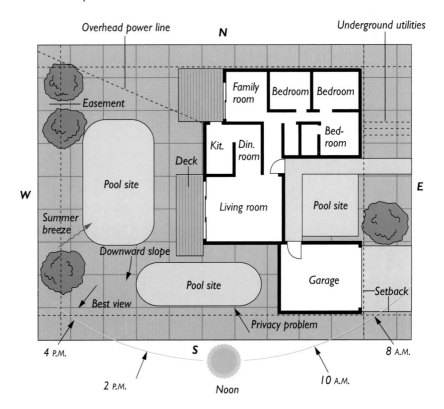

fruit dropping near and in the water will add to your cleaning chores. And a tall tree or shrub may provide unwanted shade.

In any case, these features will form an important part of the larger backyard landscape. For trees or shrubs that you want to keep, try to locate your pool so that the prevailing winds blow the debris away from the pool. In addition, plot the shadows thrown by the trees; then determine whether or not you would welcome that shade in and around your pool during the swimming season. See pages 120 through 125 for more information about planting around the pool.

See pages 120 through 125

ASSESSING THE VIEW

Pleasing aesthetics, privacy, and safety are concerns when you choose a pool or spa location. When seen from inside your home, the new

PLACING A POOL ON A STANDARD LOT

Because of the similarity in both the style of the houses and the shape of the lots in suburban housing developments, there is a tendency for the landscaping to conform to a neighborhood norm.

To show that it is possible to be original and creative even on the small, rectangular suburban lot, we have created four pool and landscape schemes. Though the lot and house are the same, each pool and garden is unique.

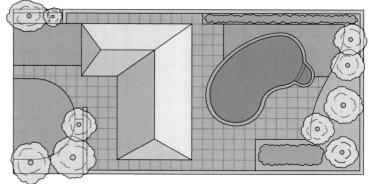

Kidney-shaped pool
Backed by a grove of trees, a kidney-shaped swimming pool conveys the feeling of graceful informality.

Angular pool
Complemented by other geometric shapes, an angular pool produces a strikingly contemporary environment in a conventional backyard.

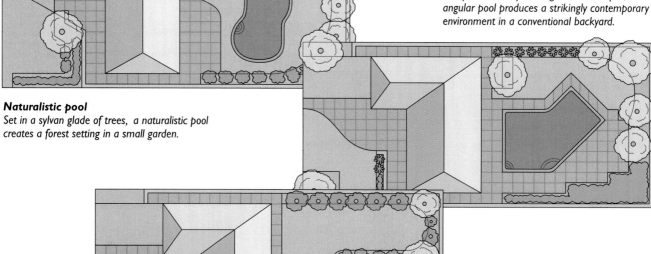

Naturalistic pool
Set in a sylvan glade of trees, a naturalistic pool creates a forest setting in a small garden.

Rectangular pool
Separated from a spacious, sheltered lawn, a rectangular pool forms one of two backyard recreation areas.

installation should be an attractive part of the landscape. On the other hand, the view from a neighbor's upstairs window may infringe on your privacy. And if there's a beautiful view from your property, try to position the pool so you will be able to take full advantage of the view from poolside.

If children will use your pool or spa, you need either a clear view of their activities from the house or, as in the case of small children, you will have to be at poolside when they're swimming. Mark the fields of view on an overlay of your plot plan. If you've already decided on a poten-tial site, use an enlarged plan of the proposed pool area to mark the fields; you will want a large plan when it comes time to mapping out your landscaping.

SLOPE, SOIL, AND DRAINAGE

Ideally, you want a pool site that's level and slightly higher than the land around it. (The same applies for in-ground spas. If you install an in-ground spa, consider the following information during planning.) The underlying soil should be stable and easy to dig. Also, you'll need a dry site, with good surface and subsur-face drainage. Good drainage conditions will depend on the slope of the land and the nature of the soil.

By analyzing a contour map of your lot, you can determine where the land slopes and how steep the slopes are. You should also be able to locate any high spots, depressions, flat areas, or drainage paths. If you don't have a contour map, wander around your property and take note of any of these features; then mark them on your plot plan.

Even if your property has no ideal level area, remember that hillsides can become sites for magnificent swimming pools and spas (page 34). ➤

LOCATING A SPA ON A STANDARD LOT

The plot plan for a spa will look much like one for a pool.
Follow the steps shown below to plan a few alternative layouts.

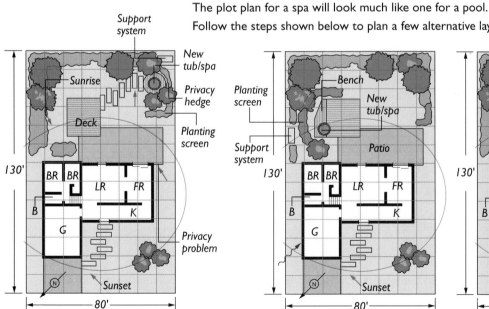

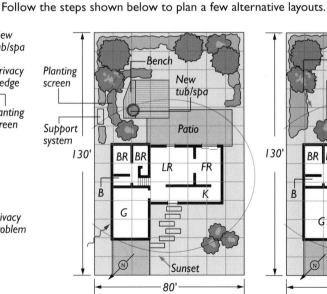

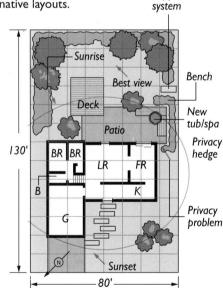

A sample plan
Located in a seldom-used corner of the lot, the spa becomes an eye-catching focal point. Screened with trees and a hedge, it is protect-ed from wind, afternoon sun, and neighbors' line of vision.

An alternate plan
This spa is connected to an existing low-level deck. Here, in an intermediate zone of the yard, the tub is near enough the house to be easily accessible, while far enough away to remain a significant visual element in the garden. With a wood lid and benches, the spa unit doubles as an outdoor entertaining area.

Second alternative
A spa located near the house shown above has the advantage of a sunny southern expo-sure, less costly installation (shorter plumbing and wiring distances), and easy access during wintry days when the tub or spa is most likely to be used. Closeness to household noise, how-ever, can make it seem less like a private retreat and reduce the spa's relaxing benefits.

Because soil conditions affect the ease of excavation and also have the potential for damaging or even destroying a concrete pool or spa shell, you must determine the type of soil underlying your property.

Once you've zeroed in on a possible site, you can have the precise nature of your soil identified by having a core sample analyzed. Gravel, sand, silt, and clay require special design features in the pool or spa. Though the pool or spa contractor may have had experience with these conditions, you may want to consult a soils engineer *(page 37)*.

Loam: Commonly called "garden soil," loam is ideal for a pool or spa site in many parts of the country since it's easy to dig. The walls of the excavation will be stable and not likely to collapse. In other areas, though, it may settle or compact causing damage to the shell.

Sandy soil: The bane of pool builders, sandy soil usually caves in during excavation. Because the walls must be shored up with wood or sprayed

LOTS WITH UNUSUAL SHAPES

An unusually shaped lot might at first look like a liability, but it can often be just the opposite. A little imagination used in designing and placing a pool can transform an awkwardly shaped lot into a very functional and appealing environment.

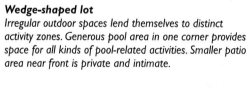

Wedge-shaped lot
Irregular outdoor spaces lend themselves to distinct activity zones. Generous pool area in one corner provides space for all kinds of pool-related activities. Smaller patio area near front is private and intimate.

Long, narrow lot
The barber-pole look of a long, narrow lot is relieved by dividing space into two distinct, offset areas. Here, the eye is carried on an arc across the large patio area into the woodsy and secluded glade with its naturalistic pool.

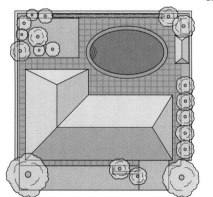

A square lot
The severe angularity is softened with an elliptical pool, forming an elegant focal point in the backyard. From the house, one may look left toward an intimate garden (accessible from main patio or master bedroom) or right across the pool to a cabana.

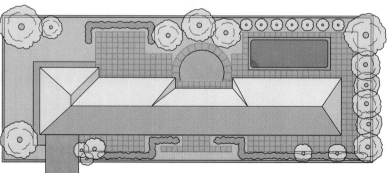

Shallow lot
An extremely shallow lot is deepened by the creation of a number of focal points across the width of the garden: a central rounded patio ringed with trees, a rectangular pool and spa on one side, and an entertainment terrace on the other.

with concrete to prevent collapse, the construction cost is increased. Sometimes, a concrete pool in sandy soil must be built with a thicker shell, or closer spacing of steel reinforcing bars, or supported on pilings.

Wet soil: Whether waterlogged from surface runoff or in an area with a high water table, wet soil is best avoided, if at all possible. Excavating for a pool in wet soil is very expensive. And the pressure of the underground water can collapse an empty pool built in such soil, or float the pool out of the ground. This is also a risk with pools built near bodies of water where tidal variation can damage or even carry away an improperly anchored pool.

Expansive soil: Known also as clay, it becomes a problem only when a significant amount of water percolates into the ground. The pressure exerted on the sides of even a filled pool can cause it to collapse.

Some communities ban pools that cannot be reinforced to withstand the pressure of wet expansive soil. A concrete pool in expansive soil may have to be built with a thicker shell; it may also require expansion joints inside the pool between the shell and coping (the lip around the edge of the pool), the coping and deck, and within the deck. A trench dug around the pool and filled with loose material can help absorb the soil expansion. Surface drainage must be directed away from the pool area and any drainage lines must be made leakproof.

Corrosive soil: Despite the advent of plastic plumbing pipe, corrosive soil can still present a problem when constructing a swimming pool. Though metal pools and the metal wall panels used with some vinyl-lined pools are treated against corrosion, special precautions may be required in highly corrosive soil. Your pool contractor or soils engineer should be aware of any problems in your area.

Other considerations: Rock beneath the soil requires drilling and blasting and may add substantially to the cost of construction.

Filled ground is unsuitable as a pool site unless the soil was compacted properly (this is difficult to assess) or unless the bottom of the pool will be deeper than the disturbed soil.

The weight of a filled pool built on improperly compacted fill compresses the soil and allows the pool to settle into the ground. If it settles evenly, the shell can pull away from the deck or, in the case of a concrete pool, from the bond beam. Uneven settling can crack the shell of a concrete pool. An expensive solution is to support the pool shell on piers or pilings that sit on solid ground.

Even though you may not see evidence of fill, dig some test holes on your potential sites. If you find layers of different kinds of soil or any man-made debris, you can be sure that the area was filled.

Dealing with drainage: Usually, any natural drainage on the surface of your property or a neighbor's property can be diverted away from a pool or spa site. Surface drainage need not be a problem if you avoid building your pool or spa in a low-lying area from which water cannot drain. During storms, muddy water collecting there can spill over into the unit.

Water running off a slope or down a drainage path can fill your pool or spa with debris. If you can't find a site free from runoff, you can landscape the area to divert the water.

Disposing of underground water and pool or spa water is another story entirely. Subsurface drainage problems—water accumulating just under the surface of your site, or a spring running under the property—is not an issue for spas, but may make the excavation for a pool more expensive; a drainage system may have to be installed under the pool to carry away the water.

Sometimes, a soggy low spot or especially lush vegetation will alert you to an area of poor underground drainage on your property. Most of the time, though, the condition is hidden until you dig a test hole or start excavating your pool.

Ask your pool-owning neighbors if they had any subsurface drainage problems; you can also consult local soils engineers, pool contractors, and building inspectors.

Water drainage involves disposing of the pool or spa water if you have to drain it, and disposing of the water from the filter when it is serviced. Dumping 30,000 gallons of chlorinated pool water in your garden would kill all your plants—not to mention the damage it would inflict on neighbors' yards. For information on correct drainage and disposal of pool water, contact the state or regional office of the U.S. Environmental Protection Agency.

SOLVING GRADE PROBLEMS

Whether you plan to install a spa or a pool, designing and building on a sloping site requires the services of experts. The steeper the hillside, the more important these experts are. The angle of the slope, the nature and stability of the soil, the design of the pool shell, and the method of anchoring the shell to the slope all must be considered.

Despite the problems, a hillside can allow a designer to create impressive designs. The pool can appear to soar into space or be nestled in a grove of trees. Few hillsides are too steep for a pool builder—pools have even been suspended from the edges of cliffs.

Support and drainage: A hillside pool needs to withstand earth pressure on one side and have well-engineered support on the other. Downslope supports for the pool should be built on a solid foundation, preferably rock. Retaining walls on the upslope side, sometimes incorporating the pool structure itself, must be sufficient to contain a possible earth or loose-rock slide and resist earthquakes.

Surface water must be routed around the pool to a lower slope, and decks must be designed to prevent water from seeping into the ground near the pool.

Special considerations: Hillside sites also pose special construction problems for spas. For a portable spa, a level cut has to be made in the hillside and a retaining wall built to hold it up. Any retaining wall over a few feet high should be engineered by a professional. A slab made of reinforced concrete is then poured to support the spa.

An in-ground spa on a hillside also requires a retaining wall, but one on the downhill side. The wall supports the spa shell and helps to contain the sand base on which the shell rests.

Depending on the lot, you may be limited in the choice of size, shape, and type of construction you choose for your pool or spa. Take the time to seek out companies and contractors with a reputation for tackling tough problems.

Pool or spa access and adequate decking can be a challenge. It's a good idea to plan the area completely on paper, including all steps, decking, and structures. If the site is too confined, any installation may be impractical.

Finally, consider the costs involved. The additional expense of building a pool or spa on a steep hillside can occasionally equal and even exceed the cost of the unit itself. But if your lot is not excessively steep, expect only a moderate increase in cost.

Hillsides can make for stunning pool sites. Here, the rolling countryside can be enjoyed from the poolside or from the water.

Indoor Spas

Some spa and tub enthusiasts prefer an indoor setting, for several reasons. There's the obvious advantage of having the spa or tub sheltered and accessible day and night, year-round. (In harsh climates, it's often necessary to have an indoor site that provides complete shelter of the support system plumbing.) And where privacy is essential but impossible to achieve in the garden, the house will provide it.

Where the safety of children—especially neighborhood children—is difficult to assure at an outdoor site, lockable doors solve all manner of legal and personal worries.

Compelling as one or more of these reasons may be, they do not make it any less difficult to locate a spa or tub inside. Integrating a spa or tub into the layout of a home takes a good deal of thought. As one side effect, these facilities are marvelously efficient manufacturers of humidity—a plus if you live in a dry climate, an uncomfortable handicap if your air is characteristically heavy with humidity. To accommodate this, your home's HVAC system (heating, ventilation, air conditioning) should be modified. **Choosing an indoor location:** As anyone who has had to fit a new bed into a well-ordered house

knows, an object 5 feet across cannot be slipped into a place unnoticed. When it is for such a singular purpose as a spa or tub is, the task of fitting it in place becomes doubly difficult.

Your first consideration should be traffic patterns. To be an oasis of calm, the spa will have to be away from the comings and goings of people in a hurry. This means putting it in a room that does not carry through traffic or serve several other purposes.

Try to locate your spa near a dressing area; trails of water across the house can be a nuisance to clean up. Consider locating it with-

A ROOM FOR AN INDOOR SPA

Under normal use spas create enormous vapor clouds; if yours is indoors you need to build a room around it that can manage a marine climate. In addition to wood, ceramic tile is often used as an indoor spa flooring material.

- Slanted ceiling to reduce glare from skylight
- Adjustable skylight lets hot air escape
- Sliding glass doors help regulate air circulation
- Opening windows improve ventilation
- Thermal blanket prevents steaming, reduces heat loss from water
- Fresh air vent
- Concrete floor and foundation (sloped toward drain)
- Exhaust vent
- Rust-resistant fixtures
- Treated wood paneling insulates and absorbs moisture
- Moisture-loving plants
- Support system (properly vented)
- Wood decking insulates and absorbs moisture, allows drainage
- Drain (from tub to main sewage line)

in reasonable reach of the outdoors. Even a nook-size deck or patio nearby can provide a pleasant place to relax.

Construction concerns: Once the problems of location are solved, the special requirements of construction must be faced. Weight and humidity are the two most complex and vital concerns.

Standard floors are designed and built to support 40 pounds per square foot. A small spa filled with water and two adult bathers can easily apply 250 pounds to the same square foot. For this reason, it's crit-

ically important to provide an adequate foundation. To support a spa safely, an existing wood frame floor usually requires re-engineering; often, even a concrete slab in the basement must be replaced with a thicker, reinforced slab.

The requirements your building code sets for an indoor spa's foundation, plumbing, and wiring—coupled with the need for efficient ventilation—explain why the best time to think about an indoor spa is prior to new home construction or room addition. Major remodeling within an existing building is

unquestionably the most problematical route to a hot soak.

In addition to the need for an adequate substructure, flooring should slope toward a drain and be constructed of such materials as ceramic tile, concrete, rubber, reinforced PVC, or masonry—materials that aren't affected by large doses of water.

Walls and ceilings must have insulation with a vapor barrier to resist moisture. (This applies to interior as well as exterior walls.) The rest of the house also needs protection from the increased humidity levels.

Controlling condensation: Efficient ventilation and a dehumidifier are your best means of controlling the condensation that can collect on walls, windows, and ceiling, even when the spa is not in use. Covering the spa with a thermal blanket or a solid spa cover will also minimize condensation.

To have the maximum control over your indoor climate, it may be necessary to back up the natural cross ventilation with a forced air system or a closed-loop energy recovery system.

In addition to ventilation, plan on double-glazed windows and skylights that improve insulation and inhibit condensation. Walls paneled with unfinished wood and moisture-loving plants are useful because they absorb excess moisture.

A Japanese motif characterizes this hot water retreat, formerly an awkward small space. Flanked by bedrooms and hallways, it's centrally located, yet very private. Simulated-marble acrylic spa is set in sand; support equipment is housed outside. Because the patio of the spa room is open to the outside, heat and humidity aren't a problem.
Design: Keith Wallach

Finding and Contracting a Professional

There are a variety of professionals who can help you plan your pool.

POOL PROFESSIONALS

Architects and landscape architects: Many homeowners retain an architect or landscape architect for projects involving a pool and the surrounding environment. These professionals are state licensed and trained to create designs that are structurally sound, functional, and aesthetically pleasing. In addition, they are familiar with construction methods and materials, understand the mechanics of estimating, and they can negotiate with and supervise the contractor, ensuring that your work is done in compliance with specifications.

Landscape designers: Landscape designers usually have the education and training of landscape architects but are not state licensed. Some landscape designers are licensed contractors, however, and can both design the landscaping for your pool and actually build it.

Soils and structural engineers: If you are planning a pool on an unstable or steep lot, in an earthquake zone, or where drainage, groundwater, fill, or clay may pose problems, your building department may require that you consult with soils and structural engineers and obtain engineering reports.

Soils engineers evaluate soil conditions on a proposed site and establish design specifications for foundations that can resist whatever stresses unstable soil exerts.

Structural engineers, often working with the site evaluation and calculations provided by a soils engineer, design pools and foundations for other structures. They may recommend soil modifications.

Pool and landscape contractors: Pool contractors specialize in pool construction, while landscape contractors are involved in garden construction. Both are state licensed. Some also have design skills and experience; their fees for designing usually are included in the price bid for performing the work.

Pool and landscape contractors are responsible for hiring workers or subcontractors, ordering materials, scheduling work, obtaining permits, scheduling inspections, and seeing that the job is completed according to the contract.

CHOOSING A PROFESSIONAL

The best way to choose a professional is to collect recommendations from pool owners and inspect the person's work. Though some excellent professionals have no professional affiliation, many belong to the American Society of Landscape Architects (ASLA), the American Institute of Architects (AIA), the International Association of Aquatic Consultants (IAAC), the National Spa and Pool Institute (NSPI), or other organizations. To locate members in your area, contact a nearby office.

It's important to check out all prospective builders. These are the principal ways to evaluate them:
• Visit their showrooms and offices.
• If you're working with a landscape architect, ask for the names of several pool builders.

• Ask the companies you're considering for names and phone numbers of their customers. Ten or so should give you a good sampling.
• Check for a company's membership in a trade association.
• Call the Better Business Bureau. The quality of the information you receive varies; it can range from an evaluation of the builder's reputation to only an acknowledgment that the company is a member.
• Some building departments sell lists of pool permits issued for the year with the names and addresses of owners and builders. Ask owners about their experiences.
• Check the records in the county clerk's or recorder's office for legal actions filed against companies you're considering. Several actions filed in a short period, or a continuous history of law suits, warrant further investigation.
• Verify that the salesperson who calls on you actually works for the company he or she represents.
• The company must be licensed by the state to build swimming pools. You may be able to check with the contractors' licensing board for specific information about the company.
• Find out whether the company uses its own men and equipment or hires subcontractors to do some or all of the work. Don't eliminate companies that subcontract much of their work for that reason alone; many small companies operate very efficiently this way.

Once you've considered all the information you've obtained, select three or four companies and ask them to submit bids on the pool you want. Unless you are certain what kind of pool you want, choose the companies that will bid on your pool based on their reputations, rather than on the type of pool they build.

Have each builder you're considering bid on the exact same package you and your consultants have prepared. If the companies are equally proficient, you can make a final choice on the basis of the bids they submit and the convenience of their construction schedules. But take your time, particularly if the bids vary widely.

If, on the other hand, the proposals don't include all the same elements, you'll have to take the differences into account when comparing bids. Neither automatically accept nor reject a bid that is unusually low. Instead, find out why. If the bidder forgot you had mentioned boulders at the pool site, and you signed the contract knowing this, he or she could probably recover the added costs in court if you did not pay.

Without a signed contract, you'll have nothing but trouble. A contract is an agreement between two parties covering the performance of certain work for a certain amount of money.

A good contract—whether it's the standard contract used by the builder or one prepared by your attorney—protects both your interests and the builder's. It must be tightly written, describing everything to be done and by whom, as well as everything not to be done.

Don't sign it until you read and understand all of it.

CONTRACT CONSIDERATIONS

A well-written contract should contain the following information:

Plans and specifications: These must be in sufficient detail so as to allow no question about what is to be built. A plan drawn to scale and attached to the contract should show the location of the pool on your property; the pool's shape, size, and dimensions; and the location of the support system, including filter and pump, solar panels (if any), heater, return lines, and main drains with pipe sizes, skimmers, and accessories.

Contracts for air-sprayed mortar (gunite) pools should contain a tolerance provision with a financial consideration for undersized and oversized dimensions. If a dimension comes out smaller than what you contracted for, you get a rebate. If larger, you pay an additional fee. The tolerances for a well-designed and well-built pool should be within 1/8 inch.

Performance: The contract should specify all the work to be done, materials to be used, equipment to be installed (including manufacturer and model number), and any optional features to be considered. The date work will start and end should be stated (unless local weather conditions don't allow it), as well as any penalties for late work. It should also note the time when the owner will become responsible for the maintenance of the pool.

In addition, the contract should lay down conditions for suspension, arbitration, and termination (under federal law, you are allowed three business days after signing the contract to change your mind).

Excavation and grading: The contract should state the costs of gaining access to the site, relocating utilities, and excavation of any

unknown underground hazards whether man-made or natural. It should also assign responsibility for final grading and for the removal of building debris and surplus earth and rock.

Costs and payment: Outlined in the contract should be the cost of the specified work and any options, the payment schedule (a series of payments based on work completed), and the question of ownership in the case of bankruptcy.

Consider the payment schedule carefully. On the one hand, to ensure that you won't have paid in full for an uncompleted pool, you may want to make partial payments as different stages of the work are completed. The builder, on the other hand, would prefer to be paid before the work is completed, in order to be paid in full by the time the job is finished.

Legal conditions: Legal provisions in the contract should include the validity period for the agreed upon price, responsibility for permits and zoning compliance, and provisions for mechanic's lien releases as the labor and materials used are paid for (these come from the contractor and any subcontractors and material suppliers involved). These releases are necessary because even though you've paid the contractor, if he or she has not paid those who have done work or supplied material on your property, you can be liable for the amount owed. In addition to requiring lien releases every time you make a payment, you can request that the pool builder post a bond assuring payment to subcontractors.

Liability for damages and personal injury and guarantee provisions for the contractor's work and any equipment installed should also be written into the contract. Under federal law, you must be advised that equipment warranties are available, and you must be given the chance to examine them.

A lap pool is surrounded by a deck with a cutout that permitted a single tree to remain, providing shade near the pool.
Landscape architect: Scott Smith

A Primer on
POOL STYLES

When it comes time to choose the style of pool for your home, there are no easy answers to the question of which size, shape, and type of construction will best meet your needs. There are a variety of factors to consider: personal tastes, pool use, the conditions of the site, the types of construction available in your area—and, of course, your budget. The following chapter will walk you through the multitude of options now available to the prospective pool owner as well as show you photos of some of the more popular designs. Supplement your research by speaking to pool owners in your neighborhood, and, if possible, visiting some award-winning sites. Many pool builders keep a photo library of their installations along with contact numbers for the owners. A visit to some of these pools will provide you with a first-hand look at styles that might suit your needs and taste.

Pool Size and Shape

Site conditions and landscape requirements will affect your decision on the size and shape of your pool. But personal tastes and how the pool will be used are the most important considerations.

PERSONAL NEEDS

The architectural axiom that "form follows function" applies particularly to a pool's size and shape. A family of happy frolickers needs a pool with a large shallow area. To satisfy those who enjoy swimming laps, the pool should feature a long, straight section with parallel ends. If your family falls into both these groups, choose a pool that can accommodate all types of swimming activity. For example, the shallow, short leg of an L-shaped pool can be large enough for the frolickers, and the other leg can be long enough for the lap swimmers.

If you plan to have a diving area, keep in mind that there is considerable debate over what constitutes safe depth and diving well size. Some experts recommend a pool depth of 9 feet that extends 25 feet for maximum safety. For more information on the subject, contact one of the following organizations: National Spa and Pool Institute; United States Diving, Inc.; National Swimming Pool Foundation.

Many pool users splash and play in shallow water and do little, if any, swimming. For this purpose, figure a minimum depth of 36 inches, increasing to 4 or 5 feet. For this type of play, any pool size and shape will do—even a converted wine barrel.

Don't be tempted to include a wading pool just because you have small children. They will quickly outgrow it and take to the main pool with the rest of the family. You can build a separate wading pool that can later be converted into a garden pond, or install a platform, available commercially, that converts spas into wading pools.

Serious swimmers—those who use the pool often for exercise—need a depth of at least 3½ to 4 feet so they don't touch bottom while swimming, and can safely negotiate tumble turns at the pool's ends.

Poolside geometry can provide new angles for a spa-pool-deck combination. This raised spa and deck conform to sloping contours of the lot; the entire pool complex fits together like a modernistic puzzle.
Design: Bob Maudsley, Peri-Bilt Pools

POPULAR POOL SHAPES

The variety of pool shapes available is limitless, ranging from the formality of a rectangle to more natural pondlike shapes. The illustrations at right feature some of the more popular shapes. Remember, select a pool shape not on its own appeal, but based on how it will fulfill your needs and complement your home and backyard.

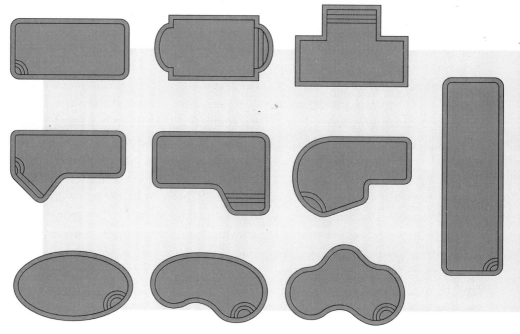

If the pool will be a training center for competitive swimmers, make the length 75 feet. Then they can develop a style usable for competitive meets. Width is not critical—some lap pools in side yards are just wide enough for one swimmer—10 feet.

There is an alternative for serious swimmers with neither the space nor desire for a long pool. You can exercise well by swimming against a current generated by a separate pumping system (see page 60).

Water fitness and therapy are other common uses for pools. If you are interested in either activity, a smaller pool will suffice. See page 9 for one possible design.

POOL SIZE

While there still are a great many residential swimming pools in the United States that range from 450 square feet (15 by 30 feet) to 800 square feet (20 by 40 feet) in size, the trend—which began in the late 1970s—is toward smaller pools.

Shallower pools are also becoming more common, with home owners opting for flat-bottomed pools (they actually have a slope ratio of 1:12) with a water depth of 4 feet. Except for diving, and some specialized uses such as some types of therapy, SCUBA, or synchronized swimming, a deep section is often unnecessary and actually increases maintenance costs and safety risks.

Industry members observing these trends attribute them not only to lower installation costs, but also to smaller lots, condominium and townhouse living, and economy of operation and maintenance. A small pool requires less water and chemicals, is cheaper to filter and heat, and takes less effort to maintain. And small can be beautiful, too, as some of the pools in the section called Enjoying Pools and Spas (page 6) illustrate.

Though the trend is to smaller pools these days, you should choose a pool that's large enough to accommodate your needs. Most experts agree that a pool measuring at least 16 by 32 feet is needed for a full range of play activities.

POOL SHAPE

The simpler the shape of your pool, the better it will blend into a landscaped setting and enhance the appearance of your property. Shapes developed from squares, rectangles, circles, ovals, and other simple geometric figures will not compete with the landscaping.

A naturalistic pool is also usually simple in shape. But making it so much a part of nature that there is hardly any delineation between the

pool and its environment usually requires the skill of a top landscape architect. Keep in mind that a naturalistic pool is not easy to integrate into a residential lot, may require more maintenance if plants are used close to the pool, and will probably be more expensive.

Unusual pool shapes are difficult to plan well because they compete with the other elements in your landscape. But sometimes an unusual shape is the best, or only, choice. If your lot is small and wedge-shaped, for example, your pool will also have to be wedge-shaped. Or to integrate a tree or other natural feature that's valuable to you, you may need to plan for a bend in one side of a pool. Whatever your situation, always plan your pool carefully before installation *(page 18)*, and remember to set aside extra space for access and poolside activities *(right)*.

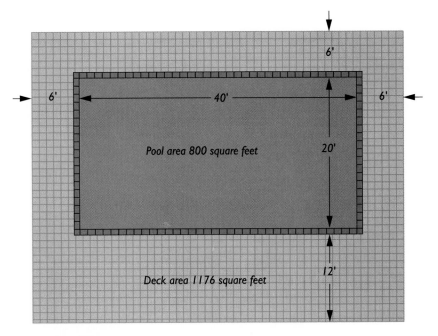

Space Around the Pool
For outdoor activities and entertainment, make sure your design provides enough space around the pool for swimmers and nonswimmers alike. Except in the case of a naturalistic pool, you will want a paved area or deck at least 4-8 feet wide on all sides of the pool. This deck allows convenient access to the pool, keeps dirt out of the water, prevents the garden from becoming waterlogged, and permits the person cleaning the pool to work unhindered. In general, the poolside area should be at least equal to the area of the pool. For example, a 20- by 40-foot pool (800 square feet) with the minimum 4-foot-wide deck on three sides would have an activity area 12 feet in width along one of the long sides.

Fitting your Pool to your Budget

Unless you have unlimited funds, your budget may impose limitations on what type of pool you install. Begin by planning the pool and surroundings you'd most like to have. Then obtain at least three bids on the same plans to learn exactly what your dream will cost. Once you have chosen a contractor, sit down together to determine how you can bring the project within reach of your budget.

Often, the solution is to defer parts of the project. Because you planned both the pool and the surroundings, you can eliminate those parts of the project that can be added later with the least amount of increased effort and cost. A gazebo, for example, can be built anytime. And with fiber optic technology, even underwater lighting is easily added after the pool has been installed.

The only absolute about the costs of the various pool types is that the portable above-ground pool with a vinyl liner is easier to install and considerably less expensive than any type of permanent pool construction.

The cost of a permanent pool varies widely, depending on a number of factors—size, shape, type and quality of construction, equipment, surface options, location, and the competitive situation among local pool builders.

Of the two most popular types of pools built in the U.S.—the air-sprayed mortar, or gunite, pool and the vinyl-lined pool—the gunite pool is the more expensive. The difference is not great in the Sunbelt states, but it is in the colder northern climes, where more steel reinforcing rods and a thicker shell are needed to withstand frost pressure. In general, building your own pool requires a lot of hard work and skill, especially for plumbing and electrical installation. It is a job that is best left to a qualified professional.

When calculating the cost of installing your pool, take into account the plantings and decking that will be needed to create the lush environment you desire, as well as the added maintenance costs these elements create.

Pool Types and Materials

Swimming pools can be installed completely or partially in the ground, anchored to hillsides, or placed directly on the surface of the ground. The type you select, as well as the availability of materials in your area, will determine the construction method you'll choose for your pool.

Most permanent pools are fully in-ground structures. They are the most accessible from patio areas and the most adaptable to unified landscape schemes. But both above-ground and partially in-ground pools can also be attractive and enjoyable.

There are conflicting claims about the merits of the various types of pool construction available today, but attractive and practical pools can be built regardless of the method used. Your main concern should be making sure the contractor you hire is knowledgeable and experienced enough to do the job. The information on page 37 will help you decide on a professional.

CONCRETE POOLS

Concrete is among the most popular construction materials used for swimming pools. Its workability, strength, permanence, and flexibility of design make it ideal for innovative and interesting in-ground and hillside pools.

The material is reinforced with steel reinforcing rods or "rebar"

Among the benefits of using concrete is the freedom to use any shape you desire. Here the pool is complemented by a boulder edging, which appears to support a redwood deck. (Actually, the deck rests on concealed piers and footings.)
Design: Lang and Wood

POOL CONSTRUCTION

Some of the more popular styles of pool construction are shown in the side-section views below.

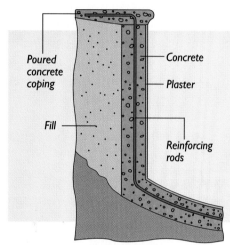

Poured Concrete

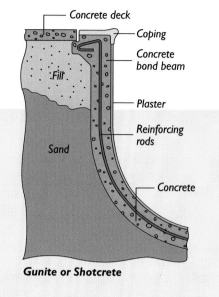

Gunite or Shotcrete

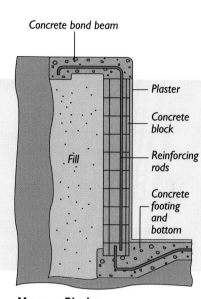

Masonry Blocks

to withstand the pressures of soil and water. The amount and size of the steel needed depends on both the geographical location and structural requirements.

The four main types of concrete construction are gunite (actually sprayed mortar), shotcrete, poured, and masonry block. Cost and availability usually determine which of these is used.

Several interior finishes are available in concrete pools. The surface may be plastered in colors ranging from white to black. Though white is still the most popular, dark colors are being used more and more in residential pools because of their attractiveness and the small solar heating benefit they offer. Instead of plastering, the concrete can be troweled smooth and painted. The most expensive finish is ceramic tile. Its

appearance can be striking and it is easy to clean. Most owners compromise on a band of tile along the water line both for its attractiveness and for the ease of removing minerals, oil, and dirt from it. Other types of interior finish include sprayed liquid vinyl, exposed aggregate, and reinforced PVC membrane. Aggregate is becoming very popular for its attractive appearance and ease of maintenance. PVC membrane is effectively used to resurface a damaged pool; it can transform an old pool into a nearly new one.

Shotcrete and gunite: These types of construction fostered the growth in pool ownership because they were cheaper than other methods of concrete construction.

Both are mixtures of hydrated cement and sand applied over and

under a grid of steel reinforcing rods directly against the soil. Gunite, a dry mix, is shot from a nozzle under high pressure while a second hose adds water. Shotcrete is premixed wet concrete applied by a hose carrying the mixture with a second hose supplying air.

In both cases, the mix must be directed behind the rebars and against the earth so that pockets of air or loose sand cannot form. The shell must be of the proper thickness throughout, with no weak spots that will be unable to resist earth and hydrostatic pressures.

Many contractors place covers over the main drainpipe, inlet pipes, and light sockets to prevent their being filled with concrete. Otherwise, all openings must be checked and cleared as soon as the crew is finished working.

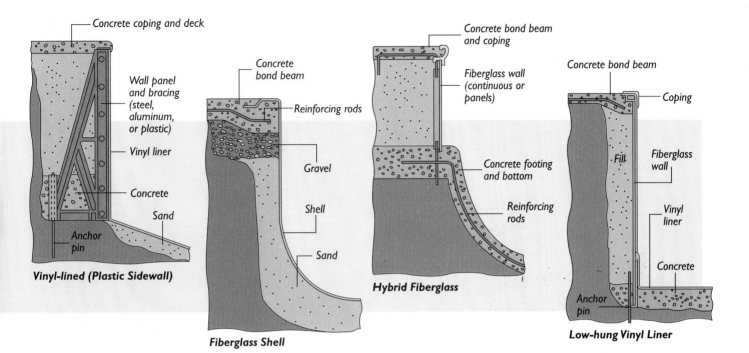

Vinyl-lined (Plastic Sidewall)

- Concrete coping and deck
- Wall panel and bracing (steel, aluminum, or plastic)
- Vinyl liner
- Concrete
- Sand
- Anchor pin

Fiberglass Shell

- Concrete bond beam
- Reinforcing rods
- Gravel
- Shell
- Sand

Hybrid Fiberglass

- Concrete bond beam and coping
- Fiberglass wall (continuous or panels)
- Concrete footing and bottom
- Reinforcing rods

Low-hung Vinyl Liner

- Concrete bond beam
- Coping
- Fill
- Fiberglass wall
- Vinyl liner
- Concrete
- Anchor pin

Gunite and shotcrete allow complete freedom of size and shape, since they follow any excavated shape. Steps and spas can be formed at the same time. The thickness of the shell and the number and size of the rebars can be adjusted to meet any structural requirement. If you have to build your pool on filled ground—not optimum conditions—a gunite or shotcrete shell supported on concrete piers that sit on solid ground may be the answer. The initial cost of gunite or shotcrete equipment makes it impractical for the small contractor who builds only a few pools a year, unless the equipment can be rented when needed. If you don't live in a densely populated area, you may find either that gunite is not available or that the cost is considerably higher than other materials.

Poured concrete: Largely replaced by gunite where it is available, the poured concrete method has been abandoned by many companies because of the labor involved in setting the forms and the time it takes for the concrete to dry. After the forms are stripped, the concrete floor is poured, spread, and then troweled smooth by hand.

The bond beam along the top of the wall is usually the last structural step, unless it is incorporated in the pour for the walls. Steel reinforcing is used in this type of pool, too. The rebars projecting from the walls are tied to the rebars in the floor and bond beam.

Masonry blocks: Some small contractors favor this type of construction because there's a minimum outlay for heavy equipment. Because the blocks serve as forms and the cores are filled with mortar, a block pool is similar to a poured pool. There are two kinds of blocks—the most common are set in mortar; interlocking blocks, available in some areas, are easier to handle.

The blocks are stacked on a poured concrete footing. Reinforcing rods in the footing extend into the walls and floor. As the walls go up, openings must be left for plumbing and underwater lights.

The floor can be poured after the walls are up or at the same time that the footing is poured. Steel is tied to rods projecting from the footing to form a solid grid. The floor is made with one pour and then troweled smooth.

The reinforcing rods projecting from the walls are bent down and wired to rods in the bond beam. ➤

Lined with trees and plantings, this vinyl-lined pool offers the same aesthetic beauty as a concrete pool—but for less money.
Design and construction: Frank L. Wall

Because of the rectangular shape of the blocks, most pools of this type have straight lines—typically rectangular, wedge-shaped, L-shaped, or T-shaped. Curves can be incorporated into the design, but they should have not less than a 10-foot radius.

An interior finish must be applied to any concrete pool to provide a waterproof surface.

VINYL-LINED POOLS

Even more than gunite, the development of vinyl-lined or vinyl pools has brought pool ownership within the budget of many people. The savings are greatest in the Northeast and Midwest, where these pools originated, because of the difficulty of building with concrete in a cold climate. Factory prefabrication from simple materials and short construction time—3 to 4 days is possible—make the difference.

Sometimes, vinyl-lined pools are known as prepackaged pools because the builder only has to specify the size and shape desired. Within a few days, everything needed for a complete pool, including the support system and accessories, is delivered at one time.

The vinyl-lined pool is actually a large, flexible container supported on the sides by walls made of aluminum, steel, plastic, masonry block, or wood. The bottom of the liner rests on a bed of sand, vermiculite, or cement. The top of the liner is secured by a special coping that both gives a finished look to the edge of the pool and serves as a border for the deck.

Some sidewall structures are self-supporting, ideal for above-ground and on-ground installations. If used for in-ground pools, the pool can be filled with water before the excavation is backfilled. The liner's lifetime is determined largely by its environment and care. It is affected both by ultraviolet light from the sun and by the chemistry of the pool water.

Fading due to ultraviolet light is prevented in some liners by the inclusion of ultraviolet inhibitors in the vinyl material. Some vinyls also have inhibitors that prevent staining by fungi in the sand underneath the liner.

Liners come in a range of colors and patterns. Rectangles and sim-

48

ple curved shapes are most popular, but special shapes can be made at a somewhat higher cost. Prefabricated steps and spas made from acrylic or fiberglass are available for vinyl-lined pools.

Aluminum sidewall: For an aluminum shell, prefabricated panels are bolted together or extruded sections are interlocked with each other. The interlocking type allows for the design of free-form pools, usually of specific shapes that fit prefabricated liners.

Steel sidewalls: Panels fabricated from galvanized steel are bolted together and supported by frames on the backside.

Plastic sidewalls: Plastic panels are strong, lightweight, and do not corrode or deteriorate in the ground. The material gives manufacturers an option against the increasing costs of steel and aluminum.

Masonry block sidewalls: These are built in the same manner as described on page 47, except that they do not have to be leakproof. The walls must be covered with smooth cement plaster to prevent tears and punctures in the liner, and they need to be built to the exact size required by the liner.

Wood sidewalls: Advances made in recent years in pressure treating wood to prevent rot and infestation make it possible now to build a long-life wood shell for a vinyl-lined pool.

FIBERGLASS AND STAINLESS STEEL POOLS

In addition to the one-piece shell, there are several hybrids combin-

ing fiberglass sidewalls with bottoms of various materials.

The biggest advantage of fiberglass pools is low maintenance: The slick surface is difficult for algae to cling to and the material is easy to clean. Color is built right into the material, and usually no other surface finish is required. In areas where the pH of the water is high, however, improperly maintained pool water can chalk the finish; the pool will then have to be painted.

Fiberglass shell: Major improvements in the construction and installation of fiberglass shells have overcome the original problems of leaking, buckling, and adverse reaction to soil chemicals.

Since the size of the shells makes long-distance transportation uneconomical, they may not be available outside of major population centers. As the demand increases, however, more manufacturing plants

are being established to extend the market for these pools. The pool is constructed on an upside-down mold. To form the smooth surface on the inside of the pool, a layer of gelcoat containing the color is applied to the mold. Then, layers of resin-saturated fiberglass are laminated over the gelcoat to the desired thickness. Necessary reinforcement is added as the glass cloth is built up. The steps are built as part of the shell.

After the excavation is completed and the plumbing installed, a bed of sand is spread in the bottom of the hole and contoured to fit the shell. A crane picks the shell off a trailer and swings it into place (right over the house, if necessary). After the plumbing is connected and the back-filling completed, the one-piece concrete bond beam and deck is poured integrally with the coping, which is part of the fiberglass shell. ➤

Preformed acrylic shells are ideal for smaller pools. This model is shaped to provide a built-in bench along one side.

Portable pools take on a look of permanence when accompanied by a deck. This type of pool is ideal for sites where deep excavation is problematic. Warning: Prohibit bathers from diving into a portable pool from the deck.

The major drawback of the one-piece fiberglass mold is the limitation in size and shape. Since molds are massive and expensive, manufacturers offer only a few models.

Hybrid fiberglass: These pools usually have 3-foot-high fiberglass sidewalls that may be made either from a continuous length or from flanged fiberglass sections bolted together with a leakproof seal. Some are designed to be installed with a concrete bottom and others with a vinyl bottom over sand—the latter type is called a "low-hung" vinyl-lined pool. The fiberglass is the same as in the one-piece shell. The sidewalls are flexible and, in the case of a concrete-bottom pool, accommodate almost any size and shape. The low-hung pool's size and shape are limited by the liner.

Stainless steel: These pools are attractive and durable but the high price of the stainless steel makes them a fairly expensive investment. The shells, assembled in panels, tend to be small and are installed in the ground.

PORTABLE POOLS

Portable pools require little excavation, cost far less than a permanent pool, and, with a bit of effort, can be assembled and dismantled by the homeowner. For these reasons, people who don't want to make a big investment, families that want to try a pool before making a commitment, and people who rent homes especially appreciate them.

Portable pools sit on the ground, and most have equal depth throughout (usually 4 feet). They may be circular (12 to 27 feet in diameter), or rectangular or oval (12 by 18 feet to 18 by 39 feet).

Construction materials consist of self-supporting walls of galvanized steel, plastic, or aluminum with interior vinyl liners. The bottom of the liner sits on a shallow bed of sand. The outer panels of the walls are often attractively colored and decorated.

You can choose a pool with or without decking. The decking can range from a sitting area on one side to one that surrounds the pool and is wide enough for patio furniture. The decks are railed for safety. Access to portable pools is by a ladder or steps supplied with the pool.

The height of the pool from the ground is a built-in safety feature—removal of the access ladder or steps to the deck or pool itself effectively keeps small children from entering the pool.

Filter units—sand, diatomaceous earth, or cartridge—are specially designed for use with these pools. The skimmer generally is built in but may float on the surface. The support system, including filter, pump, skimmer, valves, and piping, is usually supplied with the pool.

If you don't feel comfortable installing the pool yourself—portables can be a bit tricky to assemble—you can have the dealer do the work. The portable pool can also be dismantled and moved to a new location, an added attraction for mobile families. And because they're portable, these pools are usually not taxed as real property.

INTEGRAL SPAS

Whether you're planning a pool or you already own one, you may want to contemplate installing a spa. Building a spa at the same time as your pool makes good economic sense, especially when you build the spa integrally with a gunite, vinyl-lined, or fiberglass pool. Gunite pools and spas can be sprayed at the same time. In the case of fiberglass and vinyl-lined pools, some manufacturers produce fiberglass spas that can be mounted in place as the pool is being installed. Even installing a separate spa adjoining a pool can cost less than installing a spa by itself. As an added benefit, in some residential cases, you will be able to use the same support system for the pool and spa. For more information on spas, see page 52.

In this integral pool and spa design, overflow from the spa goes directly into the pool.
Design: Bill Kapranos

Choosing
YOUR SPA

People have soaked their cares away in hot baths for thousands of years. The appeal could not be more timeless— or more timely. Hot hydromassage can soothe away tensions and stress in a matter of minutes. The hot water experience we describe in this chapter relates exclusively to the most common types of spas: portables, in-grounds, and hot tubs. To soak in one of these is not really to take a bath. Ideally, you enter the water already clean from a shower. The water is kept clean with a filter and sanitizing agent, such as chlorine. There's no waiting for the tub to fill, you just step in and relax, letting the hot, soothing water replenish your body and mind as few other tonics can.

Spa Choices

Once a rare sight in homes, spas have become increasingly more common in recent years. Even if you don't own one, chances are you've experienced a pleasurable soak in a friend's spa or in one at a hotel or resort.

The hot tub was the earliest type of spa used on a wide scale by home-owners. It became popular because the first reasonably inexpensive vessels for home hot water soaking were made from wooden wine vats. These days, the term "spa" is commonly used both for wooden tubs and for the various acrylic and thermoplastic vessels on the market.

The natural way: Soft and rustic, hot tubs derive their appeal from their smooth wood surfaces. Tub-lovers often comment that the wood surrounding their soak feels good to touch. For them, it conveys a warmth and comfort that enhances the soothing, meditative experience of soaking. They also like its pleasant, musky aroma.

Whether it's made of redwood, cedar, teak, or another wood, a hot tub also boasts a classic beauty. And no wonder: The tub's simple lines reflect a barrel design that has remained unchanged for centuries. With a greater capacity than most other spas, hot tubs give a deep soak, which some people prefer. A tub that's 4 feet deep can immerse you up to your neck, thanks in part to more spartan seating options—usually just a bench around the sides—compared to the body-conforming contours typical of other spa seats.

With a hot tub, you have some flexibility in the number and place-

For an integral pool and spa combination, the easiest and usually most economical choice is to have the spa built at the same time and of the same materials as the pool, as was done above.

ment of hydrojets. Or you may choose to have no jets at all, opting instead for a gentle soak in warm, still water.

For all the natural luxury of wood, however, some hot tubs have given their owners problems after a few years, mainly due to neglect. For example, if the tub is drained and allowed to dry for more than two days, leaks can develop between the staves when the tub is refilled. This is because stave edges will no longer swell evenly to create a continuous seal. And proper water maintenance, necessary for any kind of spa, is especially important for a hot tub. When cleaning, be sure to disinfect above the waterline to remove any pathogenic organisms, such as bacteria, that spread disease.

If the wood tub attracts you but you don't want the potential problems, investigate the possibility of a lined tub. It looks like any other hot tub on the outside, but the inside is fitted with a smooth plastic, vinyl, or reinforced PVC liner.

Paradise in plastic: The sleek, contemporary whirlpool spas of today depart completely from the rustic simplicity of hot tub designs. The choices are dazzling, running the gamut from small, two-person portables to tiled and landscaped installations of splendid proportions.

Spas fall into two general categories: in-ground and portable. The first—the older and more traditional type—is sunk in the ground or placed in a deck, and the work is usually performed by a contractor. The portable, or self-contained, spa comes as a complete unit, including its support equipment, and doesn't need to be permanently installed.

Spa shells: Poured concrete, gunite, and shotcrete are the traditional materials for in-ground spas; concrete is still commonly used for a

GETTING INTO HOT WATER

For a contemporary look, choose a portable or in-ground spa. Apart from the factory molded shell shown at right, in-ground models can be made of concrete and are constructed on site. A hot tub—really just a wooden spa—offers the natural beauty of wood. Surrounded by a wooden deck, it too can have the appearance of an in-ground installation.

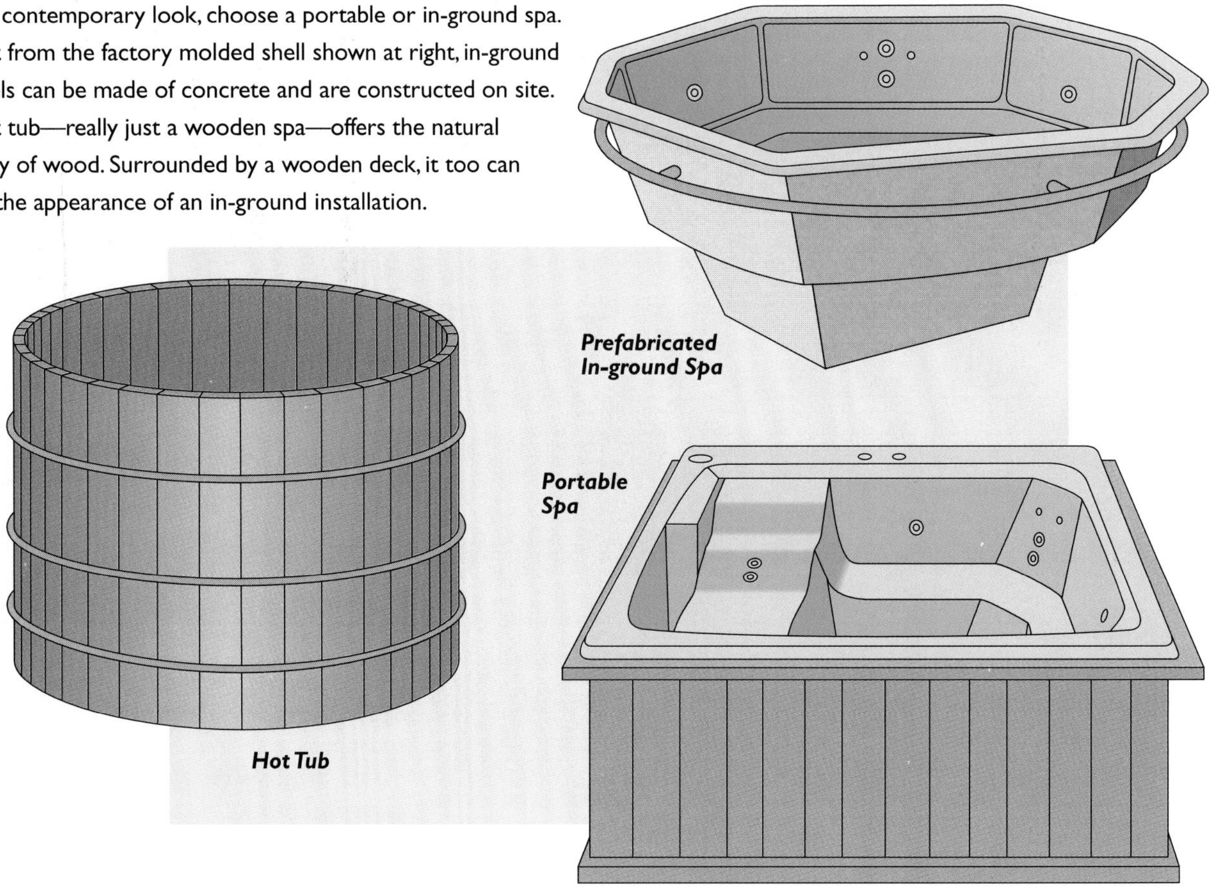

Prefabricated In-ground Spa

Portable Spa

Hot Tub

spa installed at the same time as a concrete swimming pool. But for spas that stand alone, concrete has largely been superseded by fiberglass and plastic.

Lightweight, low cost, and easily mass-produced in pleasing, one-piece shapes, molded fiberglass shells have revolutionized the home spa business. Early fiberglass spas were lined with gelcoat, a polymer resin that was sprayed onto a mold

Hot Water Safety

Although generally beneficial, spa soaking is not always good for everyone. Pregnant women and people with heart disease, multiple sclerosis, diabetes, high or low blood pressure, or any other serious illness should not enter a spa without consulting a doctor. Also, due to recent concerns regarding the contraction of diseases such as Legionnaires' disease, it's imperative that spa water is kept clean; the maintenance guidelines laid out in this book will help you do this. For more on spa safety, see page 187.

The soothing sound of falling water adds to the pleasure of a soak in this beautifully landscaped naturalistic setting. The same pump that powers the spa can recirculate the water over the falls.

of the desired shape and then backed with fiberglass. But gelcoat had its drawbacks: It tended to crack, blister, and delaminate over time in high water temperatures. It was also prone to cobalt staining, a chlorine-induced reaction which drew resin from the gelcoat, leaving black spots on the surface.

Today, spa shells are usually made from acrylic. Large acrylic sheets are heated, laid in a mold, and pulled to fit its contours with a vacuum. The cooled shell is then backed with fiberglass for strength. The result: a slick, glossy, and easy-to-clean material that is available in colors to suit any taste.

A good acrylic spa should give reliable service for years, though it may get nicked and scratched along the way. Occasionally, more serious problems develop. Unless carefully engineered and molded, an acrylic shell can become quite thin at sharp corners and susceptible to damage. And if anything goes wrong when the fiberglass backing is applied, it can lead to delamination between acrylic and backing later on. A careful visual inspection will turn up any flaws, but the surest test of quality is the manufacturer's reputation.

A SELECTION OF SHELLS

Freedom of form characterizes spas, both portable and in-ground. The options below are just some of the shapes you'll find in dealers' showrooms. With the range of choices available, it's easy to find a combination of color, form, seating arrangement, and number and placement of jets to suit your needs, taste, and budget.

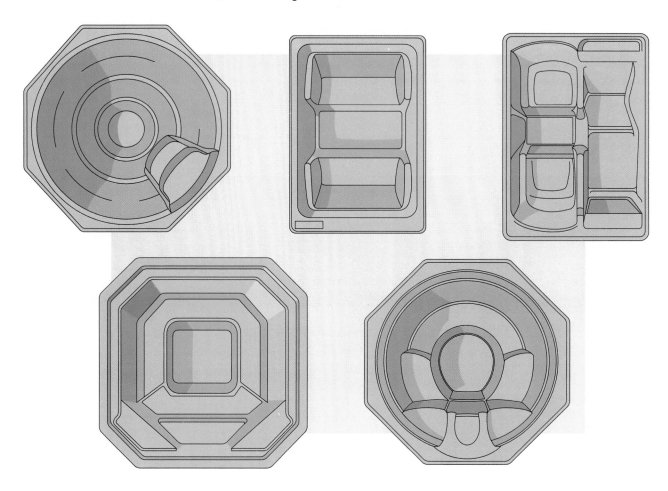

Portable Spas

A recent addition to the gallery of hot water products, the portable spa seems well in tune with today's mobile lifestyle.

Unlike other spas, a portable spa is truly self-contained. Set-up time and expense for these units is designed to be minimal. They can be installed outdoors with nothing more than a concrete slab for support and may be run on your home's standard 120-volt current. They can even be installed inside, if proper precautions are taken to support their weight and adequate ventilation is provided *(page 35)*.

Sizing up the benefits: Portables typically range in size from a 4- by 5-foot spa that holds about 125 gallons to an 8-foot one that contains 500 gallons. The smallest seats two; the largest can accommodate up to eight. With an average dry weight of 300 to 500 pounds, portables can be lifted, if you have enough helpers. And because they're relatively shallow, with a water depth of between 26 and 36 inches, they'll fit through a doorway, if turned on their side. You can move them from one setting to another, whether from a deck to a sunroom or from your old home to your new one.

Besides mobility, the other main advantage of the portable spa is its relatively low cost. An excellent one can be purchased for substantially less than an in-ground spa. And since it's a self-contained appliance rather than a property improvement, the portable spa usually requires no building permit (check with your local building department to be sure); nor will it raise your property taxes.

Operating the spa: Like the shell itself, the portable's equipment—heater, filter, pump, air blower, and hydrojets—is a smaller, less powerful version of what would be necessary to support a large, in-ground

ANATOMY OF A PORTABLE SPA

A fully self-contained unit, a portable spa is surrounded by a "skirt," typically made of redwood, which hides the underside of the shell, the insulation, and the spa's support equipment. Access to the equipment is via a small door in the side of the skirt, which may be hidden by the steps that lead up to the spa. The bottom should feature at least two drains.

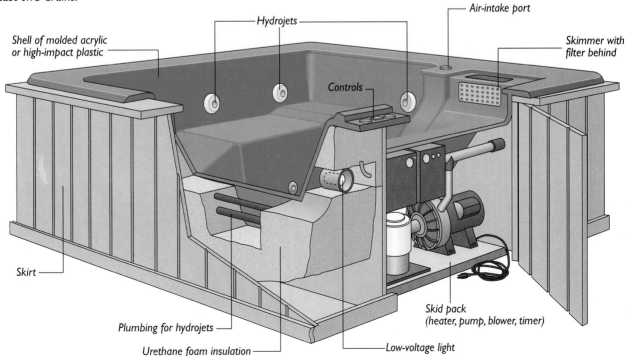

Air-intake port

Hydrojets

Shell of molded acrylic or high-impact plastic

Skimmer with filter behind

Controls

Skirt

Plumbing for hydrojets

Urethane foam insulation

Low-voltage light

Skid pack (heater, pump, blower, timer)

Integrating your portable spa in a deck, as shown at left, makes it harder to take with you if you move. But choosing a portable rather than an in-ground spa means you can enjoy it right away, and complete the project in stages as your budget allows. The deck and spa should be supported separately; neither is designed to hold the other up. *Design: Timothy R. Bitts and Associates, Inc.*

spa or hot tub. Each piece of equipment is matched to the relatively small water volume of the portable, so the spa functions more economically than a spa with larger equipment and more water to heat. The quality of equipment can vary greatly from one spa to another, so take this into consideration when deciding which model you want to buy. Also make sure that the equipment is properly sized for the volume of the spa and the number of hydrojets it features.

Many portable spas run on 120 volts. But before you bring one home, be sure to check out your home's electrical system. If you have any doubt about a circuit's capacity to support a 120-volt portable spa, have it checked out by a licensed electrician.

The outlet you use for the spa must be part of a 20-amp circuit that doesn't service any other heavy-draw appliances. Nearly all portables are now equipped with ground fault circuit interrupters (GFCI); as an added precaution, ensure that the outlet or its circuit also has GFCI protection.

Another option offered by many spa manufacturers is to run the equipment on 240 volts. This is accomplished by adding a new circuit and hard-wiring the spa directly to it. You will have to hire a licensed electrician or spa contractor for this job. Although the spa will no longer be as portable, you'll gain considerable heating speed. Also, with 240 volts you can run the heater simultaneously with the hydrojets or blower for a long

period of time, which is not possible with a 120-volt heater.

Another advantage of a 240-volt system is that you can use a 6-kilowatt heater, which will raise water temperature more quickly than a small 120-volt, 1.5-kilowatt heater—hence, a shorter wait before you can enter the spa. It also means that the spa can more easily maintain a steady temperature of 100° to 104°F. A smaller heater can have trouble keeping up with heat loss. (Air blowers, as explained on page 81, also cool down the water rapidly.)

Gas heaters, or gas packs, for portable spas are also available; the newer units no longer require remote installation. However, with gas your portable will cease being self-contained. For more information on heaters, turn to page 75.

In-ground Spas

Before the advent of the hot tub and the portable spa, the only spa available was what the industry now calls in-ground. As the name implies, these spas (made originally of poured concrete or concrete block) were placed in a hole dug in the ground. Today, the term also refers to spas set into an above-grade surface, such as a deck.

The support equipment necessary for an in-ground spa always stands a short distance away, in its own housing. Although this requires more planning and construction, it allows you more choice in types and sizes of equipment.

Shopping for an in-ground spa usually means choosing between a factory-molded shell of fiberglass-reinforced acrylic and the more expensive, longer-lasting concrete shell constructed on site. But you can even get an in-ground spa made of stainless steel. Each type offers a myriad of shapes and sizes from which to choose.

If you're having a concrete swimming pool constructed at the same time, the easiest and often least expensive choice for the spa is to have it built from the same materials as the pool. It can run on the same circulation system as the pool.

Although it's a less common and more expensive option, you can choose concrete for a stand-alone in-ground spa that's not part of a swimming pool. The spa will be formed on site by a pool contractor.

If you want to add only a spa, a manufactured shell is probably a better choice. You can buy the entire package—including equipment and installation—from a full-service dealer, who is licensed to both sell and install the spa. An alternative is to buy a ready-made spa and the necessary support equipment from a reputable dealer, then hire a contractor recommended by the dealer to install it.

Whatever type shell you choose, buy the best quality equipment you can afford, and make sure it's sized appropriately for the spa. For more on choosing equipment, see the section that starts on page 66.

Whether the shell is made of fiberglass-reinforced acrylic or concrete, an in-ground spa installation requires tearing up the garden—or deck—to some extent. Plumbing and wiring lines need to be buried or hidden, and support equipment has to be sheltered. Often the shell is fully or partially recessed into an excavation. Now is a good time to consider any other landscaping changes you want to make to your yard, since there's going to be a lot of work going on there anyway.➤

ANATOMY OF AN IN-GROUND SPA

Recessed into the ground or set flush with the top of a deck, an in-ground spa has the look of a permanent installation. The support equipment should be located close by, or you'll end up with higher energy costs transporting heated water the extra distance to the spa.

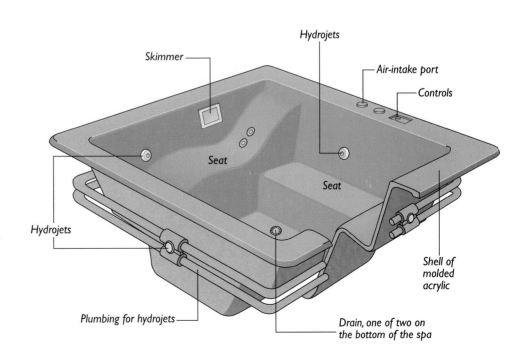

Skimmer

Hydrojets

Air-intake port

Controls

Seat

Seat

Hydrojets

Hydrojets

Plumbing for hydrojets

Drain, one of two on the bottom of the spa

Shell of molded acrylic

While most pool companies do provide a design service, if the spa is only one element of a major redesign for your entire yard, consider hiring a landscape architect or contractor who can handle everything for you.

Installing an in-ground spa involves more planning, disruption, cost, and time than purchasing and setting up an off-the-shelf portable. From the time construction starts, it may be weeks before you can enjoy your first soak. On the other hand, in-ground spas look well-integrated in their setting. They're often set in a deck or patio built expressly to surround them, their lower profile is less conspicuous, and they're likely to be professionally landscaped.

SWIMMING AGAINST THE CURRENT

If you want to work out but don't have the room for a lap pool, consider a swim spa instead. Typically between 13$\frac{1}{2}$ and 15 feet long, this practical offshoot of the spa industry looks like an elongated version of any other in-ground spa.

The difference is in the jets. In a swim spa, the water is propelled by strong countercurrent jets rather than by the hydrojets or paddle wheels that move the water in a spa. Without moving forward an inch, a swimmer can cover miles, simply by swimming against a constant current.

The water temperature in a swim spa is usually cooler, making it more conducive to an active workout. In some models, if you want a relaxing soak, you can turn on regular hydrojets and raise the water temperature. Others have a removable partition that allows you to keep the water at one end hot while the rest of the spa stays at a comfortable swimming temperature.

Generally, swim spas are about 3 feet deep, but deeper models—up to 8 feet—are available for exercising under water. They can be installed either in or above the ground. And depending on the model you buy, you can install it yourself or have a professional do it.

This fiberglass swim spa provides either a vigorous workout or a leisurely swim, depending on how you adjust the countercurrent jets at the head of the spa. *Design: S. Robert Politzer*

Hot Tubs

Although the high tide of their popularity has ebbed considerably since the 1970s, wooden spas or "hot tubs" still remain the first choice of people who appreciate the natural beauty of wood and its harmony with garden plants and trees. Tubs are also the choice of those who want a deep soak. And for traditionalists, the wooden tub still stands unrivaled for its timeless appeal.

In its heyday, the hot tub sprang up just about everywhere in the West. Hundreds of thousands were built to meet the demand. Many of these tubs have since deteriorated. Some of them simply gave in to age, but others succumbed to shoddy construction from inferior materials and poor craftsmanship.

By far the most common reason for their failure, however, has been lack of adequate maintenance. Hot tubs, like any other spas, require regular maintenance. Water chemistry must be carefully controlled, the water must be changed periodically, and the tub needs to be cleaned from time to time.

A hot tub should never be left empty for more than two days. If the unit is drained and allowed to dry out, the wood staves can twist and cup (lift at the edges), distorting the fit of the original coopering and making the tub unusable.

Choosing a wood: Sleek staves of wood, forming the watertight curves of a hot tub, are the essence of its beauty. Wood, with its comforting feel and pleasantly musky fragrance, enhances the appeal of a soak, too.

Most tubs are made from softwoods; redwood and cedar are the most common, but cypress and teak are also used. These tub woods have been chosen because they are sturdy and fairly resistant to decay and chemical damage. In addition, they also offer splinter-free surfaces.

Redwood is probably the most widely used wood for hot tubs, especially along its native West Coast. It's extremely resistant to decay, does not splinter, and swells easily to watertightness.

For strong, flawless staves and years of tubbing pleasure, make sure that the unit is built of clear, kiln-dried, vertical-grain heartwood (not the whitish sapwood). To

ANATOMY OF A HOT TUB

The tub shown here features jets—just like a portable or in-ground spa—but many tubs do not, offering instead a calming soak in still, hot water.

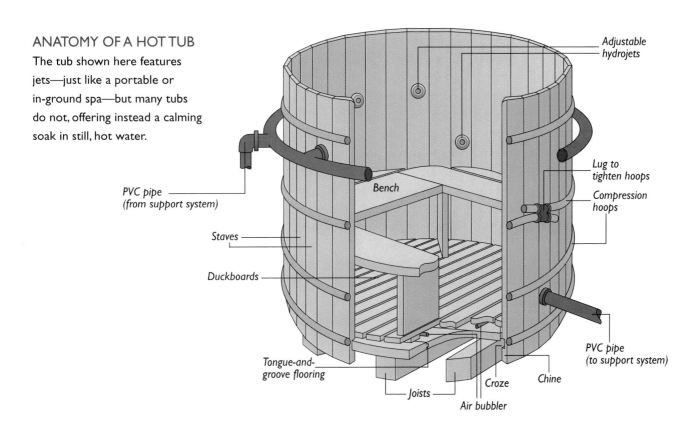

Adjustable hydrojets

PVC pipe (from support system)

Bench

Lug to tighten hoops

Compression hoops

Staves

Duckboards

Tongue-and-groove flooring

Joists

Air bubbler

Croze

Chine

PVC pipe (to support system)

A curving two-level deck and steps provide both seating and access to this pleasing hot tub.
Design: Roger D. Fiske

accept less is to risk problems in the future. A well-maintained redwood tub will last about 15 years.

Cedar, the second most commonly used tub wood, is similar to redwood. Both are porous softwoods; both are decay-resistant only if the heartwood is selected. Cedar is slightly less resistant to decay but a little more resistant to chemical damage than is redwood. However, it also has a shorter lifespan than redwood.

Hardwoods such as oak and jarrah (a hardwood grown and used in Australia for wine casks and pier pilings) have sometimes been used for hot tubs, but are rarely used by commercial manufacturers.

Coopering basics: Hot tubs are built according to the traditional craft of barrel-making, called coopering. The basic tub consists of floorboards, staves, and metal hoops, with benches and duckboards added afterward. The floorboards rest on floor joists, which, at the permanent site, in turn rest on a concrete slab. To distribute weight loads laterally, some floors use tongue-and-groove joinery, others rely on a system of dowels.

The sides of the staves are beveled to ensure a tight fit with their neighbors. A deep notch near the stave bottom, called a croze, fits it to the flooring; the lower lip of the stave is called its chine. The staves are not designed to bear the weight of the tub and should not be resting on the floor joists.

When all the staves are fitted at the croze and to each other, they're held together by from two to four steel hoops. Once the hoops are tightened and the tub is filled with water, two forces make it watertight: The wood swells as it soaks up water, tightening the joints; at the same time, water pressure from within helps to align the staves.

Filling the tub: In a newly constructed tub, the joints between the staves are not perfectly watertight, so before you can use the tub you'll need to break it in. Essentially, you keep the tub filled with water until the wood swells and seals up the joints tightly.

Fill the tub completely and let the water overflow. Wait until there is no more water seeping out between the staves. This usually takes about 24 hours. If the water continues to gush out between the staves, contact the manufacturer or your dealer; this would indicate improper milling or assembly.

Don't be alarmed when your new tub leaches tea-colored tannin into the water. Though quite harmless to people, tannin may clog the tub's filter, so don't turn on any equipment yet. Instead, let the first tubful of water darken; then drain and wipe out any residue.

Refill the tub and run the circulation system continuously for two days; scrub the insides of the tub with a stiff brush a couple of times a day. Then keep draining, refilling, and scrubbing the hot tub daily, until the tannin has all leached out of the wood and the water remains clear. This will probably take a week or so.

Clean the filter, fill the tub with fresh water, and add the appropriate chemicals to treat the water, as explained beginning on page 131.

While you're filling and draining the tub, have a look for slow, seeping leaks between the staves. Such leaks are not usually along the whole length of a stave, but just for a few inches. Monitor the rate of seepage; if it slows down from one day to the next, then the leak will probably stop as the wood continues to swell. If the rate remains unchanged, you'll need to find some other way to close the leak. You can caulk with a good grade of plastic marine putty, or try the traditional method of filling the space with a bit of wool. Contact your dealer for other techniques.

Sizes and seating: Typically, a small hot tub measures 3 or 4 feet high by 5 feet across and holds approximately 500 gallons of water. A more generous tub with a height of 4 feet and a diameter of 6 feet holds just 850 gallons. You can also buy a 5-foot-high tub, if you wish.

Seating arrangements in a tub are typically more spartan than in a molded spa shell, but they are adjustable for height, which is an advantage. A bench around the inside of higher tubs can hold from two to six people, depending on the tub's size. In shorter tubs, you sit on the floor. Benches should be attached to the tub with screws so they can be removed for maintenance and repair.

HOT TUBS: PROS AND CONS

The popularity of the hot tub in the 1970s encouraged many entrepreneurs with little or no experience in manufacturing them to start up businesses to meet the demand. When interest in hot tubs slackened, many simply went out of business as fast as they had entered it. Consequently, when owners experienced problems with their tubs, they had no one to turn to.

And, inevitably, there were problems. Many of the early hot tub enthusiasts apparently were not informed or did not understand the necessity of diligent maintenance. Even some owners who did keep up with good maintenance still found that their tubs started to leak after a few years of use. Often, the support equipment failed due to improper use of chemicals, undersized components, or poor quality.

In any case, the reputation of hot tubs has suffered over the years. Some people warn that tubs aren't sufficiently hygienic because the porous, organic wood used to make them provides lots of potential hiding places for bacteria. Because of this, some health departments require that hot tubs for public use, such as hotels and health clubs, be lined with vinyl to help prevent the spread of disease.

Proper maintenance and water chemistry can easily overcome the concerns about hygiene and chemical damage. Whether the vessel is a nonporous plastic spa or a soft, organic redwood cask, good maintenance, adequate sanitation, and oxidation will guarantee clean, safe water. None of the woods used in hot tub construction should succumb to chemical damage as long as a normal balance of chemicals is maintained.

As for leaks, once the tub's staves have had time to swell and make tight joints, a tub should not leak again if it has been built from the right kind of wood and properly assembled, installed, and maintained. If a tub does leak before the end of its expected lifetime, a good tub dealer can help out with a reliable product to fix the problem.

Buying your Spa

Because the spa and hot tub industry is still young, it's awash with changes and improvements. Although the reliability of many of its products has been proven through years of service in the swimming pool industry, the quality of its newest technology is, of course, untested. That is why it is especially important to learn as much as possible before making your purchase.

Be as cautious about buying a spa and its support equipment as you would be about buying a new car. Even more so. Selling a used spa is not an easy task.

Assessing your needs: Before you start shopping, think about your situation and your preferences. Do you want a wood tub or an acrylic shell? Talk to friends who own one or the other; visit a showroom to see the choices.

Think, too, about the number of people who will be soaking at one time. Do you plan to use the spa socially, or will it be a more private experience? The answer will guide you to the right shell size, seating arrangement, and equipment.

Which is best for you, an indoor or outdoor site? Obviously, for cli-

mate and privacy reasons, you may want an indoor spa; if so, you'll have to be prepared to deal with the resulting high humidity and the weight of a filled spa. Many homeowners have an extension built specifically to accommodate their new hot water addition.

For an outdoor spa, consider how close you want it to your house and where you will place the support equipment. Also, be sure to take into account sun and wind patterns, as explained in the chapter on planning, beginning on page 18. If you expect to do a lot of enter-

---

TIPS FOR FINDING RELIABLE PRODUCTS

The only way you can be assured of choosing quality products is to find out all you can about them first. Simply by asking thoughtful questions and listening carefully to the answers, you can often tell whether or not a dealer feels confident about a product's reliability. This is also a good opportunity to ask dealers about the services they offer, as well as specific questions about delivery, installation, and warranties. Here are some questions to get you started:

1. What kind of warranty comes with the shell and the support equipment? Ask if the dealer will back up the manufacturer's promises with a written warranty, so you'll still be covered if the manufacturer goes out of business. Ask what would void the warranty, and what's not included.

2. Does the spa carry the seal of the International Association of Plumbing and Mechanical Officials (IAPMO)? Does support equipment carry the Underwriters Laboratories (UL) listing? Is it listed with NSF International?

3. Does the dealer charge for delivery? Get a written agreement on how and where the spa will be delivered.

4. Will the dealer provide written directions and all chemicals needed for good maintenance? What services are available in the future?

5. If the spa is acrylic, how thick are the sheets used in its manufacture? A 1/8-inch thickness is the industry standard. Inspect an acrylic spa carefully for fractures, chips, or delaminated spots before you buy it.

6. If you're buying a portable spa, how thick is the wood that makes up the skirt? Look for quality of wood, hardware, and craftsmanship.

7. For a portable, how thick is the foam insulation sprayed inside? Some cabinets are completely filled, providing excellent insulation for both the spa and supply pipes, as well as greater structural stability. This insulation results in lower energy costs, but plumbing connections must be tested first, since these will be inaccessible once the foam is applied. To find out about operating costs for various models, ask to see documentation for comparison's sake.

8. What kind of heater is offered? How fast will it raise the water temperature to the desired level?

9. How big is the filter? The size you'll need depends on the size of the spa and its intended use (page 70). Is the filter easy to remove for cleaning?

10. Are the hydrojets adjustable? Are they positioned correctly for your body? Some manufacturers offer a selection of various jet positions and types. How much noise do the hydrojets and blower make when operated together?

Warranty Protection

Choosing a reputable dealer is the first step in ensuring that you'll get years of satisfaction from your spa. Your real protection, however, comes from the warranties supplied by manufacturers. Ask to see these warranties before you actually buy the product. Read them carefully and discuss them with your dealer. You should also talk about your responsibility in keeping the warranty in force. No spa or hot tub can be expected to perform trouble-free if it's abused or if proper maintenance is neglected. Most spa manufacturers warranty different parts of their spas for different periods of time.

Spa surfaces: In the past few years, most manufacturers of acrylic spas have reduced the number of years on their warranties from as many as 10 to as few as one or two. Look for the longest warranty you can find.

Remember, however, that a warranty is only good if the manufacturer is still in business to honor it. It's a good idea to speak with your dealer about the financial stability of the manufacturer and how quickly and effectively the manufacturer has responded to claims in the past.

An important point to look at with any warranty is whether the claims will be satisfied in the field or whether the product must be shipped back to the manufacturer. Another is the question of who performs the warranty service—the dealer or a factory representative? Repairing shells can be tricky and not all dealers have the capability.

It's also worth discussing with your dealer whether the manufacturer you're considering will replace the spa shell if you have a serious complaint. Obviously, no manufac-

turer will replace your spa for a minor problem such as a small blister that shows up in a few years. A large blister, however, will encourage delamination, which would require replacement of the spa.

Structural elements: Most manufacturers offer warranties of at least five years. This warranty does not cover problems with in-ground spas that shift or settle; that's part of the contract warranty you have with the person who installed your spa.

Equipment: Look for a minimum one-year warranty on equipment (pumps, filters, heaters, blowers, and controls). Be sure that this period covers both parts and labor (some manufacturers only offer 90 days on labor). Also confirm before you buy that you won't have to disconnect and send in the defective equipment to get warranty service.

---

taining, you'll probably also want to consider decking, lighting, and landscaping around the spa or tub.

Finding a dealer: To locate dealers, ask friends for recommendations, look in the Yellow Pages under "Hot Tubs" or "Spas," or turn to the reference section on page 189; contacting one of the associations listed should help you with your search. Some dealers just sell spas and tubs and their support equipment. A full-service dealer, on the other hand, actually sells and installs the equipment, and designs and sets up the

surrounding landscape. A dealer can also obtain all necessary permits required for the installation.

Keep the following points in mind:
• Spas and tubs should be the dealer's main business, not just a sideline. A full-time dealer is most likely to be knowledgeable, as well as reliable for your future service needs.
• Find out how long the dealer has been in the spa or tub business under the same name, and at the same location.
• Be sure that the dealer's products—spa shells, tubs, support

equipment, and other accessories—come from established manufacturers with proven reputations.
• Check with the Better Bus-iness Bureau in your area to find out if any complaints have been registered against the dealer.
• Ask the dealer for at least two references of previous clients, so you can see their installations and hear about their experience.
• Find out if the dealer belongs to the National Spa and Pool Institute, which establishes industry standards of quality.

Pool and Spa
EQUIPMENT

*For enjoyable swimming or soaking, you'll want a pool
filled with comfortably warm, clear water that's free from
harmful bacteria and other microorganisms and has the
correct chemical balance. That's the job of the support system:
to heat, filter, and circulate the water to achieve the warmth
and clarity you expect. In addition to the standard equipment
of pump, filter, and heater, you'll want a selection of accessories
to help clean the pool, conserve energy, and optimize your
enjoyment of your new facility. The following chapter will
provide you with all the information you'll need to outfit your
pool or spa and keep it running smoothly, providing
many years of pleasurable use.*

The Pool or Spa Support System

The support system circulates and filters the water in your pool or spa. It enables you to use the initial water supply over and over again, adding just the little bit necessary to backwash the filter, vacuum, and compensate for evaporation, splash-out, drag-off, and leaks.

Depending on what type of pool or spa you have, the circulation system is composed of many of these elements: a filter, a pump and motor,

main drains (ideally with antivortex features that prevent suction from trapping hair or limbs), hair and lint strainers, perimeter overflow system (gutters or skimmers), heater, chemical injection system and controller, flow meter, pressure and vacuum gauge, and possibly a surge chamber, a separation tank, or a neutralization tank.

The pump circulates the water through the filtration system, sani-

tizing the water and, if it is heated, distributing heated water.

All elements should be of high quality corrosion-resistant materials. Piping and fittings can be of copper or stainless steel pipe, but most pool builders use PVC or CPVC. Low cost, resistance to rust, good flow characteristics, flexibility, and ease of installation make plastic pipe practical for most pool uses. (Check codes in your area before building.)

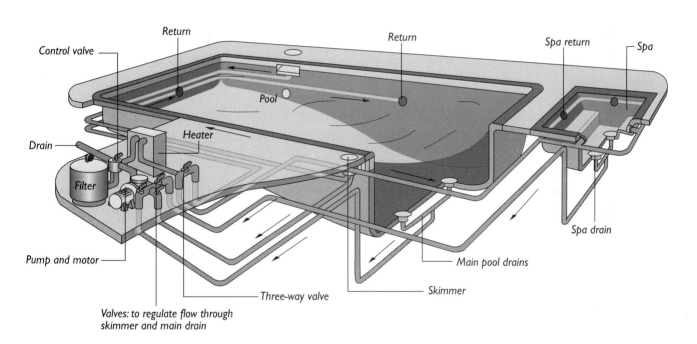

Control valve
Return
Return
Spa return
Spa
Pool
Drain
Heater
Filter
Pump and motor
Three-way valve
Valves: to regulate flow through skimmer and main drain
Skimmer
Main pool drains
Spa drain

A TYPICAL SUPPORT SYSTEM

In a pressurized support system, found on most residential pools, water is drawn from the pool through the main drains, surface skimmers, or gutters; passes through suction lines to pump, filter, and heater; and then returns to the pool via return lines. Main drains—there should be at least two, made of precast concrete, metal, or plastic—are covered with a grate or designed with an antivortex feature to reduce risk of suction entrapment. They act as collecting points for debris and allow for draining. Suction and return lines must be of adequate size. Their number and location will depend on the pool's

size and shape. Swivel fittings at the ends of the return lines allow the direction of the water coming into the pool to be adjusted, aiding filtration and ensuring a thorough mixing of the chemicals.

Some automatic pool cleaners require piping built into the pool wall or installed while the pool is being built. Decide what cleaner you will use before you build your pool or spa. If you've decided on a spa as part of your residential pool, you can use the pool support system for the spa. The drawing above shows how a spa can be integrated into the system.

Choosing the Right Filter

For residential pools and spas there are three common types of filters: high-rate sand, pressure diatomaceous earth (D.E.), and cartridge. Local code requirements will often determine the filter for your pool. If codes don't play a role, then local preferences probably will. Because of marketing, cost, and other factors, certain types of filter are more popular in certain regions, while others may not even be available. When used properly, all three types will provide effective filtration. Speaking to a pool consultant and pool-owning neighbors will help you make your final choice.

Regardless of which type you select, follow these general guidelines. Locate the filter tanks in an easily accessible position for servicing, maintenance, inspection, and air circulation. Level the unit, using metal shims if necessary, and anchor the filter to the floor. Install air relief valves on all pressure filter tanks. Finally, fit metal filter tanks with sacrificial zinc or magnesium anodes to prevent against damage from electrolysis and galvanic corrosion.

HIGH-RATE SAND FILTERS

Of the three most common styles of sand filter—including rapid sand and vacuum sand—high-rate filters are the most popular option by far. These filters are pressure vessels of fiberglass, stainless steel, or plastic with a system of drains and water distribution that maintains a nonturbulent flow through the filtering media. The media consists of special grades of sand, which should last for several years. Your filter supplier will recommend the proper sand for your unit.

The high-rate filter is based on the concept that high flow rates and pressures drive dirt particles into the sand bed, making maximum use of the filtering media.

On the down side, up to several hundred gallons of water may be used during the backwash of these filters, and must be disposed in a sanitary sewer. Check local codes to see that they permit use of a sand filter. Then check with your state or regional U.S. EPA office for more information. See page 148 for maintenance guidelines for this filter.

Sand filters are a popular option because they work effectively and are relatively inexpensive to buy and operate. And they can be easy to install. Many manufacturers supply a complete filter, pump, and motor system pre-assembled and ready to connect to the recirculating piping and electrical supply.

TYPICAL FILTER SYSTEM

The filtration system is crucial to the healthy functioning of your pool. The type of filter you select is largely up to you. Its size will be determined by various factors *(see page 70)*. A typical filter arrangement is shown at right.

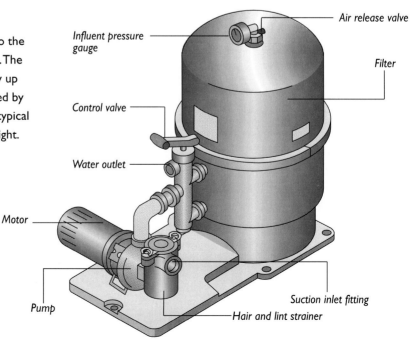

Influent pressure gauge

Air release valve

Filter

Control valve

Water outlet

Motor

Pump

Hair and lint strainer

Suction inlet fitting

POOL AND SPA FILTERS

The three different types of filters vary from model to model but they all share the main features shown in the illustrations below.

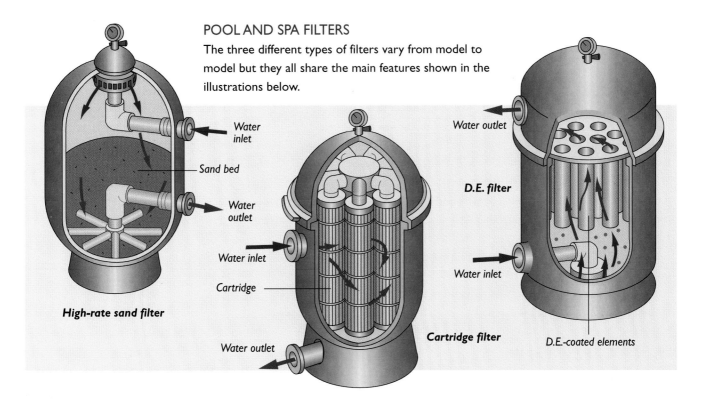

High-rate sand filter
- Water inlet
- Sand bed
- Water outlet

Cartridge filter
- Water inlet
- Cartridge
- Water outlet

D.E. filter
- Water outlet
- Water inlet
- D.E.-coated elements

PRESSURE DIATOMACEOUS EARTH (D.E.) FILTERS

D.E. filters offer a couple of key advantages over the high-rate sand variety: they are more compact and they filter out smaller particles. They are currently the most popular variety of filter in California.

The D.E. filter strains water through diatomaceous earth, a sedimentary rock composed of microscopic fossil skeletons of the diatom, a small water plant. The skeletons have a porous structure of silica, which makes them inert to most chemical action. The diatomaceous earth is mined and then crushed, washed, refined, sized, and packed as a white, chalky powder. The coarser sizes are more adaptable to pool filtration; the manufacturer will recommend the best size for your filter.

Disposing of the used D.E. after backwashing can be a problem if the use of sewers and storm drains is prohibited, as the D.E. will clog dry wells. Many D.E. filter systems come with separation tanks that hold some of the backwash water while the D.E. settles into a cloth filter. Then the water is returned to the pool and the D.E. is discarded according to local regulations. See page 150 for information on maintaining and cleaning these filters.

Cellulose fiber was introduced in 1992 as a substitute for diatomaceous earth. It can also be used as a filter aid for cartridge or sand filters, increasing their effectiveness against smaller particles.

CARTRIDGE FILTERS

Cartridge filters are rapidly becoming popular. They are safe, effective, and demand no complicated backwashing or disposal. Unfortunately, the cartridges need replacing from time to time and their cost is relatively high. A cartridge's life span is determined by the pool's use and environment. The more dirt that gets into your pool, the more often the cartridges will need replacing.

You'll need an extra set of cartridges for starting up a plaster-finished pool. The residual plaster can be removed from the cartridges only by an acid wash. Most people find it more convenient to throw them out and install new ones.

The major drawback of cartridge filters is that they are relatively difficult to clean, and will lose 25-35 percent of their effectiveness with each cleaning. They are more effective than sand filters at removing smaller particles, however.

CALCULATING FILTRATION SYSTEM SIZE

For effective filtration it is crucial that you install the correct size of filter. Filters are tested by the National Sanitation Foundation International to determine their filter design flow rate: the number of gallons of pool or spa water per minute the filter can handle per square foot of filter media (gpm/ft.^{2}). This number should be marked on the filter and on the manufacturer's instructions supplied with it. This number can also be found in NSF International's listing booklet, published four times a year. For NSF International's contact information, see page 189. Filter design rates vary between filter types. Generally, their ranges are: Cartridge: .375-1.0 gpm/ft.^{2}; High-rate sand: 12-20 gpm/ft.^{2}; D.E.: 1.5-2.5 gpm/ft.^{2}.

Given this rating, the calculations required to determine the correct-sized filter for your pool or spa are relatively easy to make. The first thing you will need to know is the volume of your pool or spa in gallons. Next, you have to calculate your system's turnover time in minutes. Turnover time is the time it takes your pump to pass the equivalent of all the water in the pool through the circulation system. This should fall some-where between 0.5 and 6 hours, or 30 to 360 minutes. Once you have these numbers, and the design flow rate of a prospective filter, you can use the formula shown below to calculate the flow rate of your pool and then determine the required surface area of filter media required to handle the chores of your pool. Filter surface area is easy to calculate. A cartridge filter, for example, with six cartridges that are 5 sq. ft. each has a surface area of 30 sq. ft. Here are the equations to help you make the calculation:

Pool volume_____ gal. ÷ Pool turnover time _____ min. = _____gpm (gallons per minute) pool flow rate

Pool flow rate_____ gpm ÷ Filter flow rate_____ gpm/sq. ft. (gallons per minute per square foot) = _____ sq. ft. (This is the required surface area of filter media to handle your pool.)

To upsize:

Required filter surface area_____ sq. ft. x 1.25 = _____ sq. ft. (This is the amount of surface area your filter should have to handle at your flow rate.)

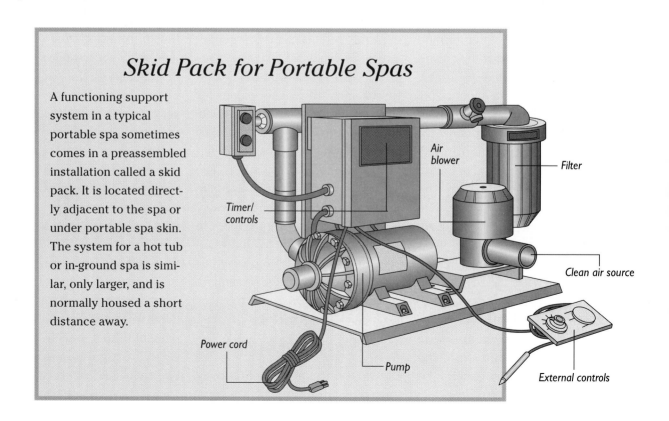

Skid Pack for Portable Spas

A functioning support system in a typical portable spa sometimes comes in a preassembled installation called a skid pack. It is located directly adjacent to the spa or under portable spa skin. The system for a hot tub or in-ground spa is similar, only larger, and is normally housed a short distance away.

Timer/controls

Power cord

Pump

Air blower

Filter

Clean air source

External controls

The structure that supports the above-ground pool shown above serves double duty, providing a deck around the pool while also sheltering the support system (*left*) stored underneath it.

The Pump and Motor

The combination of pump and motor draws water from the pool or spa, forces it through the filter and heater, and returns it to the pool or spa.

Pumps for residential pools and spas are almost always located on the intake side of the filter system so that they draw water from the pool and push it through the filter, heater, and other elements. These pumps have a hair and lint filter on the intake side of the pump to catch large particles of foreign matter before they enter and clog the pump impeller.

Most newer pool pumps are self-priming: They expel all the air from the system when they start running and thus maintain a suction. Running a pump that has lost its prime will cause the motor to overheat and damage the pump. When choosing a pump and motor,

you'll want to consider the energy-saving models. One way to compare the electrical efficiency of pumps is to compare the ratio of gallons pumped to kilowatt hours used. Just divide the gallons of water pumped in 1 hour by the pump rating in kilowatts. If the pump is rated in horsepower, convert the horsepower rating to kilowatts by multiplying it by 0.746. The higher the resulting number, the more efficient the pump. When selecting a pump, you should choose a well-established, reliable manufacturer.

Another indication of quality is the length and terms of guarantees; be suspicious of any short-term warranties. A UL listing—a listing with or recognition by the private Underwriters Laboratories—is an important indication of safety. Equipment that receives

such a listing has to pass high standards of testing.

Beware of claims emphasizing the horsepower of the pump; this is actually an incidental consideration if you expect to obtain the maximum operational economy.

To determine the best pump size for a particular system, a consultant or an engineer will perform an overall evaluation of your needs, a relatively complex task involving the following steps:
• Determine the total number of gallons in the pool (see page 76).
• Select the proper turnover rate for the pool.
• Calculate pipe sizes and layout for minimal friction losses.
• Select a pump that meets the calculated requirements. For this, the pump's performance curve, which indicates the number of gallons per minute it can pump, is used.

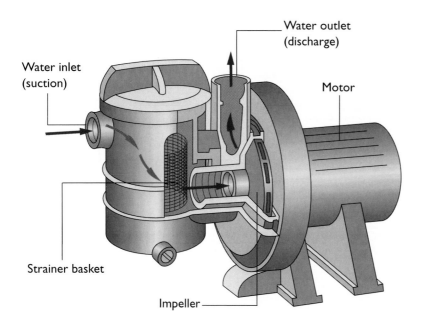

Water inlet (suction)

Water outlet (discharge)

Motor

Strainer basket

Impeller

TYPICAL PUMP AND MOTOR
Pumps are usually made of bronze or plastic and consist of an impeller (a bladed wheel) mounted on a motor-driven shaft. Because of its rotational pumping action, this type of pump is known as a centrifugal pump.

You'll want to situate your pool support equipment so that it is easily accessible, but not in such clear view that it is an eyesore. One option is to locate it behind a hedge or a row of trees as shown at right.

• Choose a filter model that will accept the number of gallons per minute that the selected pump will deliver. (The manufacturer will provide guidelines for the filter media selected.)

• Choose electrical wiring and circuit breaker sizes recommended in the pump installation manual.

• Consider the use of time clocks that precisely control the periods that pump and heater are on.

When choosing a pump, consider its pumping capacity relative to your pool or spa size, the pump's operating costs, and maintenance needs. To avoid corrosion, as many parts as possible should be made of materials that are corrosion-resistant. The motor should be water-resistant, and electrically isolated and insulated.

Installing the pump requires some care. It should be at or slightly above water level and as close to the pool or spa as possible. If it's located any distance from the pool or spa, the piping diameter must be increased to compensate for the extra pumping.

For spas, two-speed pumps have gained popularity as an energy-saving measure. For example, many portable spas use a ³/₄ hp pump that runs at two speeds. The higher speed is required to acti-vate the hydrojets, which operate only while the spa is in use. The lower speed handles water circulation through the heater and filter; it operates at significantly lower cost, keeping the water at the desired temperature, as well as sparkling clear.

Larger in-ground spas often need a pump of much great horsepower (up to 10) to handle the larger amount of water and to operate additional jets. For spas with more than four jets, a two-pump system provides the best service. The smaller pump handles regular circulation while the large one powers the hydrojets.

The Surface Skimmer

In many pool circulating systems, at least two surface skimmers connected to the pump intake pull dirt, oils, lotions, floating algae, and leaves into the filtration system. Most skimmers are built into the pool, though units that hang on the side of the pool are also available for portable or in-ground pools built without skimmers. Pools without skimmers are typically equipped with gutters extending completely around the pool. These function by handling a continuous overflow of water from the pool and collecting debris on gutter drains or grates. There are several types of gutters, both traditional and prefabricated, on the market today. They should be designed and installed according to local codes.

Built-in skimmers are also available in several varieties. Most are designed with a skimmer basket to remove large debris. You can also purchase a unit with a built-in filter cartridge, or a sensing device that automatically replaces lost water. A vacuum or suction connection may be part of the skimmer, for use when vacuuming.

A typical surface skimmer is made of precast concrete or plastic and consists of a tank with a projecting throat on its upper side. A self-adjusting floating weir performs the skimming action by regulating the amount of water that enters the skimmer. Because it adjusts to allow only a thin sheet of water to spill over, velocity—not volume—is the key to good skimming. It must have an equalizer line—a pipe that extends from the bottom of the skimmer 12 to 18 inches through the pool wall into the water—to prevent air from being sucked into the system when the water level is down.

Skimmers are most effective when located on the down-wind side of the pool; the wind helps push debris toward the opening.

Skimmers are also becoming standard on spas. Many skimmers on portable spas are combined with top-loading filters, allowing the filters to be pulled when it comes time for cleaning.

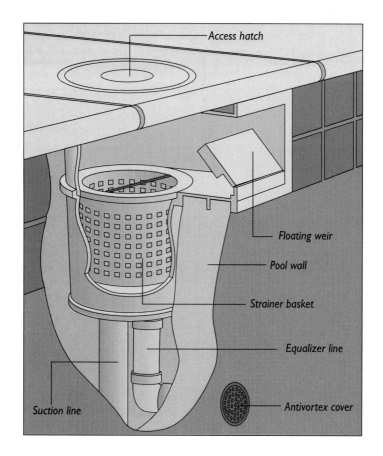

Access hatch

Floating weir

Pool wall

Strainer basket

Equalizer line

Suction line

Antivortex cover

SURFACE SKIMMER

The majority of residential outdoor pools have skimmers. For best collection of debris, there should be at least one skimmer for every 500 square feet of pool surface.

Heating your Pool or Spa

If you own a spa, you will want a heater. Over the years, people have tried everything from solar energy to chopped wood to attain the high temperatures (up to 104°F/40°C) needed for a good soak, but in the end, the vast majority of spa owners opt for a gas or electric heater. No matter what you choose, rely on your dealer to determine the correct size heater for your spa, based on the number of people who will use it regularly and how often and how long they'll be soaking.

Is it worth the considerable additional expense to heat the larger area of a pool? After weighing all the pros and cons, you will probably find that it is.

Most pools are heated to between 78°F/26°C and 98.6°F/37°C. The temperature you choose depends on the activities you do, your age, the cost of heating, and your own personal preference.

In general, the water temperature in an unheated pool is usually the average of the daytime high temperature and the nighttime low temperature. Unless you live in a very warm climate, you won't often have the chance to enjoy 80°F/27°C water. A heater will allow you to swim comfortably in early morning or late evening, and extend the swimming season.

To help you decide whether or not to heat your pool, first figure

POOL AND SPA HEATERS
The two main types of heaters for pools and spas are gas —divided into convection, tank, and coil—and electric. Shown below are some common varieties.

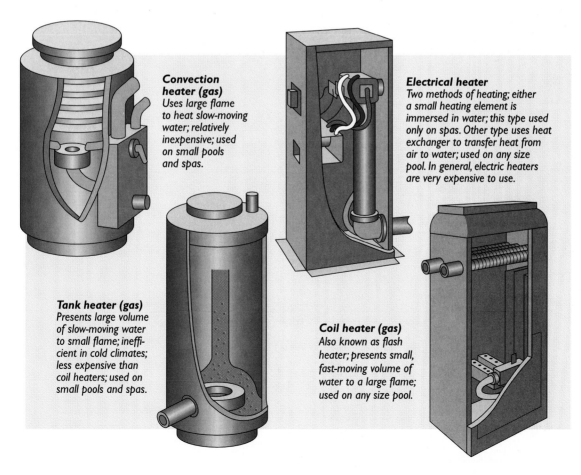

Convection heater (gas)
Uses large flame to heat slow-moving water; relatively inexpensive; used on small pools and spas.

Tank heater (gas)
Presents large volume of slow-moving water to small flame; inefficient in cold climates; less expensive than coil heaters; used on small pools and spas.

Coil heater (gas)
Also known as flash heater; presents small, fast-moving volume of water to a large flame; used on any size pool.

Electrical heater
Two methods of heating; either a small heating element is immersed in water; this type used only on spas. Other type uses heat exchanger to transfer heat from air to water; used on any size pool. In general, electric heaters are very expensive to use.

the number of weeks or months you can extend your swimming season by doing so. Then calculate the added expenses of a heater—equipment cost and installation, annual maintenance, and fuel costs—and ask yourself if the added investment is worth it.

You can heat your pool with a gas, electric, or oil heater, or you can let the sun do it for you *(see page 79)*. In many regions though, solar heating may not be practical, or you may have to supplement it with a traditional fuel.

In most areas of the country, gas is by far the cheapest heating fuel for pools and spas. For this reason, most pool heaters are gas fired. Manufacturers have developed many high-efficiency models, thanks to a variety of advances in the design of the heat exchanger (through which the pool water passes) and the combustion chamber, electronic pilots, narrow range thermostats, and other features.

In addition to cost factors, a gas heater is superior to even a 220-volt electric heater for the quickest

Calculating Pool Volume

Selecting pool equipment and water treatment chemicals depends upon a working knowledge of your pool's capacity in gallons. To find a pool's approximate volume, first calculate its area, which corresponds to the length times the width, then multiply the area by the average depth and a conversion factor (7.48). The trick is finding the "length and width" of a pool with an irregular shape. If you can't find a shape below that approximates your pool, divide the outline into units of simpler shapes, figure the volume of each chunk, and then add them together for the total.

Area: square feet of surface
Volume: gallons of water

Area = A x B x 3.14
Volume = *area x average depth x 7.48*

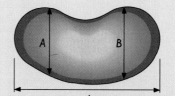

Area = (A + B) x L x 0.45 (approx.)
Volume = *area x average depth x 7.48*

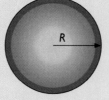

Area = R x R x 3.14
Volume = *area x average depth x 7.48*

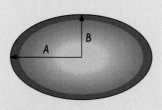

Area = (L x W) + (R x R x 3.14)
Volume = *area x average depth x 7.48*

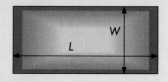

Area = L x W
Volume = *area x average depth x 7.48*

recovery—the time it takes for the water in a pool or spa to heat up—since gas heaters are traditionally much larger than their electric counterparts. For areas where gas is unavailable, propane can be used instead. Be advised, however, that for safety reasons, every gas heater must be properly vented and approved by the American Gas Association.

Electric heaters that have electric heating elements immersed in water work slowly, so they're practical only for spas.

Another heater type that is gaining in popularity is the heat pump. These units operate on the same principle as air conditioners, using refrigerant, heat exchangers, and a compressor to transfer heat from the air to the pool water.

While the up-front cost of these units is high, the payback comes with their efficiency. Whether a heat pump will be economical to operate or not depends on the climate in your area. Because the system employs the outside air to warm the pool water, heat pumps are best suited to warmer climates, or at least to warm seasons in colder climates.

WHAT SIZE HEATER?

Gas heater sizes are indicated in British Thermal Units (Btu). A Btu is the amount of heat required to raise the temperature of one pound of water one degree Fahrenheit. Electric heaters are rated in kilowatts input, one kilowatt equaling 3,412 Btu. Like air conditioners, heat pumps are rated in tons. One ton is roughly equal to 15,000 Btu.

The Btu or other heating units needed to heat your pool depend largely upon whether you intend the heater to provide temperature maintenance—keeping the pool at one temperature 24 hours a day—or intermittent heat—warming the pool water only when you plan to use the pool.

Calculating the correct size for a heater supplying intermittent heating is extremely difficult. It requires the use of a complex formula for heating a volume of water, and will involve taking into account many variables, including climate considerations, relative humidity, and how fast you want the water to reach the desired temperature. Most heater manufacturers supply charts that will help you size your unit correctly.

Calculating heater size for temperature maintenance is easier and can be performed by the pool owner. The formula is

this: Pool surface area x 15 (the number of Btu needed to raise one square foot of pool surface water by one degree) x Desired temperature rise = Btu required to maintain desired temperature. The heater you buy may need to be larger to compensate for inefficiencies. A heater with 80 percent efficiency for example should have a Btu output 20 percent higher than needed. Using this formula, an owner who wanted his 648 square foot pool (18 x 36) to be kept at 85 degrees, where the average outside temperature is 65 degrees would need a heater output of 194,400 Btu. A heater which was 80 percent efficient, would need to be rated at 233,280 Btu to provide the needed heating.

In general, avoid simply buying what your contractor suggests without further investigating your options. In areas where competition is strong among pool builders, you can end up with a heater that's too small because a builder anxious to close a sale can make a bid more competitive by selecting a marginally sized heater. For either type of heating, always consult with a professional to make the final decision—mistakes, at least fixing them, can be costly.

TIPS FOR SAVING ENERGY

As energy costs skyrocket, keeping your pool maintenance and operating expenses within your budget will become more and more challenging. Here are some ideas to help you reduce the costs of heating, filtering, cleaning, and treating your pool water.

Heating the Pool

• Use a pool cover or blanket, the single best water and fuel conservation device, and have it in place when the pool is not in use. The same can be said of spas and spa covers. The cover will reduce heating bills by preventing heat loss, save on chemicals, and reduce water evaporation. A solar cover allows the pool to collect heat from the sun.

• Set the heater's thermostat according to the activities that will take place in the pool. If it is to be used for swimming or fitness, 83° to 86°F is fine; seniors and young children will be comfortable in water that's 86° to 88°. For a spa, the temperature should never exceed 104°F. Remember that an increase of 1°F will raise your use of natural gas by about 10 percent.

• Use an accurate thermometer to measure pool or spa water temperature. When it reaches the desired level, mark the proper setting on the thermostat and allow no further adjustments. If your pool is not used at all during the week, you can reduce the thermostat setting 8 to 10 degrees during the week, moving it back to its proper setting for the weekend.

• During extended periods when the pool or spa is not in use, shut off the heater and pilot light. (This will only apply to older heaters; most newer heaters have electronic ignition systems.)

• Shelter the pool or spa from the wind with wind breaks—shrubs and other plantings, fences, or outdoor structures.

• Follow a program of regular preventive maintenance for your pool or spa heater (see page 151).

Filtering the Pool

• For maximum efficiency, follow a program of regular preventive maintenance for the pump and filter (see page 148). Remove foreign material regularly from the strainer baskets in the pump and skimmer.

• When the pool is in heavy use, turn on the filter manually. Return it to automatic operation only after all the swimmers have left the pool.

Cleaning the Pool

• If you have an automatic pool cleaner with its own pump, operate it for 3 to 4 hours a day during the swimming season but only 2 to 3 hours a day during the off-season. If this isn't enough to keep the pool clean, or if there is an abnormal amount of dirt or debris entering the pool, increase the cleaning time in half-hour increments until adequate cleaning is accomplished.

• Use your leaf skimmer and wall brush regularly and frequently.

Saving Pool Water

• Turn off the tile spray device on your automatic pool cleaner—much of the water evaporates before it even hits the tile, and scale formation will be reduced.

• Prevent water loss as a result of surge by plugging in the overflow line when the pool is in use.

Conserving Pool Chemicals

• Keep pool or spa water chemistry in balance and check it regularly. Maintain pool and spa water pH between 7.2 and 7.8.

• Maintain a maximum of 20 ppm of cyanuric acid (outdoor pools only) to reduce sanitizer consumption. (For more information on water chemistry, turn to page 128.)

• Trim back excess foliage around the pool and keep the deck areas clean to reduce chemical cleaning and filtering needs.

Solar Heating

For several reasons, solar heating and swimming pools are an exceedingly compatible combination. First, the cost of conventional heat is so high (simply because the pool loses so much heat from its broad, exposed surface every night and every cloudy day) that it makes solar costs look very inviting.

Second, the swimming season corresponds to the months of high, hot sun and long days, when plenty of solar heat is available.

And finally, because pools don't need large amounts of high-intensity heat, and because they act as their own heat-transfer liquid and heat storage, heating a pool requires only a few pieces of equipment.

Pools can be heated by the sun and the heat retained in several different ways—by positioning the pool to take the best advantage of the sun, by protecting the pool from wind, by enclosing or covering it, and by using a solar heating system.

Locating the pool where it can receive the maximum sunlight possible is the first step in solar heating your pool. If your pool is properly placed, the sun will heat the water directly; then, if you want, you can increase the heating effect by using a solar blanket, or by embedding water-heating coils in the deck.

WIND: THE HEAT THIEF

While the sun and a heater are pumping heat into your pool, the wind sets up convection currents that steal that same heat. Every square foot of the pool's surface gives up heat to the wind by evaporation, and the stronger the wind, the greater the heat loss. Evaporation alone accounts for 60 percent of the heat loss. Another 30 percent of the loss radiates into the air from the water surface and 10 percent goes into the ground. ➤

POOL COVERS

Depending on material and design, a cover prevents heat loss by evaporation and radiation; allows the pool to collect heat from the sun; helps keep the pool free of debris; and, with safety covers, prevents children or animals from falling into the pool.

Covers must be removed completely when the pool is in use. A child or even an adult surfacing under a cover may not be able to lift it sufficiently to get air.

Pool covers come in a variety of styles, from rigid to flexible. They are lifted mechanically or moved manually. Still others come in sections that float on the pool. For the most part, they are made from various forms of plastic, corrugated fiberglass and foam.

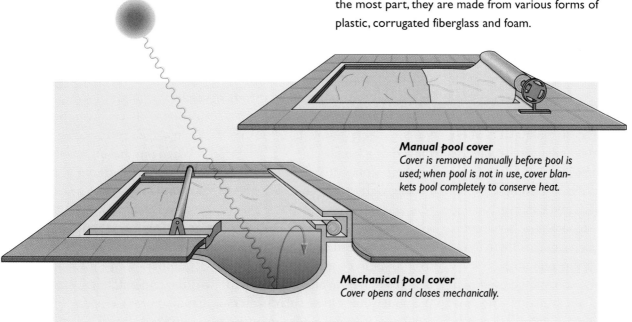

Manual pool cover
Cover is removed manually before pool is used; when pool is not in use, cover blankets pool completely to conserve heat.

Mechanical pool cover
Cover opens and closes mechanically.

South-facing solar panels are mounted on this home's roof, next to the pool's equipment enclosure. Thanks to the flexibility of solar systems, the sun-gathering panels need not face directly south and can be mounted on fences, shade structures, garage roofs, and slopes or hillsides.
Design: Sherwood Stockwell

To minimize the wind's effects, you can locate the pool where it's protected from the wind, erect screens or fences and enclose or cover the pool.

POOL ENCLOSURES

Though most pools can be used all winter, even in the snow, some pool owners use pool enclosures to control the environment. They incur the added costs of maintaining what is essentially an indoor pool. Air quality must be maintained, and a dehumidifier must be installed to control humidity.

You can either purchase one of the manufactured canopies, extend your house to include a "pool room," or improvise an enclosure to fit the pool and its surroundings.

A variety of manufactured pool enclosures are available. The most economical are air-inflated canopies;

one type even doubles as a pool cover when deflated. Some local laws regulate the use of pool enclosures. Be sure to check building codes before installing one.

SOLAR HEATERS

Put simply, solar heaters transfer the heat of the sun to the water in your pool. A properly installed unit will, in the long run, save you money off the cost of running a traditional heater by itself, although a gas or electric unit is often employed as a backup.

Most solar heaters work by cycling water through solar collectors and back into the pool. These are called open loop systems. They employ unglazed collectors—made from plastic or metal—to absorb heat from the sun and transfer it to the pool water. Other solar heaters employ glazed collectors (covered

in glass). These collectors contain an antifreeze fluid. As the fluid is heated, it is sent to coils inside a heat exchanger, which then transfers the heat to the pool water. These are called closed loop systems. A newer type of collector is made from Lexan with polycarbonate refractors. These are the most efficient units currently available.

Collectors can be installed in a variety of locations (see above). Heating coils can even be embedded in a deck surrounding the pool.

When purchasing a solar heater, deal with a company that has its own service staff. The major manufacturers train their distributors in the design, installation, and servicing of their systems.

Compare warranties and have a written understanding of where the manufacturer's responsibility ends and the contractor's begins.

The Power behind your Spa

Powered by the pump, hydrojets provide the true massage action of a spa or hot tub. In the hydrojet, a high-pressured stream of water is mixed with air, then propelled into the spa or tub water, causing it to swirl and bubble. Each hydrojet transmits a torrent of 12 to 15 gallons of water per minute.

The number of jets and sophistication of design vary from one manufacturer to another. If you're buying a hot tub and want it jetted, you can place jets almost anywhere. Given this flexibility, it makes sense to sit in the tub before it's fitted with jets so you can have them placed according to your height and preferences. Acrylic, or prefab spas, offer less choice, but the better ones do allow you to determine the spot for the jet within a larger reinforced panel.

One of the best spas can even be equipped with a hydrojet that moves up and down, creating a rippling massage, rather than focusing on just one area of the body.

Air intake in a hydrojet can be regulated by opening or closing the ports near the rim of the spa or tub. The best hydrojets are replaceable, adjustable for angle, and can be closed off completely (the spa may be fitted with four, but you may prefer to use only one, for example).

Just as some people like a gentle massage, others want a stronger one. Several manufacturers offer the option of diverting four regular hydrojets into one super, side-directed jet that spews out water at a rate of 90 gallons per minute. This transforms the spa into a version of the whirlpool bath—a form of therapy well known to athletes.

AIR BLOWERS

Some spas are equipped with a small electric motor and fan—called an air blower—that provides a gushing, tingling flow of bubbles up through the water. Air is sucked in from outside the spa, then expelled through holes or jets in the bottom of the vessel.

With proper sizing and installation, an air blower should give years of bubbling, although some maintenance is required.

One serious drawback of blowers is that most use ambient air. If air temperature is cool, a blower can put a strain on your heater—or quickly turn the water tepid. If the air is contaminated, it can cause poor water quality.

Another disadvantage of blowers is that they are usually quite noisy. Unlike a pump that works at around 3,400 rpm, a blower impeller turns at about 18,000 rpm—a speed that produces a loud, irritating whine and also some vibration.

Better-engineered blowers are quieter, but they can still be a mood-breaker when housed in hollow portables. With in-ground installations, you can place the blower and other support equipment far enough from the spa to prevent any bothersome noise. Don't forget to consider your neighbors, too, when you're planning for a blower.

SPA HYDROJET
Traditional hydrojets mix air and water to produce the massage effect in the spa. Modern models often feature several types of massaging action, with pulsating and rotating patterns.

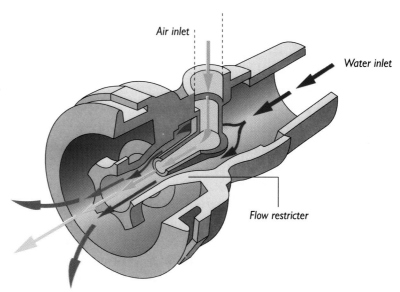

Air inlet

Water inlet

Flow restricter

SPA CONTROLS

All spas are fitted with controls to operate the support equipment. Some controls only function manually; most spas, however, have some type of automatic controls as well.

Manual controls—to engage the pump (either for circulation or to power the hydrojets), to start up the blower, or to turn on the underwater light—are typically mounted on the rim of the spa or on the edge of the surrounding deck. These controls are either air switches (the action of depressing the button sends a column of air down a thin plastic tube to activate the switch) or touch-activated electronic switches.

Most spas are also equipped with some automatic controls. The simplest automatic device is a thermostatically controlled heater. Most 110-volt portables are controlled by a thermostat: Water circulates through the filter and is heated whenever the temperature falls below the preset level. This typically keeps the water circulating for about 2 hours a day—sufficient for spas that are used a few times a week or less by just a few people and remain covered between uses.

Gas-heated spas and 220-volt portables are usually equipped with a time clock to control filtration periods, since the time it takes to heat the water is so much less than in 110-volt units. With a time clock, the heater cycles on and off in response to the thermostat within these filtration periods.

By setting the clock to cycle on about 30 minutes or an hour before the time you typically use the spa

Today's sophisticated spas include remote control units to adjust the heat and force of the hydrojets to your taste
Design: Pacific Water Works and Rob Newman

each day, you can help ensure the water is hot enough for use.

A new addition that has become increasingly popular is a dual time clock. The first clock has a 24-hour duration and is typically set to circulate the water at four different times. (Try to schedule one to follow your last soak of the day.) The second clock has a 7-day duration and controls the heater. The longer time frame on the heater clock allows you to bring the spa up to temperature at one time during the week (after work for example) and at another time on weekends.

Most 110-volt portables aren't equipped with time clocks because of their slow recovery time. But when you're away on vacation, it's possible to connect a clock to the plug-in cord of a portable, which will

assure that the water is circulated several times a day even though the thermostat is turned down.

Controls are becoming more and more sophisticated in keeping with today's electronics revolution. For example, if you have an outdoor spa, you can now install a convenient second control panel inside the house so you don't have to go outside to fire things up. These remote panels often include digital readouts indicating water temperature or water chemistry. Some spas are even wired so they can be operated by a remote controller similar to the one used for a garage door opener.

No matter how sophisticated the controls, all spas have a manual switch that can override your settings to turn the system on and off.

Pool Accessories

Slides, jump boards, and grab rails are a few of the many accessories you can add to your pool to make it more fun and easy to use. Other accessories—support system controls, chemical dispensers and automatic cleaners—reduce the time you spend maintaining your pool. Some can be added to an existing pool but most need to be incorporated into your initial pool design.

RECREATIONAL ACCESSORIES

Jump boards: Because of the danger of injury, traditional diving boards should not be installed on most residential pools. Jump boards are shorter and safer than diving boards. They must be anchored to the deck; in addition, the pool must be adequately long, wide, and deep to accept the jumpers. Check national standards carefully before installing any jump board. See page 189 for contact numbers.

Aluminum is the most common material for jump boards, though you can use wood or fiberglass as well. Be sure the top of the board has a nonslip coating or a nonslip material applied to it.

Slides: Pool slides are extremely popular among youngsters. Slides must be anchored properly to the deck and meet national standards regarding pool size and depth.

Residential slides are typically made from fiberglass with a gelcoat finish and supported on a metal frame. A straight slide 7 feet high will be about 13 feet long and may require a deck width of over 15 feet. The end of the slide should be no more than 2 inches above the water. Faux-rock slides are also becoming popular. Consult a builder specializing in naturalistic pools for more information on these installations.

Ladders and grab rails: Though your pool probably has steps at the shallow end, you'll want an easy way, or even two, to get out of the pool at the deep end. Stainless steel ladders are popular. If you have a concrete pool, build steps into the side of the pool and add a pair of grab rails. A rail near the steps at the shallow end is also convenient.

AUTOMATIC CONTROLS

Automatic controls added to your pool system can take over such

Getting out of a pool in the deep end is a lot easier with the help of a ladder—one of the many accessories that can increase the enjoyment and safety of your pool.

AUTOMATIC POOL CLEANERS

There are two main types of automatic pool cleaners that will save you the trouble of doing the work yourself. Both systems—vacuum and agitator—are shown below.

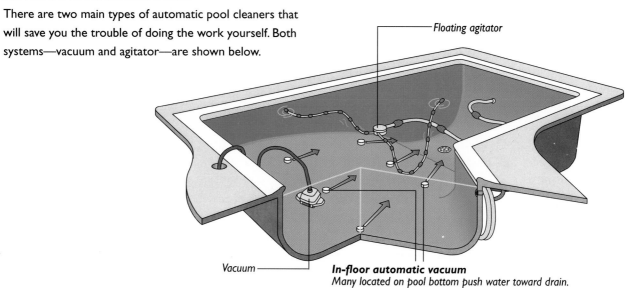

Floating agitator

Vacuum

In-floor automatic vacuum
Many located on pool bottom push water toward drain.

chores as turning the support system on and off, backwashing a filter, and maintaining the chlorine level.

Automatic timer: Basically a 24-hour electric clock with adjustable contacts, a timer turns equipment on and off at preset times. You can use a timer to turn on the heater, the pump for the filtration system, and the pump for an automatic pool cleaner. You can also control the heater with a thermostat to keep the pool water at a certain temperature. Remember, whenever the heater is on, the pump must also be running; after the heater shuts off, keep the pump running long enough to clear all hot water from the pipes.

Backwashing the filter: You can eliminate the chore of backwashing a sand filter by installing an electronic device that monitors the increasing pressure in the system due to dirt; when the pressure differential is high enough to warrant backwashing, the device activates

the necessary valves to do the job.

Dispensing chemicals: Dispensers for chemicals and disinfectants range from a simple floating type containing pellets or sticks to one that makes chlorine and dispenses it automatically. Ask your pool service company for information. Even with a dispenser, you'll need to test your pool water regularly and add chemicals as needed. ORP (oxidation reduction potential) and pH are indicators of water quality (page 130). ORP/pH controllers measure their levels and signal chemical dispensers to make adjustments.

AUTOMATIC POOL CLEANERS

Automatic pool cleaners work by vacuuming dirt off the pool bottom or agitating it so it goes down the main drain. The cleaner's pump may be separate from the filtration system or connected to it.

Vacuum system: Seemingly with a mind of its own, an automatic suc-

tion side vacuum cleaner wanders randomly across the pool bottom and sucks up dirt. The dirt-laden water is then carried through a hose into the filtration system. There are several different types of vacuum systems. Consult a pool vacuum dealer for the best one for your pool.

Pressure side sweeps: This type of cleaner floats below the surface of the pool and propels itself around. Trailing from it are two or more hoses that swirl under the force of water being pumped out of their ends. Another type of cleaner, the in-floor automatic vacuum, returns the water from the filtration system through special jets built into the bottom of the pool; the jets direct the water over the bottom of the pool and move dirt toward the main drains. Another type, so-called robotic vacuums are self-contained units which are placed in the pool and clean automatically.

Pool lighting—lighting in the pool rather than on the deck around it—has advanced considerably in the past 50 years. Long gone are the days when a pool-owner's only option was a spotlight secured to a house wall, projecting an unpleasant beam on the pool area and producing a dangerous glare on the surface of the water. Today, the prospective night swimmer has plenty of choice. Thanks to fiber-optic technology, even existing pools can be easily fitted with safe, attractive lighting arrangements.

Underwater lighting is not a requirement for every pool, but if you plan to be in the water at night, or if you will be entertaining in the pool area, it will make your pool much safer and more enjoyable. Traditionally, a single incandescent light is located at the deep end, 18 inches to 4 feet below the surface. If the pool has been designed with the deep end nearest the house, the glare from the underwater light created by waves and splashing is directed away from the house. But if the glare is directed toward the house, you can install a dimmer in the circuit—a design known as niche lighting.

You may choose to have wet-niche lights, where a watertight lighting fixture contacts the water and is cooled by it. In dry-niche lighting, underwater lights are mounted in the pool wall and separated from the water by a glass lens. These are serviced from behind the pool wall via an access tunnel. As options to traditional incandescent lights, you can use fluorescent lights or quartz-halogen lighting. Both of these use less electricity, and will save you money in the long run.

The biggest recent development in pool lighting has been the advent of fiber-optic lighting. The hardware used to install this type of lighting looks the same, but instead of electrical current being carried to a fixture, the cord that runs to the pool is made up of fibers that carry light, not electricity. A lens at the end of the cord is located in the pool and releases the illumination into the pool.

One obvious benefit of this type of lighting is added safety: No electrical current comes near the water, eliminating the risk of shock. Fiber optics also offer a great degree of design flexibility to the prospective pool owner: Retrofitting pools with fiber-optic lights is relatively easy. Design and lay-out of lights can be changed to give a new look to the entire pool setting.

Fiber-optic technology has opened up a new world of lighting possibilities. This custom pool—shaped like a musical note—is brought to life with fiber-optic lighting installed around the edge.

Spa Accessories

The heater, pump, and filter represent the serious support system of a spa. But a quantity of other equipment is also floating around in today's hot-water marketplace. Some of these items are useful; others have been created purely for fun.

PROTECTIVE COVERS

So essential is a good cover to the overall safety and economy of a spa or tub that it really should be considered basic equipment.

Covering the spa whenever it's not in use is extremely important. A cover's obvious function is protection. It keeps out curious children and pets, and prevents leaves and other debris from getting into the water and clogging the system. At the same time, a cover helps conserve the water's heat, which would otherwise rise and escape. Not covering the spa for even one night will show up in higher utility bills.

Rigid covers: The best covers today are rigid ones made of foam—typically expanded polystyrene—covered with vinyl. Their insulation value ranges from R-10 to R-14. Many are hinged at the center for easier removal; others are formed of two and three pieces and connected by elastic straps.

Foam covers are lightweight, generally weighing 25 to 30 pounds. However, over time (a good cover will last for 5 or 6 years), the foam absorbs moisture, so eventually it will weigh a lot more.

To avoid trouble early on, buy the best cover you can. A good one will cost between 5 and 10 percent of the value of a typical portable spa, but it's worth the expense.

There are many ways to judge quality in a cover. First, look at the thickness of the vinyl and the quality of its backing (avoid cotton backing—it won't stand up to the chemicals in the water). Second, check the stitching at seams and handles. Look for double or triple stitching and heavy-duty nylon zippers.

The thickness of the foam is also important. A 2-inch thickness is adequate for interior spas, but 3 inches is minimal for outdoor use. Make sure that the foam is tapered (for example, 3½ inches thick at the center of the cover, 2½ inches on the sides) so that rainwater can

TYPICAL SPA COVER

A rigid spa cover is well worth the investment. The cover will not only conserve heat and reduce electric bills; it will also reduce the evaporation of water and chemicals from the spa.

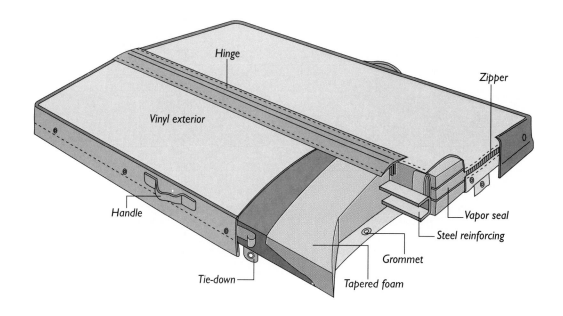

Hinge

Zipper

Vinyl exterior

Handle

Vapor seal

Steel reinforcing

Grommet

Tie-down

Tapered foam

drain off the cover before its weight breaks the foam core.

Look for metal C-channels along the hinge—they give the foam extra rigidity. Also, if the foam is sealed before it's clad with the vinyl, it will resist absorbing moisture for a longer period. Either way, there should be a grommeted drain hole on the underside of each section.

Most rigid covers come with tie-downs or other devices for securing them in place and keeping the wind and children at bay. You can also find lockable covers and even some models that have built-in alarms sound if they are disturbed.

To make your rigid cover last longer, keep it cleaned and protected following manufacturer's instructions. Also, wait at least 30 minutes after chemicals are fed into the spa water before replacing the cover.

And for safety's sake, always remove the entire cover before taking a soak. **Flexible covers:** Lightweight alternatives to rigid vinyl covers are available if security and energy savings aren't very important to you.

One, a simple bubble-plastic pad, floats on the water and can be used by itself or in concert with a rigid cover for extra insulation.

Another type forms a big plastic bubble, or tent, over the water. This cover is designed to get a boost from the sun in keeping the water warm; it's not very effective in cold or cloudy weather.

EXTRA ACCESSORIES

Though they're not necessary, cleaning gadgets sold for pools, such as special vacuum cleaners and scrubbing brushes, can also be used in a spa.

Inflatable vinyl pillows can add comfort to your soak. If you like to stretch out completely, there's even a spa lounge made of vinyl.

A number of practical items are available in buoyant form. A floating digital thermometer can provide an instant readout of water temperature. Floating plastic trays keep food and drink comfortably within reach; choose noncrumbly snacks, such as apple and cheese chunks, and nonalcoholic beverages in plastic containers. You can even buy a water-resistant hot-water floating cassette player.

For more water play, consider tinting or scenting the spa water with special additives. Using a packaged kit, you can also transform your spa or tub into a fountain. For additional ideas, visit your local spa dealer.

SPA LIGHTING

Many hot water enthusiasts prefer to indulge after nightfall or while it's raining or snowing. Also, because spas and tubs are so much fun for guests, much soaking goes on during the evening. At these times, adequate lighting is an important safety consideration.

Today, many spas come with built-in, low-voltage lights. But be sure also to light steps, deck edges, and other hazardous places. Outdoor lamps that are low to the ground are sufficient—and allow more privacy. Simple, low-voltage outdoor lighting kits work well around spas. They come with cable and a transformer.

Fiber-optic lighting can also be used in spas. Whatever lights you choose to use in your pool or spa, have them professionally installed and be sure that they come with an Underwriters Laboratories (UL) listing and comply with the National Electric Code.

Pool and Spa
CONSTRUCTION

*Once you have completed all your planning and preparation,
only one job remains. It is the largest task of all: building
the pool or spa. Think of pool or spa construction as being
divided into two main phases—the building or installation of the
basic shell that holds the water and the application of everything
that comes after it, such as the finish and trim, decking, and
landscaping. The following chapter will deal with both these
procedures for basic pool styles and for spas. Except for above-
ground pools like the one shown above, it is not meant
to provide you with a step-by-step construction manual. Rather,
it will guide you through the building process so you can
better understand what's going on while the contractors are
at work on your property. You may find variations in these
procedures because of climatic conditions, special structural
requirements, or differences among contractors.*

Pool Construction Overview

Of all the facets of in-ground pool construction, from excavation to applying the finish and trim, building the shell is by far the most crucial element; it will determine both the pool's usefulness and its longevity. The engineering, design, and workmanship required leave no room for shortcuts—maintenance problems or failure of the pool could result.

Your best guarantees of solid construction are thorough, careful planning and choosing a contractor who will do everything possible to ensure your pool is a structural success. If you have planned well and discussed the construction process thoroughly with your contractor, there should be few surprises.

One other way to ensure proper construction is to learn the essential steps in the construction of the pool and monitor the building process as much as possible to make certain they are performed correctly. The information presented in this chapter will not make you an expert in the construction process, but it will allow you to pick up on serious potential problems before they occur. It will also give you intimate knowledge of the design and structure of your pool, and will prove beneficial when you tackle the maintenance chores involved in owning it.

Although not all poolscapes are as elaborate as this one, attention to detail during construction will help ensure the result is attractive and long-lasting no matter what the scale.

Site Preparation and Excavation

Excavating for an in-ground pool or grading a level area for an above-ground pool is the first step in the actual construction of your pool. Normally, the excavated material is trucked away, but if you want to use some of the earth for landscaping, and you have a place to store it, arrange this with the builder beforehand.

LAYOUT

Working from the plan that is stipulated in the contract, the builder will establish the finished grade level, factoring in the thickness of the deck and the slopes for drainage.

The outline of the pool is then marked with stakes. A digging line, which takes into account the thickness of the walls and any additional space required, is indicated on the ground with wood strips staked into place, or with flour, lime, or powdered chalk.

ROUGH EXCAVATION

After the digging line has been marked, the rough excavation begins. Excavators normally use a back hoe or a front-end loader for this operation; the equipment needs anywhere from an 8- to 10-foot-wide access. For ease of operation, excavators usually prefer to bring the machines in at what will be the shallow end of the pool. This allows the machinery to exit the pool with less difficulty once the job is completed. In cases where adequate access is not readily available, or on hillside sites that cannot be reached safely with heavy machinery, the pool has to be dug manually, which is an expensive but a safe and effective option.

FINISHING

The backhoe or loader can cut only to within 6 inches of the pool perimeter; the final shaping and finishing is done by hand. The finishing should be done while the backhoe is making the rough cut; this way, all the dirt cut away in finishing can be moved out immediately.

There are two general types of excavations: those that follow the exact lines of the pool and must be hand-trimmed (this applies to gunite and some fiberglass pools), and those that can be overexcavated on the sides—but not the bottom—and then backfilled after the pool has been installed (poured concrete, masonry block, and vinyl-lined pools). With the latter type, the first finishing job is to establish the correct depths and slope of the pool. The excavation for a vinyl-lined pool must fit the liner exactly.

For gunite, shotcrete, stainless steel, and fiberglass pools, the finishing process is especially important. The shell follows the contours of the excavation, and errors in the finishing will show up as errors in the finished pool.

With fiberglass, the fitting of the pool into the excavation is the most critical step. Care must be taken not to over-excavate; if this does happen, a concrete mix rather than loose dirt will probably be required for backfill material.

For steel-reinforced concrete pools, walls are usually vertical for a few feet and then begin to taper into curved corners. This gives straight sides to the shallowest part of the pool and a bowl effect to the deep end.

PROBLEM SOILS

In excavating, there are only four types of problem soil—wet, rock, clay, and sand. Any of these four types will result in a cost increase.

Wet soil is a problem because the loader can't move about freely, the walls sag, and the finishing can't be done. The usual solution is to pump the water out of the hole while the loader moves in and out, the finishing work completed, and the main drain set; even then, it may be necessary to continue drawing out water through the main drain until the concrete is in.

If the wet soil prevents the loader from entering the pool at all, it may be a sign that you shouldn't build the pool, unless adequate drainage is arranged to keep water pressure away from the bottom of the pool (see page 92).

Rock requires expensive drilling and maybe even blasting; a loader must be kept on the job to move the rock as it's chipped away. But rock can be an advantage, since it provides a solid foundation.

With sand, the excavator may have trouble with the walls caving in as the hole deepens. There is usually a stopping point for cave-ins, but if the trouble persists, a thin gunite coat can be sprayed on the walls to shore them up until the shell is built. This should be done to Occupational Safety and Health Association regulations.

When the rough excavation is completed and the backhoe is gone, the wheelbarrows and shovels must come out to finish the job. Here, final excavation is being carried out for the gunite pool shown on page 94.

Dealing with Special Soil Conditions

If your pool site has any of the special soil conditions listed below, your contractor will need to take special measures to deal with it.

UNDERGROUND WATER PRESSURE

The problem of underground water pressure can exist in all pools with rigid floors. The pool can be pushed upward if enough water pressure is allowed to collect beneath and around the pool. This is particularly dangerous when the pool is empty, since there's no weight to counteract the pressure.

To avoid this problem, most pool builders install hydrostatic relief valves in the bottom of the pool and often under the main drain grate in concrete, fiberglass, and hybrid fiberglass pools. These valves open either automatically or manually to relieve the pressure by allowing groundwater to enter the pool.

Manual valves (with a handle similar to a water faucet handle) remain closed while the pool is full and there is little danger of buoyancy. When the pool is partially or completely drained, a long forked pole is used to open the valve, releasing the hydrostatic pressure. When the pool is refilled, the valve is closed.

Most hydrostatic valves today are automatic. They are equipped with a float that's raised by water pressure from below. This prevents water from leaking out of the pool. Only when the pressure beneath becomes great enough to lift the float will the valve open.

If your pool doesn't have a hydrostatic valve, it should never be drained without first contacting the contractor or an engineer. They will advise when the water table is low enough to avoid a dangerous pressure buildup. You will probably be required to sign a release anytime the pool is drained.

Where valves are not used (and in cases where heavy underground water buildup is likely), a subgrade drainage system should be installed. The pool can be ringed with a line of drain tile, placed on a definite grade for good drainage. The floor of concrete and fiberglass pools should rest on a bed of crushed rock if surrounding soils are slow-draining.

EXPANSIVE SOIL

Expansive soil generally resists absorbing water, but when it finally does, it expands a lot. As a result, heavy pressure builds up against pool walls, which may crack.

Pool builders typically have two sets of steel plans, one for normal soil and one for expansive soil. The latter calls for more and thicker reinforcing steel, thicker walls, or both. But since the walls are rigid, there is still a danger of cracking if the soil expansion is uneven or is greater than anticipated.

An expandable water stop can be installed to prevent water from seeping into the soil. Made of rubber or plastic, the stop can take several forms. The usual type, called a compressible expansion joint, is poured as a liquid into a gap made for it between the deck and coping when the deck is laid (opposite, bottom). When the joint dries, it forms a tight, flexible seal. Your contractor can take additional measures, often used together to insure protection.

• A 6-inch lip can be poured on the back edge of the surrounding walkway to provide extra support for the bond beam.

• A trench, 4 feet deep and 12 inches wide, can be dug around the pool, 5 to 10 feet from the walls. This is filled with loose material that can absorb the soil expansion; the top of the trench can be covered with decking later.

FILL

A few feet of fill on the top layer of an excavation, or perhaps a thin layer deeper in the hole, is not a problem. But if the entire excavation is loose fill, the pool will not have a footing in solid earth and will float in the fill. When the fill settles, the pool settles with it. If the settling is uniform, the pool pulls away from the bond beam—the top of the pool wall—and cracks; if it's uneven, the pool will crack crosswise at approximately the 5-foot-depth mark.

ROCK

Normal granitelike rock requires expensive excavation but makes a fine bed for a swimming pool. Holes are drilled in the rock for explosive charges. After the explosion, the shattered rock is removed from the excavation.

Slate, shale, and gravel, on the other hand, tend to move and slide when wet and can impose great forces on the pool. To eliminate these forces, you'll need extra retaining walls and perhaps a backfilling of solid earth.

SOLUTIONS TO NEGATIVE SOIL CONDITIONS

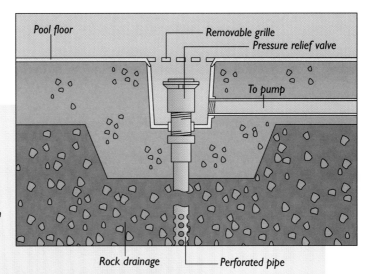

Pool floor — Removable grille — Pressure relief valve — To pump — Rock drainage — Perforated pipe

Hydrostatic relief valves
Every pool built into the ground should be equipped with a hydrostatic valve. It is designed to allow groundwater to enter the pool when empty to relieve water pressure from below.

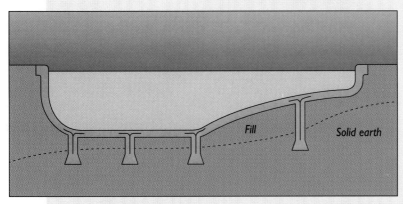

Fill — Solid earth

Caisson construction
To give the pool a solid footing in deep fill, the contractor can use caisson construction, building the pool shell on piers or pilings sunk into solid ground. The piers are made of concrete and reinforcing steel rods. The rods extend into the pool shell and are fastened to the reinforcing steel in the shell. Even though the fill may compact and leave a space under the shell, the integrated construction of the piers and the pool shell prevents any damage or movement.

Dealing with expansive soil
An expansion joint between the pool coping and the deck is essential to limit the soil's effect on the deck and pool edge. Another popular option for dealing with expansive soil is to replace the top 3 feet of soil around the pool with compacted fill; this lessens the problem by removing the cause.

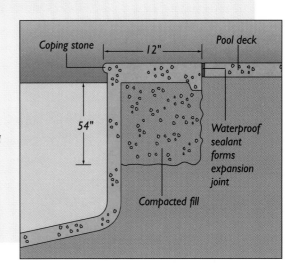

Coping stone — 12" — Pool deck — 54" — Waterproof sealant forms expansion joint — Compacted fill

Builder's Guide

Building a Gunite Pool

Cheaper than poured concrete but offering the same degree of durability and flexibility, gunite pools are an extremely popular option across the country. The broad steps discussed below also apply to the construction of poured concrete and shotcrete pools, though the details will differ.

CONSTRUCTION STEPS

The following are the general construction steps that your contractor will follow after the excavation has been completed:

• Plumbing pipes and conduit that will be inaccessible once the gunite is sprayed are installed.

• A gravel bed is laid on the bottom of the excavation.

• The reinforcing rods and tie wires, along with the blocks and forms for the bond beam are installed.

• The main drain, skimmers, in-wall cleaner (if used), and stubs for the return inlets are set down.

• Niches and electrical conduit for underwater lights are put in place.

• Bonding gunite is sprayed on walls and floor, and on steps, seats, and connected spa (if any).

• Gunite is cleaned out of light niches, main drains, return inlets, and all other blocked openings.

• Gunite is troweled to a smooth finish.

• Coping is built around the rim of the pool. The coping may be precast, brick, flagstone, or tile. *(See page 100.)*

• Tile is applied to the waterline and, depending on plans, to the steps, spa, coping, ledges, sides, and bottom of the pool.

• After gunite has cured for a week, plaster or exposed aggregates are applied to a smooth finish, or gunite is painted, fiberglassed, or tiled.

• After plaster is cured or paint is dry, support equipment is hooked up, the pool is filled with water, and water is treated with chemicals.

This gunite pool—the same one shown being excavated in the photograph on page 91—was sized to take advantage of all the space in this small yard. The result is a stunning backyard setting which naturally has the pool as its focus.

APPLYING PLASTER

Plaster is applied by hand, using a nonmetallic float like the one shown at right.

Bonding gunite is sprayed to form a pool. The gunite must be directed behind the rebars and against the earth so that pockets of air or loose sand cannot form. It is crucial that the shell be of proper thickness throughout, with no weak spots.

Builder's Guide

An Above-Ground Pool

An above-ground, or portable, pool can be installed by the homeowner following the manufacturer's instructions, but you are better off having it installed professionally. The work, while it appears relatively simple is more difficult than it looks.

CONSTRUCTION STEPS

Though the details of installation may vary widely between manufacturers, the general steps to erecting an above-ground pool are as follows:

• Site is excavated flat and even. Perimeter is graded level.

• Track for wall is installed around pool perimeter according to manufacturer's specifications.

• Pool wall is inserted into track (it may be a continuous sheet or paneled like the model shown below and opposite).

• Sand is spread evenly within the excavated area.

• Sand is screeded level in the area.

• Holes are cut for any rough plumbing, and piping, such as the main drain, is set down.

• Liner is installed and temporarily fastened around perimeter of pool.

• Liner is smoothed in place as water is added to pool.

• Liner is properly fastened in place.

• Plumbing and electrical work is completed and the support system is hooked up.

An above-ground pool doesn't take up much space, making it perfect for a smaller yard. And depending on the model, professionals can install such a pool in as little as half a day.

Assembling the wall

Wall panels are often plastic or metal and come in a length that can be unrolled and held in place by a sand wedge. The panels shown at left are assembled by joints on the edges. Helpers are needed to hold the wall upright at several points until it is entirely assembled.

Leveling the sand

A straight 2-by-4 serves as a level as it is swept around pool interior, razing high areas and filling in low ones.

Installing the liner

Several hands are needed to install the liner. Working from one starting point, it is pulled over the edge of the pool. It is then secured temporarily using the liner clamps supplied with the pool so that it can be smoothed.

Builder's Guide

Building a Vinyl-Lined Pool

The advent of vinyl pool lining, less expensive than concrete, has made pool ownership a real possibility for many homeowners.

CONSTRUCTION STEPS

Design and installation specifics vary between manufacturers of vinyl-lined pools, but the general steps are roughly the same. Expect your contractor to follow these procedures in constructing your vinyl-lined pool:

• The footing for the sidewall panels is leveled.

• The sidewalls are bolted together, and anchored in place with concrete, following the manufacturer's guidelines.

• Rough plumbing for the main drains, skimmers, return inlets, and automatic cleaners (if used) is installed; lights are hooked up.

• Sand or other suitable material is spread in bottom and leveled or contoured as required.

• Excavated area around sidewalls is backfilled with earth removed in pool excavation.

• Liner is spread over sidewalls (as shown for an above-ground pool on page 97), lowered into position, and fastened to top of sidewalls.

• The coping is attached (see page 100).

• While pool is being filled, liner is smoothed out, openings cut, and main drains, skimmers, return inlets, and lights are installed.

• Plumbing and electrical work is completed and support system is hooked up.

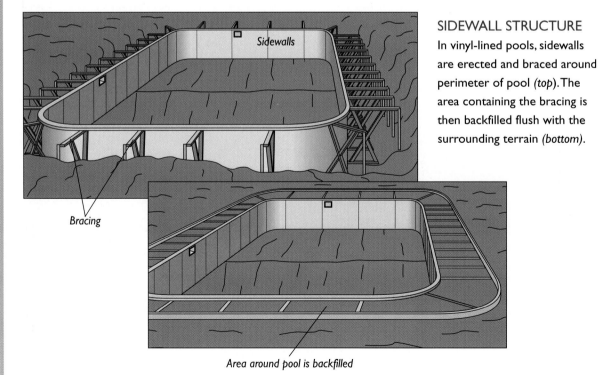

Sidewalls

Bracing

Area around pool is backfilled

SIDEWALL STRUCTURE

In vinyl-lined pools, sidewalls are erected and braced around perimeter of pool (top). The area containing the bracing is then backfilled flush with the surrounding terrain (bottom).

Installing a Fiberglass Pool

Fiberglass pools enjoy popularity in certain regions of the country. If you are installing a steel shell, the following broad guidelines also apply.

CONSTRUCTION STEPS

The site for a fiberglass pool is excavated before the shell makes its dramatic appearance. The work proceeds as follows:

• The rough plumbing under the pool is installed.

• Sand is spread in bottom of excavation and contoured to fit the pool shell.

• Shell is lifted off truck and lowered into excavation.

• Shell is leveled and adjusted to proper grade; temporary braces supported on wood rails on each side of pool hold shell in position.

• Rough plumbing is connected to main drain, floor-type cleaners (if used), skimmers, and returns.

• Excavation is backfilled with sand, and at the same time, pool is filled with water.

• Plumbing and electrical work is completed and support system is hooked up.

• Backfilling is finished, sand is compacted, and deck is graded.

• Forms for deck are prepared.

• Concrete for the deck is poured and finished.

FIBERGLASS POOL INSTALLATION

Fiberglass pools are unwieldy; a crane will likely be used to lower it in place. Once within the excavated site, the shell is cross-braced according to the shell manufacturer's instructions.

Pool Finishes and Trims

Depending on the type of pool you're building, you may have a choice of materials and colors for pool finishes and trims, including paint or plaster, tile, and coping.

INTERIOR FINISHES

Vinyl-lined and fiberglass pools need no interior finish. All others must be plastered, painted, fiberglassed, tiled, or coated in an exposed aggregate such as pebble or quartz. All interior surfaces have advantages and disadvantages, so you should discuss the options with your pool contractor before you decide.

Plaster, which must be applied by a professional, is the most common finish used on concrete pools; it gives a smooth waterproof skin to the pool, and provides a nonskid walking surface. Though most concrete pools are finished in white

plaster, a mixture of white cement and white marble dust, now other colors are increasing in popularity. In mild climates, a well-kept plaster finish may last indefinitely, but generally a pool must be replastered every seven years or so.

Paint can be applied by the homeowner and is less expensive, but must be reapplied every one to three years, a distinct disadvantage. Paint applied to a surface that will be underwater must be chosen and handled carefully. Consult a reliable paint manufacturer before deciding whether to do your own painting.

Fiberglass can be applied by hand or sprayed. For either method, the surface must first be properly cleaned and patched.

Fiberglass is long-lasting, relatively inexpensive, and easy to maintain. It doesn't leak and will inhibit

algae growth. On the negative side, it may not bond properly if the surface is not prepared and it can suffer cobalt staining. Fiberglass can leach chemicals and exposed fibers into the water.

Ceramic tile is an attractive option. While it is expensive to install, it will last for the life of the pool, requires little maintenance, and feels smooth underfoot. Installation can be difficult, however—tiles can chip or crack and they must be set perfectly level because the slightest variances are visible.

For the decorative effect of tile at a much lower cost, you can choose plaster for the main interior surface of the pool and add just a few rows of tile at the waterline.

Exposed aggregate finishes, either quartz or pebble, are becoming more and more common, and

COPING

Coping provides the finished edge to the pool and prevents water from getting behind and damaging the pool shell. Coping stones can be set flush with the deck and extend slightly over the pool wall (below) or you can simply extend the decking to or slightly over the edge of the pool (right).

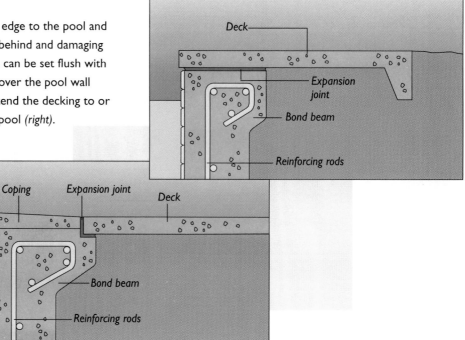

Large stone decking does double duty as coping. These oversize, flat stone pavers provide a rounded edge to the pool and a comfortable walking surface.
Design: Don Brandeau

it's easy to see why. They are natural looking, come in a wide range of designs, and last a long time. They are slip-resistant and absorb solar energy. On the other hand, exposed aggregate can be expensive to install and the surface may be uncomfortable on your bare feet.

COPING

Coping covers the round concrete edges of the bond beam, conceals the steel projecting from pool walls into the deck, prevents water from getting behind the pool shell, and integrates the finish and tile of the pool. Coping also serves as a non-skid surface for walking, a handhold for swimmers, and a smooth sitting bench or shove-off point into the water. When coping is correctly installed, water splashed out of the pool or carried out by dripping swimmers should flow away from the pool and down into deck drains.

Precast coping stones in straight lengths, corners, and curved sections are the most economical type of coping. The stones are usually made from grayish white concrete and have a porous finish. When choosing stones for pool coping, make sure to check that they are colorfast. If they are not, the color can leach into the pool, causing discoloration of the water and, over time, of the pool shell itself.

Instead of using coping stones, you can simply extend a concrete or wood deck to the edge of the pool and even slightly over the edge. Or you can use flagstone, brick, or other masonry materials. Be sure to trim and buff the edges of any naturally rough stone to a smooth finish. Make the overhanging portion thin enough for a comfortable handhold.

Spa Installation

Regardless of which type of spa you plan to build, the installation will not be vastly different from that for a pool of the same kind.

Both gunite and shotcrete construction are ideally suited to the free-form curves and custom shapes that are required for spas. Many spa contractors and landscape architects favor these techniques over the alternatives because of their ease of installation and their durability. Due to its ability to hold sharp corners, poured concrete is still the favored method of construction for more elaborate spas with these types of details.

The installation process for all types of concrete spas roughly follows the steps listed on page 94 for gunite pools. See the illustration below for a cross-section view of a typical installation.

The most popular in-ground spas are made of acrylic reinforced with fiberglass. One important concern—how the spa will be framed—must be dealt with before any installation of this kind takes place. Whether it will sit in a deck or a masonry patio, an acrylic spa requires a level site with support in as many locations as possible. Work with your general contractor or with a subcontractor specializing in deck work or masonry to create the location for the spa.

Acrylic spas are much like their larger cousins (*page 99*). Molded in a factory, they are brought to the site, and lowered into position. The steps for installing a pre-formed spa are roughly the same as those for a fiberglass pool. Remember, at some point you may need to repair or service plumbing or patch leaks on the backside of the spa; make certain the excavation is sufficiently oversized so that a technician can get behind the spa walls for these chores. See the illustration below for a look at a shell installation.

TYPES OF SPA INSTALLATION

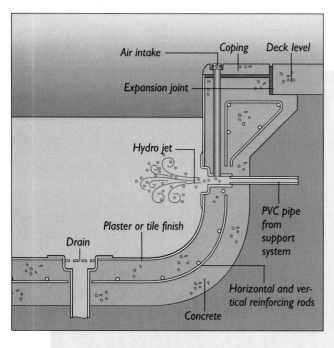

Acrylic spas
The spa shell (right) is supported by a bed of sand lining the excavation. The lip of the spa is connected to the decking which frames the spa. The sand can be excavated to service the plumbing or to repair leaks in the spa.

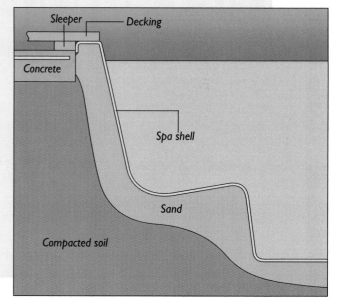

Concrete spas
A concrete shell (left) follows the contours of the excavation and is reinforced with rebar throughout. An expansion joint connects coping to decking. Note: As a safety precaution, all spas should be equipped with two drains.

Raised decking provides a stable, balanced setting for an acrylic spa, while integrating it nicely into the landscape. The deck must be specially constructed to support the spa's weight.

Landscaping
AROUND YOUR
POOL OR SPA

*Whether you're landscaping a pool or spa from scratch,
remodeling what's already in place, or just contemplating the
task for the future, designing a successful landscape demands
the same careful planning that went into building your
pool or spa. There's more to a pool or spa setting than just
the pool, a lawn, and a few scattered plants. Good pool and spa
landscaping involves arranging and integrating
many diverse elements—plantings, fences, walls, pavements,
structures, and lighting, as well as the pool or spa and its
decking. Ideally, the final result should reflect your personal
tastes and accommodate your needs. The following chapter will
provide a primer in some key principles of landscaping and
offer some suggestions for the elements that will eventually
make their home in your pool or spa landscape.*

Basic Landscaping Principles

Landscape architects and designers rely on several fundamental principles when they're establishing a landscaping plan for a client. You, too, can master the same principles and then use them when it comes time to developing your own pool or spa landscape.

LANDSCAPING GOALS

A successful landscape scheme has several goals, including beauty, privacy, comfort, safety, convenience, flexibility, and ease of maintenance. Though you may not be able to achieve them all, you'll succeed if you design with these goals in mind.

Beauty: You may consider a beautiful pool or spa setting almost as important as a good swim. Create this environment by blending the pool or spa and other landscape elements with the house to achieve an aesthetic balance throughout the whole area.

Privacy: If privacy is your primary concern, include trees, fences, walls, screens, or hedges in your plan to block the view of the pool or spa area from outside your yard.

Comfort: For swimming, soaking, sunning, or entertaining, you'll be happier in a setting that's been adjusted for particular climatic con-

ditions. You'll need room for lounging, as well as the right combination of design elements to modify sun or wind *(page 110)*.

Safety: Planning a safe pool area—not only for your own family but for your neighbors as well—needs to have high priority. Self-closing, self-latching, and self-locking gates and safety fencing around the pool (required by law in many communities) or yard will help keep children, animals, and even adults out of the pool when you are not around. Passageways near the pool need to be well-defined, lit at night, and not slippery or obstructed.

The seclusion of a naturalistic pool is accentuated by surrounding plantings. A pool house provides a spot for changing and a place to store equipment and chemicals.

Convenience and flexibility: Try to incorporate areas for pool-related activities like cooking, eating, entertaining, showering, and changing into your plan. The more convenient to the pool or spa these facilities are, the more you'll enjoy them without worrying about traffic in and out of your house.

Give landscape elements multiple jobs: design built-in benches that also store furniture, sports gear, or garden equipment; install adjustable screens that add shade and block the wind; build a covered firepit that doubles as a sunning deck or low table. Easy access to your pool from more than one of your main living areas also gives flexibility, but will probably require an alarm or self-closing doors for safety reasons.

Ease of maintenance: With ever-rising maintenance costs, you'll want to choose materials very carefully. Consider using wood that is naturally water-resistant, such as redwood, masonry surfaces that need no painting, rustproof furniture, and trees and shrubs that drop a minimum of leaves and flowers.

LANDSCAPING GROUND RULES

As you plan the setting for your pool or spa, keep four basic landscape goals in mind: unity, balance, variety, and proportion *(see below)*.

Unity in a pool or spa setting is achieved when everything looks as though it belongs together. No landscape element stands out; each blends with the other parts, as well as with the house and the lot.

To achieve unity, avoid designing too many distinctive units that will have to be tied together. The more units you divide your landscape into, the harder it will be to create unity.

Balance—not to be confused with symmetry—does a lot to make a setting pleasing. Most likely, your pool or spa will be the focal point of your landscape design. Achieve balance by combining elements that produce the same visual weight on either side of this center of interest. A large tree or structure on one side of a pool, for example, can be balanced with a grouping of smaller trees on the other.

But don't try to make these relationships too equal. Remember that mass isn't the only expression of visual weight; it can be expressed with color, form, or interest, as well.

Variety breaks up what could be monotonous unity. Differing but complementary grade levels, textures, colors, and shapes arouse visual interest both horizontally and vertically. You might vary an expanse of pavement with different paving materials, for instance, or plant shrubs in groupings of various heights and colors.

LANDSCAPING PRINCIPLES

This illustration highlights the four essential landscape design principles in action.

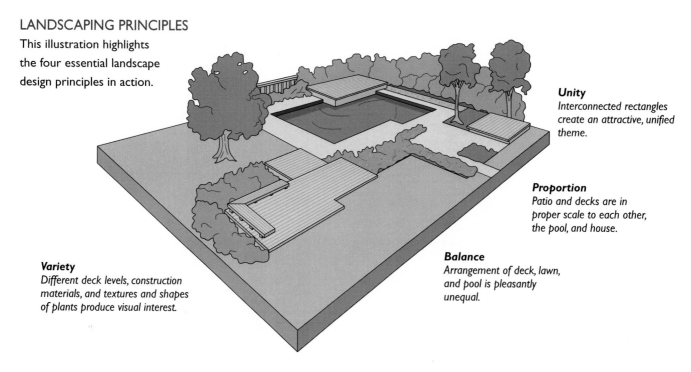

Unity
Interconnected rectangles create an attractive, unified theme.

Proportion
Patio and decks are in proper scale to each other, the pool, and house.

Balance
Arrangement of deck, lawn, and pool is pleasantly unequal.

Variety
Different deck levels, construction materials, and textures and shapes of plants produce visual interest.

The interplay of similar shapes creates unity in a pool landscape. Here, the curve of the pool is echoed in circular deck areas.

Proportion demands that the various forms, materials, and open spaces of your landscape be in scale with one another. Nothing looks more out of place than a small pool in a yard as flat and expansive as a football field, or a patio that looks more like a parking lot than an entertainment area.

Landscape elements need to be in scale not only with each other, but also with your house, lot, and pool or spa. If your lot is extremely large, try breaking the space up into several distinct areas. Screens, plantings, patios, or walks become borders or barriers that can divide your yard into intimate areas.

To maintain proportion in a small lot, keep things simple and uncluttered. Tall vertical screens used to enclose a small area will actually make it seem larger, as will solid paving. Use plants with restraint—overplanting adds clutter.

When selecting plants, keep their ultimate sizes and shapes in mind. Though a young plant may suit the proportion of your lot, within a few years it may grow so tall that the effect is spoiled.

BASIC DESIGN TECHNIQUES

Landscape architects and designers use some basic design techniques that you can borrow in thinking about your own plan. These can make the difference between a visually pleasing landscape and an awkward, jarring one.
• If the relationship between elements in your landscape is either too equal or extremely unequal, the result can be visually disturbing.

• When organizing space, remember that most people find a sense of order in well-known, simple shapes, such as squares, rectangles, triangles, and circles.
• Arrange plantings and structures to satisfy the need for privacy, but don't carry the design so far that it will produce a cooped-up feeling.
• You can create pleasing variations in the landscape design and yet maintain unity by carrying a recognizable shape through a main theme. A theme with variations creates a unified landscape.
• In grouping shapes or masses, make them seem unified by joining or interlocking the units, rather than separating them.
• The safe way to create a unified landscape is to make a rhythmic pattern of the landscape elements.

Challenging Sites

Like everything else in nature, lots are not all perfect. One of the secrets of landscaping—whether you're starting from scratch or rearranging and restoring a well-worn yard—is knowing how to turn liabilities into assets.

Small sites: Function needs to be your foremost consideration when you are landscaping a small area. Besides swimming, or soaking, you may want to use the space for entertaining, sunning, or play; it might also just be admired for its aesthetic qualities.

Even in a small site, careful planning can create the illusion of space. Brick paving, with its small-scale, repetitive pattern, gives an expansive feeling. To save space, display plants in small beds, containers, or hanging baskets.

Built-in storage and seating are practically a must where space is limited. Choose furnishings that don't overpower their surroundings, and avoid clutter at all costs.

Sloping sites: Whether your lot is gently sloping, extremely steep, or somewhere in between, you will have to consider special design requirements. The illustrations below should provide some help.

A shallow slope can be converted with a minimum of grading into two or more level areas. Steps and a raised planting bed serve as retaining walls. Steps, ramps, or both can provide the transition from one level to another. (Exercise caution when moving from level to level so as to reduce slips and falls.) Grass or ground cover can be used to prevent erosion in large unpaved areas.

A medium slope can be graded to form a series of gradual levels, each marked by a retaining wall and planted with ground cover.

A steep slope can often be conquered by a deck built beside the pool. Steep slopes often require the attention of professional landscape architects and engineers, however.

Besides their purely functional use in providing a connection between different levels, steps and ramps play a major role in both grading the site and integrating buildings into the landscape. They also separate areas, direct foot traffic, display plantings, and on occasion, even provide extra seating.

Odd-shaped lots: For tips on landscaping your pool or spa on odd-shaped lots, see the illustrations on the facing page.

SLOPING SITES

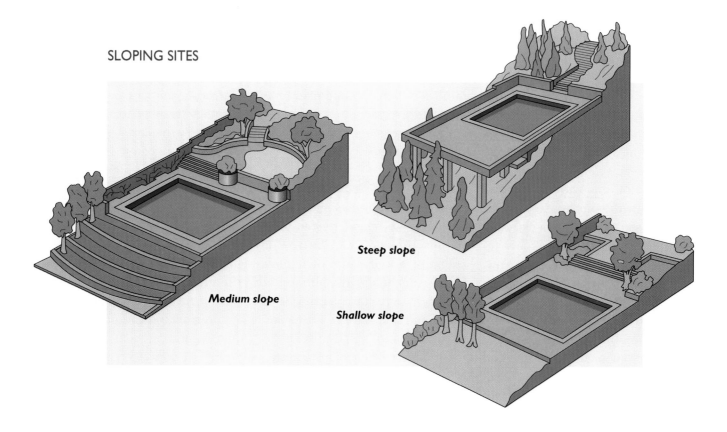

Medium slope

Steep slope

Shallow slope

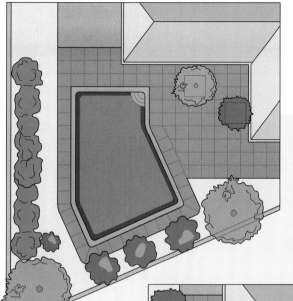

ODD-SHAPED SITES

The four basic types of odd-shaped lots are square, wedge-shaped, wide and shallow, and long and narrow. See pages 31-32 for additional ways to handle odd-shaped lots.

Wedge-shaped lot
A wedge-shaped lot's primary drawbacks are its sharply angled corners and unequally divided spaces. Plants can camouflage the sharp corners. Locating the swimming pool in the large open area contributes to the secluded nature of the adjoining smaller garden.

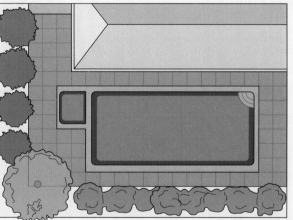

Wide, shallow lot
This lot appears deeper when the area behind the house is broken up into a series of outdoor living areas: a long, narrow pool, a large patio for entertaining, and a circular sitting area shaded by trees.

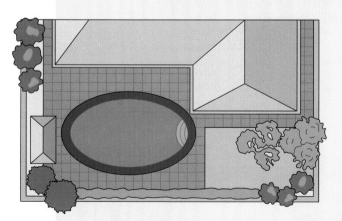

Square lot
A square lot's symmetry is softened by an elliptical pool and a separate landscaped area behind the house.

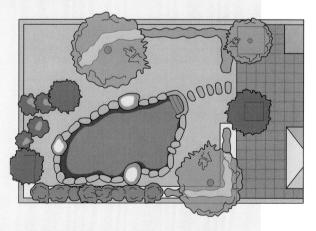

Deep, narrow lot
This type of lot can be divided into two distinct areas—a large patio and a very private, naturalistic pool site beyond. A modest grade adds visual interest.

Landscaping Design Elements

When landscaping the area around your pool or spa, you'll quickly discover that the scope of landscaping elements available is very broad. The following few pages present those that are most crucial—plantings, fences, masonry walls, vertical and horizontal screens, decks and pavement, poolside structures, and final touches such as lights.

Many of these elements can be used in different ways—some will work for you, others won't. Let your needs, your budget, and your personal taste determine your final choices. Be sure to follow all codes and be open to professional advice.

Combining the elements wisely is as important as choosing them in the first place. Remember that they should not only complement each other, but also harmonize with the lot, and the house itself.

FENCING YOUR POOL

Enclosing a pool with a fence is good pool insurance. It helps keep children, animals, and nonswimmers out of the water when there's no one around, and also provides security and privacy when you're swimming. Many communities require fences with self-closing and self-latching gates around pools. Check with your local building department early in the landscape planning stages. Consider that even if there's no code to this effect in your area, a fence is a good safety measure for your own children and those of your guests—even for nonswimming adults. Most safety experts agree that fences should be at least six feet high with vertical members spaced no more

A simple but attractive solid fence of concrete blocks provides privacy, security, and a windbreak for this pleasant pool setting. The raised spa in the foreground is designed and situated to allow users to take in the view while they soak.

than 4 inches apart to prevent entry. Turn to page 180 for more information on using barriers to create a safe pool or spa environment.

Besides being an important safety feature, fencing can be used to separate your lot from your neighbor's, to designate space, to conceal pool support equipment, and even to hang maintenance equipment. A fence near the pool can keep debris from blowing into the water and reduce maintenance. It also provides more specific climate control in the immediate pool area; you can orient the fence panels to block out cool winds and admit the sun when you want it.

Safety or property line fencing should not be less than 4 feet from the edge of the pool; that's the minimum width required to permit safe passage around the pool.

The type of fence you build will be dictated by cost, location, the style of your home, zoning requirements, and the visual effect you want to achieve. Some examples are illustrated below.

Whether you purchase a prefabricated kit, build the fence from scratch, or have a professional do it, you'll find that advice from a landscape architect or fence contractor can help you decide what type of fence is best suited visually and functionally to your pool landscape.

Fencing materials include wood, chain link, wire mesh, wrought iron, and various forms of masonry. For fences around pools, you should choose pressure-treated wood or rust-resistant, noncorrosive metals.

The style of your fence can affect the amount of wind protection you receive. For example, wind rushes over a solid fence like a stream of water. Such a fence provides little or no wind protection past the distance equal to its height. ➤

A HOST OF POOLSIDE FENCES

Grapestake

Solid panel

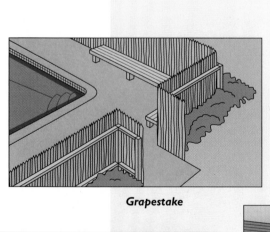

Louver

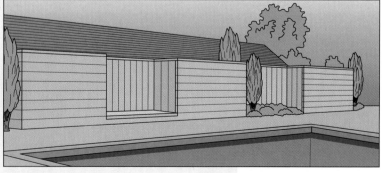

Solid board

Angling a baffle 45° into the wind extends maximum wind protection to a distance almost more than twice the fence height. Or, you can eliminate the downward crash of wind by using a baffle angled 45° with the wind. You'll feel warmest in the pocket below the baffle and at a distance equal to a little more than the fence height.

To reduce wind flow, use fencing with openings at least $\frac{1}{2}$ inch but no more than 4 inches wide, or use plant screens *(page 120)*. Dense plants offer even more protection.

POOL SCREENS

Screens may be lightweight partitions made from bamboo or reed, canvas, wood, safety glass, or translucent plastic; or they may be living screens composed of plants and trees. Either way, they help control unwanted sun and wind while contributing to an attractive outdoor setting. Screens can be portable or stationary, simple or elaborate.

You can position screens to block the sun's heat and glare, the

A COLLECTION OF POOL SCREENS

Wood

Reed

Plastic panels

Safety glass

112

EXAMPLES OF MASONRY WALLS

Brick

Stone

Adobe

wind's chill, and the view of neighbors. Screens can also define space for showering and dressing, lounging, and entertaining. Trailing, climbing, or espalier-type plants grow well on such screens.

MASONRY WALLS

Masonry walls—constructed from concrete block, brick, stone, adobe, or poured concrete—are, for the most part, solid, sturdy, permanent, and practically maintenance-free.

Masonry walls are excellent barriers to sun, noise, and intruders. Because they store and reflect heat, masonry walls can heat or cool the area directly around them. Low masonry walls are also effective retaining walls for raised plants, beds, terraces, or embankments.

Masonry walls do have two major drawbacks: high cost and a tendency to give a closed-in feeling. You can cut costs by tackling some of the construction yourself. To make the area feel more inviting, make the wall the minimum height required by code, usually 5 feet, and at a distance of at least 4 feet from the pool. Arches, wrought iron panels, gates, or grilles created with bricks or concrete blocks can be incorporated in the wall to open up the space.

Plants can soften the lines and texture of masonry walls; the wall itself provides excellent support for climbing plants. But since masonry both absorbs and reflects heat, delicate plants may not fare well near a sunny wall.

DECKS AND PAVEMENT

The deck around the pool and any paved surfaces such as walks, patios, or steps are functional and versatile landscaping tools. They add usable space, provide a transition from one area to another, allow for drainage, and cover up barren soil.

Decks: Most pools and spas are surrounded by a symmetrical or free-form deck. Besides creating a frame for the pool, the deck provides a safe walkway around the edge of the pool, and, if enlarged, provides enough space for pool furniture and lounging.

In choosing a decking material, remember that the deck must be safe underfoot and not slippery, coarse, or uneven; using a heat-reflective material will keep the deck's surface cooler. To prevent hose or rain water from draining into the pool, or water that has splashed onto the deck from re-entering the pool, the deck should drain away from the pool's coping by $1/4$ to $3/8$ inch per foot.

Be sure the deck is easy to clean or hose down—it forms the barrier between the pool and your plants and will catch falling leaves, grass clippings, and other debris. Deck maintenance information is provided in the chapter on Protecting Your Investment *(page 140)*.

Choose a decking material that blends with or matches other paved areas and is resistant to acid, algae, bacteria, chemicals, frost, and funguses. It should also be non-slippery and cool under your feet. Brick, flagstone, tile, pavement block, and finished, colored, and exposed aggregate concrete are excellent decking materials. Other interesting materials are rubber, broom-finished concrete, and cool-type concrete decking for hot climates. A selection of materials is illustrated below and opposite.

Pavement: Paved surfaces in the pool area include patios, walks, low-level decks, steps, and special activity areas.

A patio can function as an entertainment or lounging area, as well as a transition between the house and pool. Walks permit passage from one area to another, provide a border for plantings, and can break up the straight lines of an angular lot. Low-level decks add more surface space on problem grade sites such as hillsides. Steps not only link one level to another, but also separate areas and levels.

Interlocking concrete pavers blend nicely with pool coping while providing an even, nonslip surface *(left)*. Bricks lend a rustic appeal to pool decking *(right)*.

Combining decking materials can provide very attractive results. Here, wooden decking and flagstone paving blend to create a striking naturalistic pool setting.

Porcelain tiles impart a clean, orderly appearance to this pool and spa area, but their advantages don't end there. They are also durable, water-resistant, and able to withstand extreme cold.

Brick, concrete (finished, colored, or pebble surfaced), tile, flagstone, adobe blocks (use only the type with a burnt finish), and wood are durable and reliable pavement materials for the pool landscape. Again, consider surface texture and color, ease of maintenance, weather resistance, and drainage capability.

POOLSIDE STRUCTURES

Chances are you won't want pool traffic going in and out of your house, you'll need storage space for pool equipment, and you'll want to be outside by the pool as much as possible. The answer to all is to build a structure near your pool— a pool house or cabana, a storage facility, a sauna, a gazebo, or some other enclosed or semi-enclosed area. Such a structure will add immeasurably to the comfort and attractiveness of your pool's landscape.

Though your house and poolside structure can differ in style, their scale, texture, and material should be compatible. Remember that your structure must conform to local building codes, and you must have a building permit.

Shade structures: Adding a shade structure such as a gazebo, patio roof, horizontal screen, or overhang makes for a more versatile pool environment. It can become a shel-tered play area for children, a shady spot for relaxation and reading, and a place for eating and outdoor entertaining.

A gazebo, fine for entertaining, has storage and dressing rooms in the rear. A pool house can simply be a place to change in privacy and hang wet towels and bathing suits, or it can include a shower and lavatory. Some pool houses are a lot more elaborate, designed as warm-weather retreats complete with sauna, living and sleeping areas, and storage space.

A simple approach is to incorporate a dressing area into your garage by erecting a few panels in a corner.

Areas of sun and shade dapple the decking area just a few steps away from the pool thanks to an overhead shade structure, while the water and poolside spaces enjoy full sun throughout most of the day.

An intricate wooden roof structure provides an attractive overhead for a spa. The wooden arbor in the background supports plants to provide poolside shade.

A stunning poolside gazebo lends old-world charm to a backyard pool. The structure does double duty, providing storage space below and a seating area above.

Some pool houses have room for a shower and bath, sauna, changing area, and small kitchen.

Saunas: A Finnish sauna and a swimming pool are a perfect complement. After relaxing those tired or tense muscles in the hot sauna, you'll find a dip in the pool feels totally invigorating.

Your sauna can be a freestanding structure in a private, unused corner of your yard near the pool, or it can be incorporated into your pool house. You can purchase saunas in kits, either prefabricated or precut, or custom-made. For more information on saunas, see page 170.

Storage structures: You'll need considerable storage space for the support system, vacuum, leaf skimmer, brushes, and chemicals. You'll probably also need space to store poolside furniture, game and fitness equipment, and other accessories during off seasons.

Sheltering pool support equipment in a well-ventilated, covered area prolongs its life. If the support equipment is installed near a fence, garage, house wall, or garden storage shed, only a simple windscreen or fence extension with a lean-to roof is required. Allow a clearance of 3 feet for air circulation and maintenance access. Check zoning requirements before building.

Long-handled cleaning equipment can be hung neatly on hooks in a wall or fence. Just be sure they don't block access to the pool support equipment. Keep pool

A well-designed storage facility adds beauty as well as utility to the poolside area. Equipped with hangers for plants, wood shutters, and visually linked to the raised deck, this building becomes a pleasing element of the pool landscape.

A small cabana provides ample space for a changing room, and handles the storage of pool and garden equipment while adding an attractive touch to the pool area.

chemicals locked in a cool, dry, dark place.

Protect pool or patio furniture, game equipment, and other pool accessories from the elements by storing them in the garage, in storage boxes that double as benches or in utility storage areas.

GETTING THE WORK DONE

There are several ways you can approach the design and development of your pool landscape providing you have the experience, time, skill—and the energy.

You can create the landscape design and then carry it out yourself, or you can design it and hire a contractor to do the actual work. You can even complete certain parts of the project yourself and then hire subcontractors who have the skill, and the equipment, you don't have—maybe for the electrical wiring, paving, or excavation.

No matter how you choose to do the work, you'll benefit from consulting professionals during the design stage. A professional can offer sound advice and make sure your landscape design conforms to local building regulations.

With a project as involved as developing or remodeling a pool landscape, you may find it best to rely completely on professionals— architects, landscape architects, landscape designers, contractors, nurserymen, or gardeners.

Putting your ideas on paper: Whether you're designing the landscaping yourself or retaining a professional to do it for you, you'll want to draw up some plans based on your own ideas first. If you've already made a plot plan to determine your pool location, you can use that for your landscape design. If not, you'll want to make one *(page 29)*.

Use tracing paper laid over the plot plan to sketch the various approaches; inexpensive computer programs for landscape design are also available. Plan for what you'd most like to have, then add up the costs. Creating a strong design will help you distinguish between the more important and less important elements of your plan. See page 22 for information on choosing a site and making a plot plan.

Try to think in three dimensions to help you balance the design elements and visualize the results.

Planting around the Pool or Spa

Plants around the pool or spa add color, texture, shape, and interest to the landscape, as well as creating a beautiful, natural setting for your enjoyment. Moreover, plants provide privacy and security. Trees, dense hedges, or vines, when grown over a support, hide unwanted views. Tough plant borders or barriers can prevent animals and people from walking across lawns or plant beds. Prickly or thorny plantings can discourage trespassers from climbing the walls or fences, but you won't want them near the pool, spa, or lounging areas.

Plants are thermal tools that insulate the area surrounding the pool or spa: grass and ground covers cool; trees, plant screens, and hedges cool and shade; deciduous trees provide protection from summer sun and wind and allow winter sunlight to filter through branches; evergreen trees provide year-round shade and wind protection.

Plants are even good coverups. Use them to soften severe architectural lines, hide construction flaws, camouflage pool equipment, and fill in odd angles or spaces on your lot.

Plants must be suited to their climate zone. For examples of poolside plants that will thrive in your climate, see pages 122-124.

Planting considerations: If you've ever had to pluck plant debris out of a pool, you'll understand the reluctance of many pool and spa owners to plant anything next to the water. But plants play a vital role in the environment. Choosing plant materials and the location of planting beds very carefully will produce the attractive landscape you want and ensure minimum maintenance.

Successful plantings require adequate drainage. Water from the pool or spa, from rain, and from the hose you use to clean off paved areas may run off into your plantings, though you should make every effort to route drainage elsewhere.

Lawns, ground covers, and other plants can absorb quantities of water, but the first foot or two of space adjacent to paved areas often

Nestled among surrounding trees and plants, a feast of sights and sounds awaits all soakers in this backyard spa.

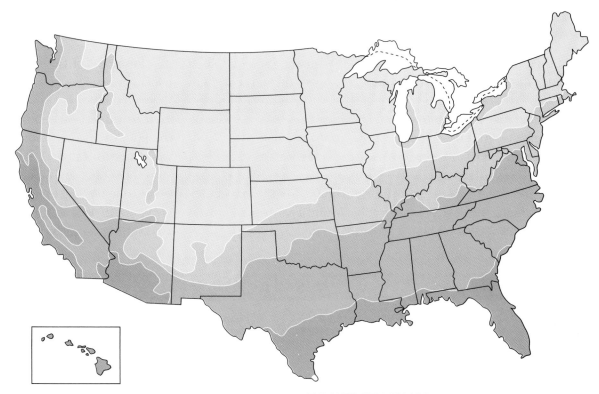

CLIMATE ZONE MAP

The plants listed beginning on page 122 are some that are happy growing near swimming pools. The map above indicates climate zones keyed to the plant list. If you want a more detailed map of your growing area, you can obtain the Plant Zone Hardiness Map from the United States Department of Agriculture. This map divides the United States and Canada into 10 temperature zones and shows the boundaries of all U.S. counties in relation to those zones. To determine the precise growing requirements of the plants for your area, consult your local nursery or a regional growing guide.

AVERAGE ANNUAL TEMPERATURE	
Zone 1	Cold
Zone 2	Cool temperature
Zone 3	Warm temperature
Zone 4	Subtropical

receives more than its share. To protect this area from becoming saturated and boggy, channel the water before it reaches the plant materials by using deck drains.

Selection of plants: Installing a pool will affect the climate in your yard—the expanse of water, especially if it is heated, produces high humidity. Plants susceptible to mildew are likely to be affected. In making new selections, choose plants that will withstand this extra moisture.

If your pool or spa site is surrounded by eucalyptus trees, pines or other conifers, all of which shed year-round, you might go so far as to consider a screened enclosure for the entire pool, spa, and deck area. Otherwise you'll have to accept the debris problem. Sometimes those who want the benefits of trees plant deciduous varieties, preferring a big leaf drop once a year to the small but continuous dropping of many of the evergreens.

Keep any new tree plantings away from the pool or spa, if possible. Also, be sure you know how far their root systems are likely to spread, so you won't get roots in your water pipes.

Don't plant any fruit-bearing shrubs or trees near the deck. The dropping fruit becomes slippery and can stain the deck; it also acts as a magnet for bees, yellow jackets, and other insects that can spoil your enjoyment of the pool or spa.

Around the pool or spa, choose plants that drop a minimum of leaves, seeds, resin, and other debris; avoid any that attract birds or stinging insects. And if you're fond of shrubs with thorns or barbs, plant them well away from the area.

Unhappily, some of the worst litterers are also among the best looking plants around a pool—bamboo and pampas grass, for example. If you want to use them, plant them on the side of the site away from the wind or where they're best sheltered from wind, to prevent litter from blowing into the water.

As in any garden setting, choose the right plant for the particular location. In small gardens where the pool or spa and its pavement occu-

py almost all of the garden, container gardening comes into its own. Where a baffle fence is used for privacy or wind protection, or where the pool or spa is enclosed with a wire fence for safety reasons, these structures offer an opportunity for interesting vine plantings.

Where there's an existing woodland setting, let the pool or spa imi-

LOW SHRUBS

PLANT NAME	COMMON NAME	CLIMATE ZONES	REMARKS
Abelia (dwarf forms)	Dwarf Abelia	2-4	Evergreen. Use for borders, space dividers, banks.
Camellia sasanqua	Japanese Camellia	3, 4	Evergreen. Good for espaliers, hedges, containers.
Chamaecyparis	False Cypress	1-4	Evergreen. Needs fast drainage—use for containers, rock gardens, hedges.
Cistus	Rock Rose	3, 4	Evergreen. Good plant for hot, dry banks.
Euonymus alatus 'Compacta'	Dwarf Winged Spindle Tree	1-4	Deciduous. Background plant for screens, hedges.
Juniperus	Juniper	1-4	Evergreen. Use for screens, windbreaks, borders.
Myrsine africana	Cape Myrtle	3, 4	Evergreen. Rounded form; good for hedges, backgrounds, foundations, narrow beds.
Philodendron selloum	Tree Philodendron	3, 4	Evergreen. Tropical jungle effect; plant against walls, glass, or in pots.
Phoenix roebelenii	Pygmy Date Palm	4	Evergreen. Use in containers in sheltered locations.
Pinus mugo	Mountain Pine	1-4	Evergreen. Variable growth, from low to pyramidal tree of moderate size.
Pinus mugo mugo	Dwarf Mountain Pine	1-4	Evergreen. Excellent container plant; good in rock gardens.
Pittosporum tobira 'Wheeler's Dwarf'	Japanese Pittosporum	3, 4	Evergreen. Good for foregrounds or low boundaries, even small-scale ground cover.
Podocarpus macrophyllus	Bigleaf Podocarp	3	Evergreen. Plant in tubs or as screens or hedges; will espalier.
Podocarpus nivalis	Alpine Totara	4	Evergreen. Dense; attractive as ground cover or in rock gardens.
Raphiolepis	Indian Hawthorn	4	Evergreen. Good for backgrounds, ground cover, dividers, informal hedges.
Taxus cuspidata 'Nana'	Dwarf Japanese Yew	1-4	Evergreen. Use for hedges, screens; plant grouped, single, or potted.
Viburnum burkwoodii 'Chenault'	Arrowwood	1-4	Deciduous. Fragrant flowers; will espalier.

tate a small lake or spring in a mountain meadow—a situation that neither requires nor benefits from a lot of additional planting.

When selecting flowering plants, aim for good design with beauty—if not bloom—the year round. Remember that in some areas early spring flowering varieties may bloom long before the pool or spa is in maximum use. Plants that bloom during summer months, when the facility is being used, will brighten tubs, boxes, or insets in the pavement.

Color and fragrance grace the entryway to this above-ground pool. You can arrange plantings to provide blooms throughout the swimming season.

TALL SHRUBS			
PLANT NAME	**COMMON NAME**	**CLIMATE ZONES**	**REMARKS**
Abelia *grandiflora*	Glossy Abelia	2-4	Deciduous, evergreen. Good for borders, dividers, screens.
Camellia	Japanese Camellia	3, 4	Evergreen. Use in containers or for espaliers, hedges, screens, ground cover.
Euonymus *alatus*	Winged Spindle Tree	1-4	Deciduous. Dense, flat-topped appearance; use for backgrounds, screens.
Euonymus *japonicus*	Japanese Spindle Tree	1-4	Evergreen. Heat-tolerant group as hedge or screen.
Euonymus *kiautschovicus*	Spindle Tree	1-4	Evergreen. Showy fruit, hardy to cold.
Fatsia *japonica*	Japanese Fatsia	3, 4	Evergreen. Tropical appearance; shade loving.
Griselinia	Kuputa Tree	4	Evergreen. Well-groomed appearance; use for screens, windbreaks.
Juniperus	Juniper	1-4	Evergreen. Pyramidal form; good for screens, windbreaks.
Nandina *domestica*	Heavenly Bamboo	2-4	Evergreen. Delicate foliage with flowers, fruit; use for hedges, screens.
Pittosporum *tobira*	Tobira Pittosporum	3, 4	Evergreen. Use for screens, backgrounds.
Podocarpus *macrophyllus*	Bigleaf Podocarp	3, 4	Evergreen. Good for screens, hedges, backgrounds.
Xylosma *congestum*	Fragrant Wood	4	Deciduous, evergreen. Handsome, versatile, graceful spreader; easily trained as espalier.
Yucca	Adam's Needle	1-4	Evergreen. Tough, sword-shaped leaves; keep away from traffic areas.

Plantings are the final ingredient to creating a naturalistic pool environment. On the down side, the leaves from plants and shrubs close to the edges of a pool can be a maintenance and safety concern.

TREES			
PLANT NAME	**COMMON NAME**	**CLIMATE ZONES**	**REMARKS**
Acer *buergeranum*	Trident Maple	1-3	Deciduous. Low-spreading maple; good for patios.
Acer *davidii*	David Maple	1-3	Deciduous. Handsome, upright maple; use on patios, lawns.
Chamaecyparis *obtusa*	Hinoki False Cypress	1-3	Evergreen. Plant in containers; use at entryways.
Chamaerops *humilis*	European Fan Palm	3, 4	Evergreen. Mass for hedges or use in containers.
Cordyline	Cabbage Tree	4	Evergreen. Often sold as Dracaena; good for tropical backgrounds, containers.
Cornus *florida*	Flowering Dogwood	1-3	Deciduous. Eastern dogwood; spring flowers.
Dracaena	Dragon Plant	4	Evergreen. Dramatic, palmlike silhouette; good in containers on patios.
Ensete	Ethiopian Banana	3, 4	Perennial. Palmlike appearance; plant in containers and protect in winter.
Ficus *lyrata*	Fiddle-leaf Tree	4	Evergreen. Dramatic form; needs protected location.
Ginkgo *biloba*	Maidenhair Tree	1	Deciduous. Autumn color; leaves drop all at once.
Juniperus	Juniper	1-4	Evergreen. Dense columnar form; good for screens, wind breaks.
Livistona	Fan Palm	4	Evergreen. Oriental appearance; slow growing.
Magnolia *grandiflora*	Southern Magnolia	1-4	Evergreen. Good for lawns, trees, espaliers, containers.
Magnolia *quinquepeta*	Lily Magnolia	1-4	Deciduous. Strong vertical effect; attractive flowers.
Musa	Banana Tree	3, 4	Perennial. Tender, needs protected location.
Pinus	Pine Tree	1-4	Evergreen. Good for large rock gardens, containers.
Schefflera	Umbrella Tree	4	Evergreen. Use for tropical effect.
Stenocarpus *sinuatus*	Firewheel Tree	3, 4	Evergreen. Dense foliage, showy flowers; use on patios, terraces, lawns.
Strelitzia *nicolai*	Bird of Paradise	4	Evergreen. Litter-free; withstands splashing.

GROUND COVERS

PLANT NAME	COMMON NAME	CLIMATE ZONES	REMARKS
Agapanthus 'Peter Pan'	African Lily	4	Evergreen. Good for containers, borders.
Ajuga *replans*	Carpet Buglewood	1-4	Perennial. Fast-spreading; makes thick carpet.
Cerastium *tomentosum*	Snow-in-summer	1-4	Perennial. Cascades in rock gardens, patterns, fillers, borders.
Cotoneaster *adpressus*	Creeping Rockspray	1-4	Deciduous. Slow-growing; follows contours of ground, rocks.
Dianthus *deltoides*	Maiden Pink	1-4	Perennial. Use for borders, rock gardens.
Helianthemum *nummularium*	Sun-rose	1-4	Evergreen. Rambles in rock gardens, on slopes.
Hypericum *calycinum*	Creeping St. John's Wort	2-4	Evergreen. Controls hillside erosion.
Iberis *sempervirens*	Edging Candytuft	1-4	Evergreen. Good for borders, rock gardens, containers.
Juniperis *chinensis sargentii*	Chinese Juniper	1-4	Evergreen. Slow-growing; use for borders, rock gardens; controls erosion.
Pachysandra *terminalis*	Japanese Spurge	1-4	Evergreen. Transition between walks, lawns, shrubs.
Sagina *subulata*	Pearlwort	1-4	Perennial. Useful between paving blocks.
Santolina	Lavender Cotton	3, 4	Evergreen. Attractive foliage; use on banks.
Sasa *veitchii*	Kuma Zasa	2-4	Evergreen. Oriental, tropical effect.
Sedum	Stonecrop	1-4	Perennial. Succulent used in rock gardens, borders, containers.

VINES

PLANT NAME	COMMON NAME	CLIMATE ZONES	REMARKS
Antigonon *leptopus*	Coral Vine	4	Deciduous, evergreen. Fast growing; tolerates heat, needs winter protection; use on patios, terraces, fences, walls.
Beaumontia *grandiflora*	Nepal Trumpet Flower	4	Deciduous. High-climbing, flowering; good for trellises and eaves.
Campsis	Trumpet Creeper	1-4	Deciduous. Flowering, invasive, clings to wood, brick, stucco.
Cissus	Grape Ivy	4	Evergreen. Use for trellises, walls, banks; controls erosion.
Clematis	Virgin's Bower	1-4	Deciduous. Attractive flowers; climbs trellises, trees.
Euonymus *fortunei*	Spindle Tree	1-4	Evergreen. Dense; good for shaded walls, fences, or as ground cover.
Hydrangea *anomala*	Tibetan Hydrangea	1-3	Deciduous. Flowering vine for shade.
Polygonum *aubertii*	Russian Vine	1-4	Deciduous, evergreen. Fast-growing; good for screens. fences, arbors, hillsides.
Solandra *maxima*	Chalice Vine	4	Deciduous. Grows well on walls, arbors, eaves.
Tetrastigma *voinieranum*	Chestnut Vine	4	Deciduous. Fast-growing; good for screens, eaves, lattices.
Wisteria	Wisteria	1-4	Deciduous, evergreen. Adaptable; attractive flowers.

Lighting the Pool Area

Swimming pools and spas can offer you and your family and friends more than the chance to swim or soak. They also provide pleasant backdrops and tranquil settings in which to entertain. At night, with the addition of tastefully arranged outdoor lighting, the view of your pool or spa and landscaping can be especially appealing.

The safety and the level of illumination within the pool—the underwater lighting—is of primary importance. A dim glow is all that is necessary to delineate the edge of the pool and provide a soft background setting for late-evening swimming. Use full brilliance when children are swimming or when you are hosting late parties or cocktail hours. The extra light is necessary for guests who have been drinking or for those people who have poor eyesight or poor night vision. For more information about underwater lighting for your pool or spa, including new fiber-optic technology, see page 85.

Good outdoor lighting is both functional and aesthetic. On the practical side, it offers the right kind of light when and where you need it for entertaining, outdoor cooking, or just relaxing. At the same time, proper lighting adds to the beauty of the pool or spa area by highlighting architectural features and background plantings. For example, when incorporating lighting into the

Pretty, useful path lights follow the brick border and beam low-voltage light onto flowers beds. In addition, they illuminate the spa's surroundings. *Landscape design: Rogers Gardens/ Colorscape*

landscape around a pool or spa, you can arrange the lights to reflect the pool's surface so you can see the shimmer from inside the house.

If you're designing your own outdoor lighting, experiment with lights in various locations. Buy several inexpensive clamp-on lights and reflectors and extension cords. (Keep in mind that according to the National Electric Code, extension cords that are used around pools should not exceed 3 feet in length.) Place the lights in the areas you want to highlight or illuminate and observe the results at night. If you're not satisfied, move the lights around until you get the effect you want. Then have the permanent lights installed professionally or do the work yourself.

TRADITIONAL OUTDOOR FIXTURES

Outdoor lighting fixtures for around the pool or spa come in many variations, some depicted below. Regardless of what you choose, you'll want to avoid glare. An opaque covering on a fixture will create a warm glow rather than a hot spot of light. You can also use lower light levels.

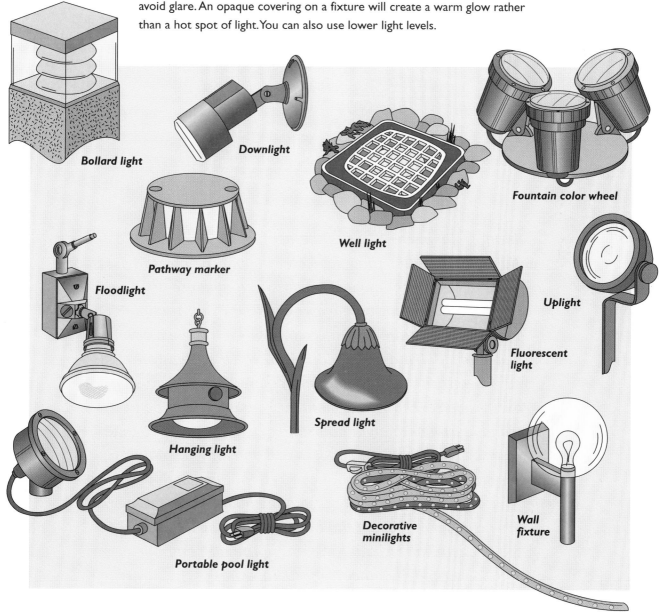

Bollard light

Downlight

Fountain color wheel

Well light

Pathway marker

Floodlight

Uplight

Fluorescent light

Hanging light

Spread light

Wall fixture

Portable pool light

Decorative minilights

Keeping the
WATER
HEALTHY

Filtration, chemical treatment, and cleaning are the three
essential methods of keeping the water in your pool or spa clear,
clean, and free of pathogenic organisms that cause disease.
The job of maintaining safe water continues year-round. For
a pool, you can hire a service company to do the work,
or do it yourself. For a stand-alone spa, you'll probably do the
work yourself. The amount of time required depends to some
extent on use. During the summer, you'll likely have to
spend at least four to eight hours a week; winter chores take
far less time if the pool is not in use and may be almost
nonexistent if you keep the pool covered. Automatic devices for
chemical treatment and pool vacuuming help reduce the work.
This chapter will cover the basics of filtering the water
and chemically treating it. For information on pool
maintenance, turn to page 140.

Filtration and Circulation

The circulation system serves many purposes—it moves hot water from the heater and disperses it throughout the pool or spa, it keeps the water from stagnating, and it allows the filter to do its job, namely, removing solid material that clouds the water. This material may be dirt or leaves blown into the pool or spa by the wind, or dirt and impurities brought in by bathers. A properly designed system should pass all the water through the filter within a given period of time, usually between 30 minutes and 6 hours. This is called the turnover rate.

One factor in determining how much you need to circulate the water is bather load, or the number of people using the pool or spa.

Bather load has a much higher impact on the relatively small volume of a spa than it does on a large pool; see the box below for details.

Apart from dealing with bather load and the need to filter out wind-blown debris, proper circulation is necessary to keep the water heated and chemically treated (if you're using a chemical feeder), and to keep it from stagnating. The best method of determining how long to run the pump is to start by running it 24 hours a day, then cut back in 1-hour increments until you notice a degradation in the water quality. As a rule of thumb, it's better to run the pump on and off for shorter periods of time, say an hour on and two hours off, than to let it run for 8 consecutive hours and then shut it down for 16.

Always be sure to maintain adequate sanitizers *(page 134)*. Whenever poor water clarity or chemical imbalance becomes apparent, increase the filtration time. Because you see the water every day, you may not notice a gradual decline in clarity. A quick and easy test is to toss a quarter into the water (in a pool, toss it in the deep end). In properly filtered and treated water, you should be able to tell whether it's heads or tails. At the very least, you should be able to clearly see the drains in the deep end. If you can't, don't use the pool until the problem is corrected.

BATHER LOAD

In spas, bathers have a significant impact on water clarity. Depending on the number of bathers present, you'll need to adjust the length of time you run your pump to compensate.

For example, suppose you have a 300-gallon spa and your pump circulates water at a rate of 25 gallons per minute. (Check the flow meter to see how many gallons per minute your pump actually moves.) If you run the pump 24 hours a day, then 36,000 gallons of water are circulated (25 gallons/minute x 60 minutes x 24 hours). To compensate for the impact of each bather, you need to circulate 1,400 gallons of water per day. (This covers the impact of bathers on the water. You may need to circulate a higher volume to remove other debris.) To determine the number of bathers that can use the spa in a day, divide 36,000 by 1,400 to arrive at 25.71, or 25 bathers. If you run your pump for 6 hours per day, for example, you're only circulating 9,000 gallons (25 gallons/minute x 60 minutes x 6 hours). At this rate, 6 people could use the spa in a day (9,000 ÷ 1,400 = 6.43).

So if you're planning a party, adjust your circulation accordingly. Remember, it never hurts to circulate the water more frequently, and it can be unhealthy to circulate it less than you need to.

A TIMELY INVESTMENT

Perhaps the smallest expenditure you can make for your pool in return for the biggest convenience is a timer. Once you determine the filtration schedule, set the timer and allow it to turn the pump on and off for you. Some timers will even reduce the time during the week and lengthen it on weekends if that's when the pool load is heaviest. You can buy a timer at your local pool supply store and have it wired to your system by an electrician.

Water Chemistry Basics

Clear, healthy water is the goal of every pool or spa owner. But getting water to that state—and keeping it there—can prove difficult for novices. This section will explain the basics of water chemistry, so that you can obtain maximum enjoyment from your pool or spa.

Aside from filtration and circulation, the major factor in keeping your water clean and healthy is water chemistry. Treating the water with chemicals maintains the chemical balance, disinfects the water,

and helps keep it clear. It's not hard to do this job yourself—you'll need to test the water regularly for various characteristics and then make sure the correct amounts of certain chemicals are added, if required.

Because the formulation of chemicals varies from one manufacturer to another, follow the instructions on the containers of the products you buy. Or, hire a service company to test and balance the water and perform regular maintenance procedures.

Even if you aren't making the adjustments yourself, you'll still need to test the water between visits from your service technician. For that reason alone, you'll find it valuable to acquire an understanding of the factors involved.

The main issues in water maintenance are chemical balance, sanitation, and oxidation. Water is balanced if it contains just the right amount of pH, total alkalinity, calcium hardness, and total dissolved solids at a given water temperature.

TYPICAL TESTERS

There are various water-testing instruments on the market; a few of the most common ones are shown below. For more elaborate tests, or help in resolving specific water problems, you can take a water sample to a pool or spa dealer for testing.

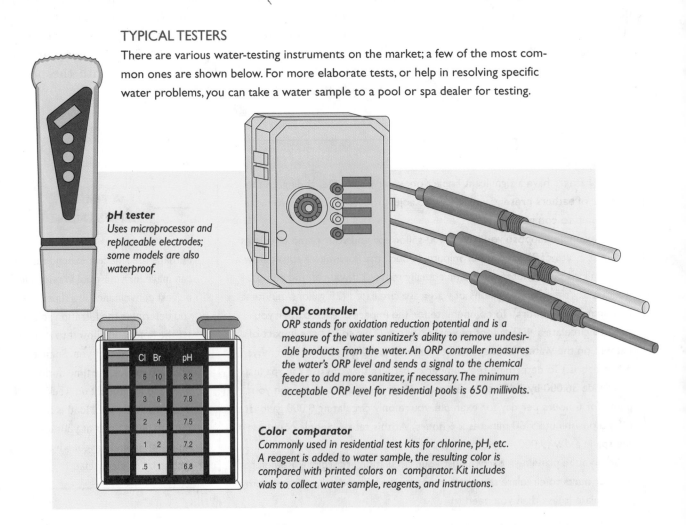

pH tester
Uses microprocessor and replaceable electrodes; some models are also waterproof.

ORP controller
ORP stands for oxidation reduction potential and is a measure of the water sanitizer's ability to remove undesirable products from the water. An ORP controller measures the water's ORP level and sends a signal to the chemical feeder to add more sanitizer, if necessary. The minimum acceptable ORP level for residential pools is 650 millivolts.

Color comparator
Commonly used in residential test kits for chlorine, pH, etc. A reagent is added to water sample, the resulting color is compared with printed colors on comparator. Kit includes vials to collect water sample, reagents, and instructions.

Cl	Br	pH
5	10	8.2
3	6	7.8
2	4	7.5
1	2	7.2
.5	1	6.8

Sanitation and oxidation are achieved by adding chemicals, such as chlorine, which kills pathogens and removes organic debris by oxidizing it. These aspects of pool chemistry are interrelated. For example, if the water is high in dissolved solids, you'll need more chlorine to achieve the same level of sanitation.

BALANCED WATER

Water must be kept in balance to prevent corrosion of metal parts, scale deposits, and etching of plaster surfaces. Water that's out of balance can cause expensive damage to the pool or spa. Let's look at the various aspects of water balance one by one.

pH: Water has an acid-alkalinity balance that's measured on the pH scale. The scale runs from 0 to 14, with the center, 7, indicating a neutral state.

Numbers above 7 represent varying degrees of alkalinity; lower values stand for degrees of acidity. For example, muriatic acid has a pH of about 0, vinegar is 3, distilled water is 7, and lye solutions are close to 14. The ideal range for pool or spa water is slightly on the alkaline side, between 7.2 and 7.8.

Controlling the pH of pool and spa water is vital. If the pH is too high (alkaline), disinfectants are less effective in destroying bacteria and algae; water will be cloudy; scale can develop on heater coils, in the circulation pipes, and on pool surfaces; and the filter might become blocked. If the pH is too low (acidic), chlorine dissipates rapidly, the metal parts of equipment will corrode, and surface materials will etch or crack.

Total alkalinity: This term refers to the measure—in parts per million (ppm) of water by weight—of the carbonates, hydroxides, bicarbon-

Testing the water

Using a color comparator test kit

Proper procedures will ensure the accuracy of your test results. Inaccurate results can lead you to add the wrong levels of chemical, and can contribute to unhealthy water.

To test the water, first rinse out the sample vial in pool water. Then hold the vial open-end down, plunge your arm into the water up to your elbow, and turn the vial up. Cap the vial under water. Don't cover the opening with your finger, because your body acids can affect the results. Take the sample indoors, to a well-lit room. Ideally, the water should be at room temperature when it's tested.

Pour the water into the comparator and, holding the bottle of reagent at eye level in a full vertical position, add the specified number of drops of reagent (right). (Holding the bottle on an angle can change the size of the drops and thus the quantity of reagent administered and the accuracy of the test.) Shake or swirl the sample according to the instructions. Hold the comparator at eye-level, preferably against a white background, and compare the color of the sample with the printed color scale. For accuracy, the results must be read within 4 or 5 seconds.

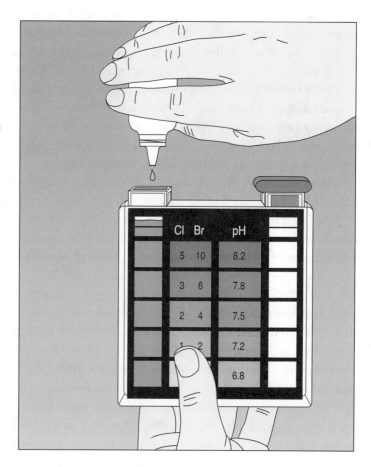

Cl	Br	pH
5	10	8.2
3	6	7.8
2	4	7.5
1	2	7.2
		6.8

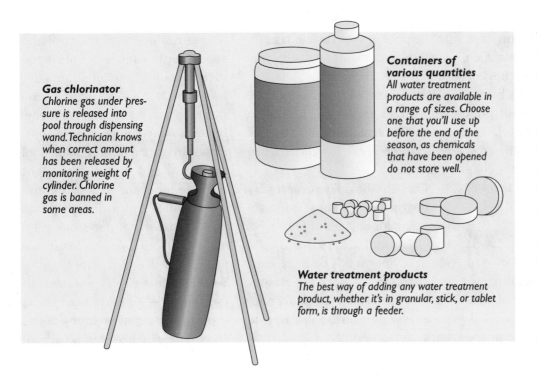

Gas chlorinator
Chlorine gas under pressure is released into pool through dispensing wand. Technician knows when correct amount has been released by monitoring weight of cylinder. Chlorine gas is banned in some areas.

Containers of various quantities
All water treatment products are available in a range of sizes. Choose one that you'll use up before the end of the season, as chemicals that have been opened do not store well.

Water treatment products
The best way of adding any water treatment product, whether it's in granular, stick, or tablet form, is through a feeder.

WATER TREATMENT PRODUCTS

Some common forms of chemicals for water maintenance are shown at left. Chlorine gas must be administered by a professional service company, but the other products can be applied by the homeowner. If you have a chemical feeder (page 139), use only those products designed for it. Be sure to adhere to safety guidelines.

ates, and other alkaline chemicals in the water. Total alkalinity (TA) refers to the ability of the water to neutralize acid or "buffer" the pH of the water.

The pH tends to fluctuate rapidly, and having the right level of total alkalinity helps reduce this fluctuation, also called "bounce." There's a range of acceptable levels of total alkalinity: 80 to 150 ppm is acceptable; 100 to 120 ppm is ideal.

After you test for pH, you may also need to test for acid demand (if pH is high) or base demand (if pH is low); the results of these tests tell you how much chemical you need to lower or raise pH.

Calcium hardness: A measure of the calcium ion content of water, calcium water hardness should be maintained at between 200 and 400 ppm in most pools. Water that's too hard can raise the pH, cause scale to form, and cloud the water; water

that's too soft can end up softening or etching plaster, cause tile grout to dissolve into the water and tiles to pop off the walls, and lead to cracks in vinyl liners. Some homeowner test kits don't include tests for calcium hardness, but the more complete kits do. An alternative is to take a water sample in to a pool store for testing.

To raise calcium hardness, add calcium chloride dihydrate; to lower it, add sodium hexametaphosphate (10 pounds per 250,000 gallons of water to start, then 2 pounds per 250,000 gallons of water every other week), dilute the water, or have a professional come in with a nanofilter, which can remove particles as small as 0.001 of a micron from the water. Cellulose fiber will also remove calcium from the water. You can add it to a sand or cartridge filter, or, if you have a diatomaceous earth filter, use cellulose fiber in

place of the diatomaceous earth.
Total dissolved solids: As its name suggests, total dissolved solids (TDS) is a measure of all the products dissolved in the water, including chemicals, bather impurities, pollution, debris, etc. As the amount of total dissolved solids increases, the water becomes cloudy, sanitizers become less effective, and algae growth increases, as does scaling, corrosion, and staining. There is no chemical way to reduce TDS but nanofiltration by a professional will lower it. Or, the pool or spa can be drained and refilled. To determine how often you need to drain and refill to control for TDS buildup, you can use this calculation: Volume of water ÷ 3 ÷ average number of bathers per day = number of days between drainings.

An 18,000-gallon pool that 6 people use per day will need to be drained just once every 1,000

Developed in the 1930s by W. F. Langelier, the Langelier Saturation Index (SI) is a formula based on the water's pH, total alkalinity, calcium hardness, temperature, and total dissolved solids (TDS) that indicates whether or not the water is balanced. Except for pH, each of these components is represented by a factor; for pH, you use the actual reading. The chart at right gives the factors. The formula for SI is: pH + Alkalinity factor + Calcium factor + Temperature factor - TDS factor.

A well-balanced pool has an SI of 0, but +0.3 or -0.3 is acceptable. If the result is a negative number, the water is likely to be corrosive; if it's a positive number, the water's likely to be scale-forming.

A typical example will help illustrate how the index works. Suppose you have a spa with a pH of 7.6, a total alkalinity of 140 ppm, a calcium hardness of 300 ppm, a temperature of 104°, and a TDS reading of 850 ppm. Looking up the factors in the chart (taking the next highest factor if the number isn't there), we get the following calculation: SI = 7.6 + 2.2 + 2.1 + 0.9 - 12.1. Since the SI = + 0.7, this water is likely to form scale; therefore, the total alkalinity and pH should be lowered.

If you don't know your pool's TDS, buy a TDS meter to measure it, or take a sample to a pool store, where they'll measure it for you.

Some companies offer a conversion chart that makes these calculations unnecessary. You test the water as usual and then use the chart to determine whether the water is balanced.

SI FACTORS

TOTAL ALKALINITY PPM		CALCIUM HARDNESS PPM		TEMP. F°		TDS PPM	
50	1.7	75	1.5	66	0.5	< 1,000	12.1
75	1.9	100	1.6	77	0.6	> 1,000	12.2
100	2.0	150	1.8	84	0.7		
150	2.2	200	1.9	94	0.7		
200	2.3	300	2.1	105	0.9		
300	2.5	400	2.2				
400	2.6	800	2.5				
		100	2.6				

days—every 3 years—to control TDS. A 300-gallon spa used by only 2 people per day, however, would have to be drained every 50 days. **Temperature:** Water temperature has some effect on water balance, but is not adjusted just for the sake of the water chemistry: You want your pool or spa to be comfortable. Still, you should know the water temperature to factor it into your calculations. Multi-use pools are usually between 83° and 86°; spas have a maximum temperature of 104°. Calcium is less soluble in warm water, so spas and other warm water pools have more of a problem with scaling (the calcium precipitates out of solution).

The Langelier Saturation Index: An overall indicator of water balance, the Langelier Saturation Index *(above)* was developed for closed water systems, like boilers, rather than an open system such as a pool or spa. Nonetheless, it still gives an indication of the water's tendency to be corrosive or scaling.

Adjusting the balance: Not only do you need to determine what the levels of these various elements of pool and spa water chemistry are, you may also need to adjust them. The charts on pages 134 and 135 tell you which chemical to add, and how much, to adjust total alkalinity.

Always adjust total alkalinity before pH, because once TA is in the proper range, pH will fluctuate much less, requiring only minimal adjustments. Mechanical feeders are best, but if you choose to apply chemicals by hand, the following guidelines should help.

Sodium carbonate (soda ash) is an inexpensive, effective, and quick-acting option for raising TA and pH. To determine how much to add, use the following formula: (pool volume ÷ 113,231) x number of ppm change desired = number of pounds of sodium carbonate required.

To raise alkalinity, sodium bicarbonate (baking soda) is inexpensive and easy to use but is only half as strong as soda ash. Use as needed to increase total alkalinity and pH. To determine how much to add, see the chart opposite, or calculate: (pool volume ÷ 71.425) x number of ppm change desired = the number of pounds of sodium bicarbonate that are required.

If you need to raise TA but pH is already high enough, choose sodium bicarbonate; sodium carbonate will raise pH more.

Muriatic acid (liquid) can be used to lower alkalinity; it will also lower pH somewhat. However, if it is incorrectly applied, it can be very damaging. Handle it carefully to avoid splashing yourself, and wash off any spillage immediately.

It's best to use a mechanical feeder, but to add muriatic acid by hand, pour the acid while walking around the pool. Do not add muriatic acid through the skimmer.

To determine how much to add, use the following formula: (pool volume ÷ 125,000) x number of ppm change desired = number of quarts of muriatic acid required.

Sodium bisulfate (dry acid) is the best chemical to use to lower TA. It's easier to store than liquids and is especially good for small pools that require small quantities. To use it, get a mechanical feeder or dissolve the acid in water and spread it around the pool. For proper

amounts, see the chart below, or calculate: (pool volume ÷ 47,058) x number of ppm change desired = number of pounds of sodium bisulfate required. It should be premixed with water (always add acid to water, never water to acid). Wear protective gear (gloves, goggles, etc.) and handle it carefully.

SANITATION

Pathogenic organisms, such as bacteria, viruses, and protozoa, are the main cause of unsanitary pool water. These microscopic organisms invade pool water by means of carriers—mostly people. Particularly in smaller pools that sustain heavy use—including children's wading pools and warm water pools and spas—it's essential that you control these organisms.

Proper water treatment involves both sanitation and oxidation. Sanitation is the killing of path-

LOWERING TOTAL ALKALINITY WITH SODIUM BISULFATE							
DECREASE TA				**GALLONS IN POOL**			
in ppm	1,000	5,000	10,000	15,000	20,000	25,000	50,000
10	0.21 lbs.	1.06 lbs.	2.13 lbs.	3.19 lbs.	4.25 lbs.	5.31 lbs.	10.63 lbs.
20	0.43 lbs.	2.13 lbs.	4.25 lbs.	6.38 lbs.	8.50 lbs.	10.63 lbs.	21.25 lbs.
30	0.64 lbs.	3.19 lbs.	6.38 lbs.	9.56 lbs.	12.75 lbs.	15.94 lbs.	31.88 lbs.
40	0.85 lbs.	4.25 lbs.	8.50 lbs.	12.75 lbs.	17.00 lbs.	21.25 lbs.	42.50 lbs.
50	1.06 lbs.	5.31 lbs.	10.63 lbs.	15.94 lbs.	21.25 lbs.	26.56 lbs.	53.13 lbs.
60	1.28 lbs.	6.38 lbs.	12.75 lbs.	19.13 lbs.	25.50 lbs.	31.88 lbs.	63.75 lbs.
70	1.49 lbs.	7.44 lbs.	14.88 lbs.	22.31 lbs.	29.75 lbs.	37.19 lbs.	74.38 lbs.
80	1.70 lbs.	8.50 lbs.	17.00 lbs.	25.50 lbs.	34.00 lbs.	42.50 lbs.	85.00 lbs.
90	1.91 lbs.	9.56 lbs.	19.13 lbs.	28.69 lbs.	38.25 lbs.	47.81 lbs.	95.63 lbs.
100	2.13 lbs.	10.63 lbs.	21.25 lbs.	31.88 lbs.	42.50 lbs.	53.13 lbs.	106.30 lbs.

ogenic organisms. Oxidation is the removal from the water of organic matter; it's essentially burned up with oxygen. Oxidation usually has to happen before sanitation can take place. A good water treatment product for a pool or spa must be able to both oxidize and sanitize. Or it can be used in conjunction with another method.

Chlorine, available in gas, liquid, powder, and tablet form, is by far the most popular disinfecting agent for residential swimming pools in the U.S. It is both a good sanitizer and a good oxidizer.

Methods used in the commercial pool industry and in scientific laboratories to disinfect or sterilize water are now gradually being adopted for residential swimming pool use. Such new methods include electrolytic chlorine generation, ultraviolet sterilization, and ozone oxidation.

Bromine is often used in spas because it is less affected by fluctuations in pH than chlorine, and it is believed to evaporate less quickly at high temperatures than chlorine. It is a good sanitizer, but not a good oxidizer. The form in which it is usually sold for home use (BCDMH) includes some chlorine as an oxidizer. It is also more effective if used in combination with an ozone oxidizer.

Some experts prefer chlorine over bromine because bromine tends to form compounds, making it less effective as a sanitizer. Bromine is not an effective algicide; nor is it as effective at killing various pathogens such as *Pseudomonas aeruginosa*, which causes spa rash, ear infections, and other medical problems.

The use of chlorine: Common forms of chlorine for residential use are sodium hypochlorite (liquid chlorine) and calcium hypochlorite and chlorinated isocyanurates (dry chlorine). Lithium hypochlorite is another dry form of chlorine that is sometimes used in pools, but it's less common because it is much more expensive than either sodium hypochlorite or calcium hypochlorite. It dissolves very quickly, making it a good choice for vinyl-lined or dark-colored pools that might be stained by undissolved chlorine.

Automatic feeders dispense the proper amount of disinfectant in the water. They're considered the best choice for home pool maintenance, especially when combined with an ORP controller.

Chlorine residual: Whenever you add chlorine, it immediately goes to work killing algae and pathogens, and oxidizing organic matter. But in the process some of the chlorine itself is destroyed. The amount of chlorine used up in this manner is

INCREASE TA	GALLONS IN POOL						
in ppm	1,000	5,000	10,000	15,000	20,000	25,000	50,000
10	0.14 lbs.	0.70 lbs.	1.40 lbs.	2.10 lbs.	2.80 lbs.	3.50 lbs.	7.00 lbs.
20	0.28 lbs.	1.40 lbs.	2.80 lbs.	4.20 lbs.	5.60 lbs.	7.00 lbs.	14.00 lbs.
30	0.42 lbs.	2.10 lbs.	4.20 lbs.	6.30 lbs.	8.40 lbs.	10.50 lbs.	21.00 lbs.
40	0.56 lbs.	2.80 lbs.	5.60 lbs.	8.40 lbs.	11.20 lbs.	14.00 lbs.	28.00 lbs.
50	0.70 lbs.	3.50 lbs.	7.00 lbs.	10.50 lbs.	14.00 lbs.	17.50 lbs.	35.00 lbs.
60	0.84 lbs.	4.20 lbs.	8.40 lbs.	12.60 lbs.	16.80 lbs.	21.00 lbs.	42.00 lbs.
70	0.98 lbs.	4.90 lbs.	9.80 lbs.	14.70 lbs.	19.60 lbs.	24.50 lbs.	49.00 lbs.
80	1.12 lbs.	5.60 lbs.	11.20 lbs.	16.80 lbs.	22.40 lbs.	28.00 lbs.	56.00 lbs.
90	1.26 lbs.	6.30 lbs.	12.60 lbs.	18.90 lbs.	25.20 lbs.	31.50 lbs.	63.00 lbs.
100	1.40 lbs.	7.00 lbs.	14.00 lbs.	21.00 lbs.	28.00 lbs.	35.00 lbs.	70.00 lbs.

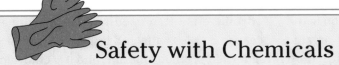

Safety with Chemicals

Because swimming pool maintenance involves chemicals that can be harmful if not handled properly, it is very important to follow certain procedures in using them.

• Never use someone else's pool water test results or filtration procedures as a guide for your own pool.

• Never use reagents from one test kit with comparitors from another. You won't get accurate results because the concentration of the reagents varies.

• Never mix any pool chemicals together unless so directed by the manufacturer on the label of the container. Common household bleaches, if used to clean pool areas, must never be mixed with or used simultaneously with household drain cleaners— the combination will form poisonous chlorine gas.

• Keep all pool chemicals and cleaning agents sealed, and store them in a well-ventilated, dry area out of reach of children. The space should be locked and the key available only to adults familiar with the use of the chemicals.

• Never store muriatic acid and calcium hypochlorite next to each other. The combination of the two (in fact, of any acid with calcium hypochlorite) will cause an explosion. Calcium hypochlorite can combust if it gets wet (even with water) while in storage.

• Do not store chemicals in enclosed support system rooms, since even covered containers can emit corrosive fumes that can damage the support system equipment.

• Wear gloves and any other protective gear recommended by the manufacturer.

• Handle all acids with extreme care. Follow the manufacturers' directions carefully.

• Always read the labels of chemicals, both in buying and using them. Labels sometimes look similar; adding the wrong chemical can lead to harmful conditions. Ask for and read the material safety data sheet (MSDS) for any chemicals you use.

• When possible, use sanitizing agents and algicides registered with the Environmental Protection Agency for pool or spa use. The package should carry an EPA registration number. Some pool products, such as chlorine enhancers, aren't registered with the EPA.

the chlorine demand of the water. The amount of disinfectant left in the water is referred to as the chlorine residual or the total available chlorine (TAC).

Pool and spa water also contains ammonia and other compounds of nitrogen, particularly ammonia nitrogen. Nitrogenous compounds come from human wastes, bird droppings, and source water. Chlorine and ammonia combine to form chloramines (also called combined available chlorine or CAC), which are not effective sanitizers. The characteristic smell that we associate with chlorine is actually the smell of chloramines.

The form of chlorine that is an effective sanitizer is free available chlorine (FAC), which is practically odorless. So if you can smell the chlorine, the combined chlorine level is too high, and there probably isn't enough free available chlorine in the water to do the job. CAC should not be allowed to exceed 0.2 ppm. If it does, you'll have to superchlorinate or "shock" the water, as discussed on the next page.

WATER PROBLEMS AND SOLUTION

PROBLEM	CAUSE	SOLUTION
Algae	One-celled aquatic plants that thrive in sunlight and warm water—especially shallow water. The water may have a greenish or mustard-colored tint, and there may be green, yellow, brown, or black spots on pool or spa surfaces.	Good maintenance—constant circulation, proper chlorine levels, frequent brushing of walls, and regular removal of debris from water, skimmers, and filter baskets—should keep algae problems from starting. Adjust the pH to between 7.2 and 7.4, then superchlorinate. For persistent colonies, pour liquid chlorine directly on them; or place dry chlorine in a nylon stocking and suspend it next to the colony. Black algae should be scrubbed first to remove the protective waxy coating.
Colored water	May be caused by suspended dirt or minerals in the water or by algae (see above). Hazy or turbid water may be too alkaline, lack sufficient filtration or chlorination, or may need a clarifying agent, or some combination of these things. Green, green blue, or milky water indicates a chemical imbalance, poor filtration, or both. If the balance is normal, the water may contain iron or any dissolved minerals.	Start by running the filter continuously, which will solve problems caused by dirt and may clear hazy or turbid water. Balance the water; in particular, test and adjust pH and total alkalinity. Monitor chlorine levels and adjust if necessary. If none of this helps, test for minerals in the water. Add a chelating agent (pronounced "key-late-ing"), or a sequestering agent, which prevents metals from precipitating out of solution.
Stains	May be caused by debris, metal objects, algae, or mineral deposits. Yellow or reddish stains may be caused by iron in the water. Too much acid added to the water at one time can cause stains.	Any metal objects dropped in the water should be removed immediately to prevent rust stains. To prevent acid stains, maintain the proper pH and water balance. For iron stains, use a chelating agent. On a plaster finish, ordinary stains can be buffed with fine sandpaper or a pumice stone. In a painted pool, try scrubbing with a chlorine solution.
Scale	Mainly caused by an accumulation of calcium salts. It will appear first on heater coils but may also appear as a white, gray, or brownish crust on pool surfaces.	Balance the water. Add a chelating agent. You may be able to remove new scale deposits with a pumice stone or sandpaper. For well-developed scale, you'll need to have a professional drain, sand, and acid wash the pool.

Chlorine levels, both TAC and FAC, should be tested regularly. A good idea is to test them every time you swim. Many home kits test chlorine levels using orthotolidine (commonly called OTO). These kits are not recommended because OTO doesn't distinguish between free available chlorine and combined chlorine; you'll end up with a reading for total chlorine, but this doesn't help because much of the chlorine may be already combined, and thus unavailable for sanitizing. With a test based on diethyl-p-phenylene diamene (or DPD) you can test for TAC and FAC; subtracting the FAC result from the TAC level will tell you CAC, so you'll know when you need to shock the water.

Many water maintenance manuals suggest a set range of FAC, such as between 1.0 and 3.0 ppm for pools, and between 4.0 and 5.0 ppm for spas. Obviously, a certain amount of sanitizer is required at all times to keep the water healthy. But setting a maximum amount of sanitizer is unnecessary. Having more than you need admittedly wastes the chemical, but is not harmful to bathers and may help keep pool water sanitized during periods of heavy use.

The best indicator of how much sanitizer is required is a measurement called the oxidation reduction potential or ORP. An ORP sensor measures the conductivity of the water, taking into consideration all the constituents in the water (chemicals, pH, temperature, body oils, sweat, etc.). The resulting number, expressed in millivolts, is an indication of what's called the "potential generated for oxidation" or "work potential." When this work potential is at a certain minimum level (for residential pools and spas, that level is 650 mV), you know that there's enough sanitizer in the water. If you have a chemical feeder, you can also add an ORP controller, which will both monitor pH and ORP levels and send a signal to the chemical feeder to add sanitizing chemicals as required.

Chlorine stabilizers: Chlorine tends to dissipate when exposed to the ultraviolet light of the sun's rays. Adding cyanuric acid to an outdoor pool or spa can help prevent this; indoor pools and spas don't need it. But only a small amount is required: 10 ppm provides 85 percent chlorine retention; there are diminishing returns at levels over 20 ppm, and higher levels may even damage the pool or spa. The EPA sets acceptable levels at 100 ppm, but this standard is based on the health of the bathers, not the health of the pool. To remove cyanuric acid when levels become too high, the pool usually has to be drained and refilled.

Rather than adding cyanuric acid directly, you can use a sanitizer that includes both chlorine and a stabilizer, such as sodium dichloro-s-triazinetrione (called dichlor) or trichloro-s-triazinetrione (called trichlor). It's best to use a chemical feeder for these products.

Shocking: Also known as superchlorinating or breakpoint chlorinating, this involves adding many times the usual dose of chlorine to the water to break up combined chlorine and burn out nitrogen compounds and human wastes. The amount required depends on the level of combined chlorine in the water (7.6 molecules of free chlorine are required to break up 1 molecule of combined chlorine), and on the sanitizer you're using (different sanitizers have different percentages of available chlorine). Some test kit manufacturers provide instructions for superchlorinating or follow the instructions on your water treatment product.

You'll want to superchlorinate when the combined chlorine reading is higher than 0.2 ppm, or about every week during the swimming season, whichever comes first.

Superchlorinate after sundown, since the ultraviolet sun rays are likely to destroy some of the chemical. Close the pool or spa to bathers until the residual level drops to normal for your water or as indicated by an ORP reading of at least 650 mV.

Forms of chlorine: Sodium hypochlorite, a liquid, is an inexpensive form of chlorine. It disperses quickly in water and leaves no residue to add to water hardness. It has a lower chlorine content than dry forms, but requires careful handling to avoid splashing and potential damage to clothes.

It's best to buy a pump that attaches to the container to inject the chemical into the return line. If stored too long or allowed to get hot, liquid chlorine can deteriorate. Sodium hypochlorite raises the pH of pool water.

Calcium hypochlorite, a dry form of chlorine, is available in granulated or tablet form. It is inexpensive and stores well but disperses more slowly than liquid chlorine. It contains 65 or 75 percent available chlorine. It's best to choose the tablet form and use an erosion feeder or an erosion-soaker feeder to dispense calcium hypochlorite. The granulated type is also often used for spot treatments of clinging algae. But if added directly to the pool, it leaves a calcium residue that can clog diatomaceous earth filters, turn the water milky, ruin the surface of the pool, and sometimes cause the grains of sand in sand filters to cement. Calcium hypochlorite, like sodium hypochlorite, raises the pH of the water.

Chemical Feeders

The best way to add chemicals to your pool is through an automatic chemical feeder. (In commercial pools, this is the only legal way.)

Chemical feeders have many advantages. In the first place, you know that chemicals are being added whenever the pump is running, so if you're running the pump constantly—or on an hourly on-off basis—the level of sanitizer in the pool should remain fairly constant. Or you can use a controller to regulate the chemical feeder. Secondly, the chemical is added after the water has gone through the pump, filter, and heater, so by the time the water returns to the support equipment, it will be sufficiently diluted not to cause damage. And lastly, there will be no areas in the pool with high concentrations of chemicals, as there are when you hand feed, because although the treated water enters the pool in one location, it contains a much lower concentration of chemicals. This is better both for bathers and for the pool.

But make sure you're using the chemicals that the feeder is designed for. Chemical substitutions can be very dangerous.

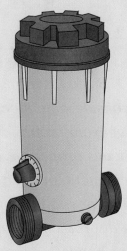

The in-line erosion feeder for chlorine at left dispenses chemicals whenever the pump is on. All you need to do is ensure that there's always some chemical in the feeder.

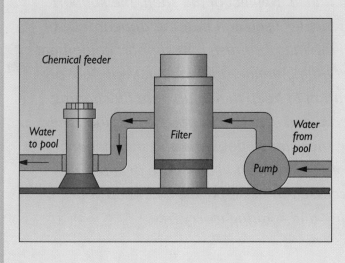

Schematic hookup diagram for in-line feeder
Whatever type of feeder you use, it's important that it be installed after the support system, so that the chemicals are added to the water after it goes through the pump, filter, and heater. Otherwise, the chemicals can damage your equipment.

Protecting YOUR INVESTMENT

Since installing a swimming pool or a spa involves a considerable investment, you'll want to make sure that you get your money's worth and protect your investment. That means proper maintenance. Neglect of the shell, the support equipment, or even the water itself can mar the appearance of a pool or spa and ruin the interior finish and support equipment in a surprisingly short time. Summer and winter, your pool or spa needs some attention to keep the equipment functioning smoothly, the water clean, and the shell in good condition. There are no real "tricks" or shortcuts to pool and spa maintenance. Regular cleaning of the water and basic care of support equipment, as discussed in these pages, will keep you swimming and soaking worry-free.

A Clean Pool

Pool maintenance doesn't require a great deal of backbreaking labor, but rather a regular schedule of routine work intended to ward off serious problems and make your pool a pleasant place in which to swim. In general, you can count on spending four to eight hours a week working around the pool during the summer, if you do the maintenance yourself. Winter chores will be far easier and may be practically nonexistent if you cover the pool during the coldest months.

In many areas, pool service companies will maintain and chemically treat your pool. The monthly charge varies, depending

TOOLS OF THE TRADE

Some of the common choices in pool cleaning tools are shown below. You may not need all of them every time you clean, but you will probably use each one at one time or another.

Algae brush and extensions
Stainless steel bristles help remove algae from plaster- or tile-finished pool walls. Telescopic handle can be used with other cleaning tools.

Vinyl liner pool vacuum head
Bristles loosen dirt, which is sucked back to filter.

Wall and floor brush
Nylon bristle brush for general cleaning of walls and floor is all you need for vinyl, painted, or fiberglass pools. Plastered pools may also require an algae brush.

Leaf skimmer
An aluminum, stainless steel, or plastic frame with a mesh skimmer attached, for scooping out leaves and debris.

Concrete pool vacuum head
As with vinyl liner vacuum, dirt is sucked back to filter.

Tile brush
Handheld brush for cleaning tiles.

on the geographical area, the competition, the number of service calls per month, and the pool's size. Most companies will visit the pool one or two times a week during the swimming season and once a week or less during the off-season. You may want to skim debris out of your pool every day and test the water between visits from the maintenance person.

Maintenance procedures outlined here are based on a concrete pool with a plaster finish. If you have a vinyl-lined or fiberglass pool, maintenance of the interior surfaces will be easier, since the nonporous finishes resist algae growth, calcium deposits, and dirt accumulations. But water treatment, as described in the previous chapter, is about the same in all pools regardless of their construction method or the interior finish.

A vacuum is an important tool for maintaining your pool. Instead of the manual vacuum shown in the tool inventory on page 141, you may prefer to have an automatic pool cleaner such as those shown on page 84. Whether manual or automatic, there are a number of ways to run a pool vacuum. It may run off a separate line with its own pump, it may be connected to the circulation system via the clean water return lines, or it may be connected to the circulation system via the skimmer. In pools with only one skimmer, the last option is the least desirable because the skimmer is out of operation while the vacuum is working, allowing debris to fall to the bottom before it is skimmed.

Keeping the pool clean

1 Skimming out debris
Use the leaf skimmer to collect debris floating in the water or lying on the bottom. It's much easier to skim the surface than dredge the bottom, so use the skimmer often—every day if the wind is blowing—to remove debris before it can sink.

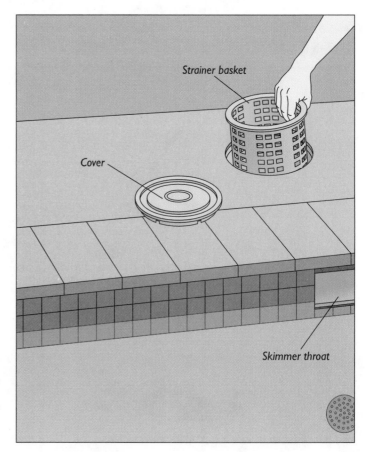

2 Cleaning strainer baskets
Clean the strainer baskets in the skimmer (right) and pump. During the swimming season, clean the skimmer daily. If you're using a vacuum that connects through the skimmer, it's especially important to remove debris regularly in order to maintain maximum suction for vacuuming.

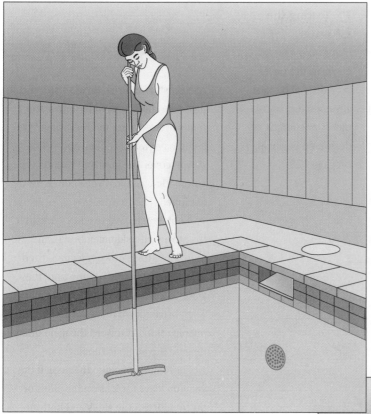

3 Cleaning the walls

On a vinyl-lined or fiberglass pool, use cleaners recommended by the pool manufacturer. Waterline tile scum can be removed with a nonabrasive chlorine-based liquid and a sponge. Use a white nylon scouring pad for tough spots and avoid steel wool as it can stain the plaster.

When brushing the walls, overlap your strokes so the surface gets an even scrubbing. Using a nylon brush, work down to the floor, brushing toward the main drain so some of the dirt is pulled into the filter. Start at the shallow end. Ten to 15 minutes of daily brushing will make the weekly cleaning easier. Use a stainless steel brush to remove algae, stubborn dirt, and scale from plaster.

4 Vacuuming the pool

Vacuum the pool at least once a week. If the vacuum is attached to a filtration system outlet, and uses the filter pump for power, it's important to keep air out of the lines. Fill the hose with water before attaching; submerge the line to eliminate any air. Keep the vacuum head under water while in use.

For maximum suction, the only line open to the pump should be the vacuum inlet; consult your filter manual. The vacuum head should be about $1/8$" off the wall or floor. Work it back and forth, overlapping each stroke. Check the clearance and adjust the position of the wheels, if any. If a nylon brush is part of the head, adjust it so it will touch the floor and dislodge embedded dirt. Clean the filter after vacuuming, if necessary.

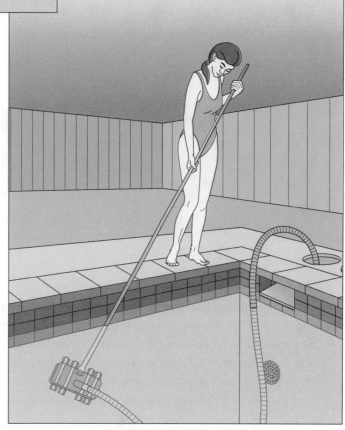

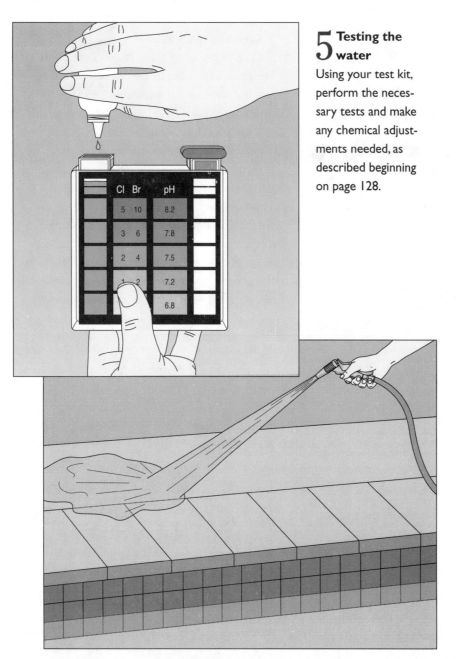

5 Testing the water

Using your test kit, perform the necessary tests and make any chemical adjustments needed, as described beginning on page 128.

6 Hosing the deck and coping

Always hose the pool area after cleaning the pool. Otherwise, dirt blown into the pool from the deck will spoil your efforts. Keep spray directed away from the pool to prevent silt from washing into the water. Always hose the deck before swimmers arrive to prevent dust and dirt from being tracked into the water. Scrub the decking occasionally with a stiff brush and a solution of trisodium phosphate and water, following manufacturer's directions. Disinfect with a 1:20 mix of chlorine and water to kill bacteria.

EXTRA CLEANING

After a storm: A rain or wind storm can turn sparkling clear water into water that's littered and unfit for swimming. If you have warning of an approaching storm, cover the pool and turn on the automatic cleaner, if your pool is so equipped.

If not, you'll have to go to work after the storm with skimmer, brush, and vacuum. First, hose down the coping and the deck. Remove all debris from the water surface with your leaf skimmer. Then brush down the walls and bottom, pushing the dirt toward the main drain. Be sure the pump is running.

Thoroughly vacuum the pool. If the vacuum leaves tracks on the sides or bottom, brush the sides and bottom again (with the pump running), while you push the dirt toward the main drain. Let the dirt settle before making another pass with the vacuum.

Pool accessories: The chrome-plated brass, stainless steel, and aluminum used for pool accessories require only minimum care to retain good appearance. The surfaces that are out of water can be cleaned and polished with a chrome cleaner; underwater sections probably won't need more than a wipe with a soft cloth from time to time.

TROUBLE-SHOOTING TIPS

SYMPTOM	SOLUTION
Cloudy, milky, or turbid water	• Operate filter for a longer time • Backwash sand filter, recoat D.E. filter, or replace filter cartridge • Check and adjust pH, total alkalinity, and chlorine • Check for air leak in intake lines to pump • Make sure filter control valve is in filter position • Check skimmer and pump strainer baskets for debris • Add water clarifying agent, enzymes, or absorbent foam (see pool supply or service company)
Sudden decrease in water flow rate	• Shut pump off immediately • Check for restrictions in suction lines (before pump) • Check pump and skimmer strainer baskets for debris • Be sure proper valves are open
Gradual decrease in flow rate with increase in influent pressure	• Time for regular filter cleaning
Reduced time between filter cleaning	• Clean sand filter with sodium bisulfate or commercial filter cleaner, available from pool supply or service company, to eliminate mudballs • Open D.E. filter and clean elements (*page 152*)
Heater cycles on and off	• Low water flow rate; may be time to clean filter • Check high temperature control (see owner's manual)
Gas burner won't light, though pilot is on	• Check all furnace controls • Check that pilot flame properly heats thermocouple • Check water pressure in heat exchanger • Check main electric gas valve
Pump motor doesn't start	• Blown fuse or tripped circuit breaker • Loose electrical connection or broken wire
Pump motor noisy	• Loose connections between pump and motor • Worn bearing in motor • Impeller damaged (call a service technician)
Pump runs but doesn't pump CAUTION: If pump is hot, immediately shut off motor to avoid damage.	• Low water level in pool; add water • Clogged filter—backwash sand filter, recoat D.E. filter, or replace filter cartridge • Air leaks in intake lines • Loose pump impeller • Impeller damaged (call a service technician) • Pump has lost its prime

Cleaning Your Spa

Spas, like swimming pools, require regular maintenance. In addition to the chemical testing and adjustment outlined in the previous chapter, your spa needs regular cleaning and checking.

At least once a week, and more often if necessary, empty the skimmer basket of any collected leaves or other debris.

With a spa that's used infrequently (only on the weekends, for instance), the filter will probably be able to go without cleaning for a few weeks; filters on higher-use spas will require cleaning more frequently. The best indicators are flow meters and pressure gauges. For more on cleaning filters, see the section on equipment maintenance beginning on page 148.

Occasionally, you will need to drain and clean the spa. This is necessary because of the natural increase of total dissolved solids over time, as discussed on page 132. These particles, which can't be filtered out, make the water less responsive to chemicals and, as a result, less safe for bathing. The formula for determining when to drain is: volume of spa ÷ 3 ÷ daily bather load = the number of days between each draining.

Be careful of draining an in-ground spa at times when the ground is very wet—if your spa's not equipped with a hydrostatic relief valve, the pressure can force it right out of the ground.

While you are cleaning, lubricate gaskets and O-rings with specified products. After the last rinsing, refill the spa or tub with water, test the water and make all the necessary chemical adjustments (*page 130*).

Generally, good water maintenance and regular cleaning of strainer baskets and filter is the best overall protection against mechanical failures in a spa or tub.

How long you run the pump depends on how often you use the spa. To find the optimum running time, see page 129. If you have a chemical feeder attached to the spa's circulation system, remem-

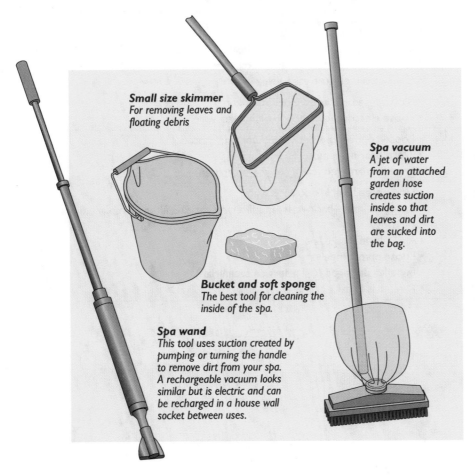

Small size skimmer
For removing leaves and floating debris

Spa vacuum
A jet of water from an attached garden hose creates suction inside so that leaves and dirt are sucked into the bag.

Bucket and soft sponge
The best tool for cleaning the inside of the spa.

Spa wand
This tool uses suction created by pumping or turning the handle to remove dirt from your spa. A rechargeable vacuum looks similar but is electric and can be recharged in a house wall socket between uses.

TOOLS FOR A HEALTHY SPA

Cleaning a spa is much like cleaning a pool, only many of the tools are smaller. The selection at left will serve you well in your maintenance tasks.

ber that the chemicals are only dispensed when the pump is running. You may need to run the pump for longer periods to ensure good water quality, even if you don't use the spa heavily. Check and clean the pump's hair and lint strainer at least weekly—and perhaps more often—depending on how much use the spa gets. Cleaning too frequently is better than not cleaning often enough.

If you have a gas heater with a pilot light, be particularly careful about lighting the pilot light or making any adjustments; follow the manufacturer's directions—printed on the heater—to the letter. Or choose a gas heater with an electronic ignition system to avoid potential pilot light problems.

Equip all equipment with proper housing to ensure trouble-free

service. For spas other than portables, be sure to allow for good ventilation on all sides and adequate protection from water, dirt, and the elements. A roof overhead and a floor that is raised above the decking or concrete will help prolong the life of your equipment. When you clean and drain the spa, check the pipe joints for leaks. Using the cover between soaks indirectly protects equipment by keeping out leaves and other debris, which could clog the filter. It also keeps the water hotter, so the heater has less work to do, reducing wear and tear, and cuts down on evaporation of the chemicals.

SPA MAINTENANCE TIPS
Regular maintenance will keep your spa in tip-top shape. But once in a while, some specialized tasks are in order to prolong the life and appearance of your spa.
• Apply oil to the exterior of a wooden tub two to four times a year, to preserve the finish.
• Check the metal bands or hoops of your hot tub for signs of rust or corrosion.
• Add a coat of special wax—available from a spa dealer—twice a year to restore the luster of a fiberglass spa.
• Have the heater checked annually for corrosion or scale damage.

Cleaning a spa

Washing the inside

Clean the spa surface with a mild, nonabrasive detergent or with a special cleanser from a water-care product line. Use a sponge, soft cloth, or very soft brush. Rinse thoroughly, then wipe with a household disinfectant. This is especially important for wooden tubs, since the porous wood tends to harbor organisms that cause disease. Be extra thorough with the disinfectant above the waterline, because that area of the tub is not exposed to the sanitizing chemicals the way the rest of the wood is.

Equipment Maintenance

Maintaining the support system— pump, filter, heater, and the like— involves keeping everything in working order and watching for and correcting small problems before they develop into expensive repairs.

Follow manufacturer's instructions and specifications when you're checking the components of the support system. If you don't have manuals for the equipment, obtain them from the manufacturers. These manuals will tell you what needs to be done, how often, and what repairs, if any, you can make yourself without voiding the warranty.

Usually with a new pool, the support equipment sits on a concrete slab without an enclosure. If you enclose the equipment for protection or for aesthetics, leave room for good ventilation and accessibility.

To prolong the life of your equipment, sweep the enclosure out and wipe down the equipment each time you clean the filter.

Use the following information to establish a maintenance routine and to supplement the recommendations of the various manufacturers. Eventually, you'll be able to work out your own schedule to keep your water in pristine condition.

Considered a single component, and most often called simply "the pump," the pump and motor are usually purchased already assembled on the same base. The type most frequently used for home pools has self-lubricating bearings and seals.

The owner's manual for your pump outlines the maintenance required. Usually, you'll only need to remove hair, leaves, and other debris from the strainer basket when you vacuum the pool *(page 143)* or when you've shut off the pump to clean the filter.

Have an extra basket ready to install when you remove the dirty one. Then you can clean the dirty basket at your convenience (it's easier to clean after the hair and other debris have dried). Extra gaskets and O-rings are also useful.

Though most home pool pumps are self-priming, they may lose prime when the basket is cleaned or when there's an air leak under the basket cover or elsewhere in the line from the pool to the pump. To prime the pump, remove the hair and lint strainer lid, fill the pump to brimming with water, keep the water hose running, and start the pump. Within a few seconds it should be pumping water free of air bubbles. If not, try the priming procedure again.

If it doesn't work, call a service technician. Running a pump dry or with air entering the system can cause overheating and seriously damage both pump and motor.

Cleaning a pump

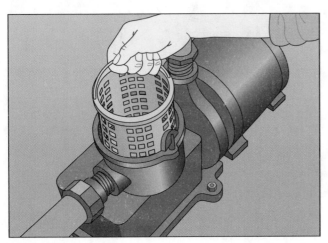

Cleaning the pump's hair and lint strainer
To remove the basket, shut off the pump; if the pump is below water level, turn off the valves on the pipes from the skimmer and main drain, otherwise, you'll be doused with water when you remove the basket cover. Then remove the cover, lift out the basket, and either clean it or replace it with a spare.

After the clean basket is in place, replace the gasket or O-ring, position the lid and tighten it securely. Open the valves on the skimmer and main drainpipes and turn the pump on. If it does not pump water immediately, shut the pump off and prime it *(see above)*.

No matter what kind of filter your pool has, the filtering media must be cleaned periodically or replaced to keep your pool water in good condition. The various types of filters are cleaned in different ways, as described below and on the following pages.

The obvious time to clean the filter is when the water is no longer clear. The ideal time, though, is before the quality of the water deteriorates. The best indicators of when to clean are pressure gauges and flow meters. Ideally, you should have two pressure gauges—one on the line into the filter (the influent line) and one on the return line out of the filter (the effluent line)—and a flow meter, as described below.

Don't clean your filter if the pressure gauges and flow meter reading say you don't need to. Contrary to expectation, a slightly dirty filter usually does a better job of filtering small particles out of the water.

High-rate sand filters: To clean a sand filter, water is circulated through it in the reverse direction, a process known as backwashing. This reversed flow of water through the filter raises the sand bed and cleans it, carrying the dirt and debris out through the waste line.

These filters have a valve that controls the flow of water. Two common types, a multiport valve (also called a rotary valve) and a slide valve, are illustrated on page 151.

In many parts of the country, it is illegal to send backwash water directly into the sewer system or storm drains. If this is the case in your area, you'll need a neutralization tank to hold the water until it's safe to release it.

The multiport valve has some additional positions, which you may find useful occasionally. The "recirculate" position bypasses the filter and can be used until a leaky filter is repaired. The position marked "waste" discharges water from the pool directly into the waste line. Use this position to lower the water level or to get rid of a lot of dirt when you're vacuuming the pool.

Use the "closed" position when the system is not running, such as during a shutdown for the winter. Never run the pump with the valve in this position.

Open your filter and inspect the sand every year. You may find channeling and mudballs, as illustrated on the following page. If you do,

HELPFUL INDICATORS

Pressure gauges and flow meters can tell you when you need to clean your filter. If you have two pressure gauges, record the difference in pressure between them when the filter is clean. As the filter gets dirty, the difference between the two readings will increase. Clean the filter when the difference increases by 10 to 15 psi. If you only have one pressure gauge, it will be attached to the filter itself. Again, record the starting pressure, and clean the filter when the gauge shows an increase of 10 to 15 psi.

A flow meter measures the number of gallons of water per minute flowing through the system. Record the flow when starting up with a clean filter. Flow will decrease as the filter gets dirty. Clean the filter when the flow decreases by 10%.

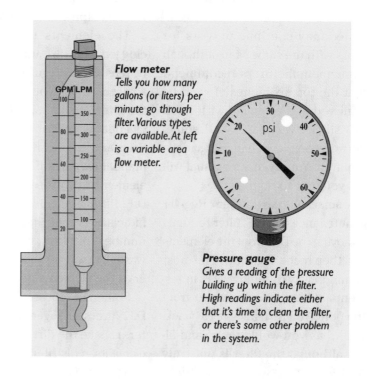

Flow meter
Tells you how many gallons (or liters) per minute go through filter. Various types are available. At left is a variable area flow meter.

Pressure gauge
Gives a reading of the pressure building up within the filter. High readings indicate either that it's time to clean the filter, or there's some other problem in the system.

FILTERING IMPEDIMENTS

Inside a sand filter, mudballs and channels may form, as illustrated at right. You'll probably notice a decline in water quality, because the water passes so quickly through the sand that impurities are not filtered out.

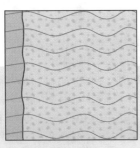

Normal water flow
Sand particles well separated; water passes in many streams through most of the sand.

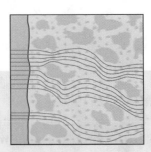

Partly impeded water flow
Mudballs beginning to form; water forced into fewer channels.

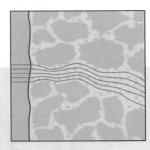

Impeded water flow
Multitude of mudballs forces water through one large channel; filtering capacity of sand is greatly reduced.

clean the sand with a commercially available sand-cleaning solution or sodium bisulfate. This should break up mudballs and channels inside the sand. Also check for scale, which indicates water that's improperly balanced. If you've noticed sand in the pool, especially near the return line, it may indicate that the laterals inside the filter are broken. Call a service technician for assistance.

A filter that's been properly maintained may continue to work for years with the same sand, although some manufacturers recommend that the top six inches of sand be removed and replaced with fresh #20 silica every year. And sometimes, a complete change of sand is required. Your owner's manual will tell you how to do the job.

Diatomaceous earth filters: Regular maintenance of a D.E. filter requires removing the D.E. from the elements and then recoating them. The most common way to remove D.E. in residential filters is to use water from the pool. You turn a valve to "backwash," as you would for a sand filter, although the filter is not truly backwashed the way a sand filter is.

After you've backwashed, follow manufacturer's recommendations for the amount of D.E. to add. Turn the valve to "precoat," mix D.E. with water and add it to the D.E. slurry pot, if your system has one, or into the skimmer with the pump running. Once the D.E. is added, turn the valve to its normal operating position. CAUTION: Inhaling D.E. can cause serious lung disease; always wear a respirator when handling it.

The elements themselves get clogged with dirt and oil that can't be removed by regular maintenance, so occasionally you'll need to drain the filter, open it, take it apart, and clean it, as described on page 152, then add new D.E. Your owner's manual explains how to clean the elements in your particular type of D.E. filter and how often. A good indicator is that the filter run (the number of days between backwashings) will get shorter and shorter as the elements get dirtier.

Some D.E. filters (called bump D.E. filters or regenerative D.E. filters) shake the dirt and D.E. off the elements, redistribute it, and replace it, rather than backwashing and adding new D.E. The idea is that since the D.E. gets dirtiest on the surface, if you move it around you'll take advantage of the cleaner D.E. underneath. After a few bumps, though, you'll still have to thoroughly clean the elements and replace the D.E.

In some communities, there are restrictions on the use of D.E. filters. Usually, the regulations apply to the disposal of the used D.E. and water containing it. In these communities you're required (and elsewhere it's recommended) to include a separation tank in your circulation system. When water is drained from the filter for cleaning, it is sent to the separation tank. There, the D.E. is strained out of it through a mesh bag. The water can then be returned to the pool, and the used D.E. can be removed and disposed of as a hazardous waste.

If you replace the D.E. with cellulose fiber, you'll have to clean your filter more frequently than you're used to at first because the fiber does a better job.

Cartridge filters: The most common filter for spas, cartridge filters are relatively easy to clean. You remove the filter, hose it off, and soak it to remove oils, as described on page 152. Check your owner's manual for instructions specific to your model.

If you're using a cartridge filter on a newly plastered pool, the plaster dust will clog the cartridges. Many pool builders supply extra cartridges for start-up so you can throw away the first set after the plaster dust is removed from the water.

Owning a spare set of cartridges is a good idea anyway. That way, you can remove the dirty ones, replace them with spares, and still use the pool or spa while you're cleaning the first set. Some spa dealers will clean cartridges for you, for a small fee. Store clean spare cartridges submerged in a barrel of water or in dark garbage bags out of the sun to keep them moist and to prevent algae growth.

THE HEATER AND SKIMMER

Maintenance of pool heaters varies depending on the type. Check your owner's manual for the maintenance needs of your model.

Generally, open-flame and electric heaters should be checked out by a service representative before you start up the pool in the spring. It may be necessary to disassemble the heater and clean the tubes of scale with a wire brush or acid.

During the swimming season, you'll need to clean the strainer basket in the skimmer frequently. If debris is allowed to accumulate, it will stop the skimming action that helps keep the water surface clean. Be sure to include cleaning the strainer basket of the skimmer as part of your regular maintenance routine, as discussed on page 142.

Backwashing a sand filter

To regulate the flow with a multiport or slide valve, turn off the heater and the pump and clean the pump strainer basket. Close the valve on the pool return line and open the valve on the discharge line to dispose of the dirty water. Turn the multiport valve *(near right)* or raise the handle of the slide valve *(far right)* to the backwash position.

Turn the pump on and let it run until the water passing through the sight glass on the discharge line is clear; usually between 2 and 10 minutes. Turn off the pump, close the valve on the discharge

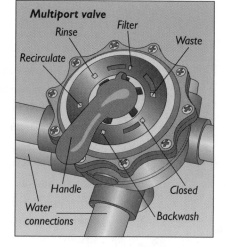

Multiport valve
Rinse
Filter
Recirculate
Waste
Handle
Closed
Water connections
Backwash

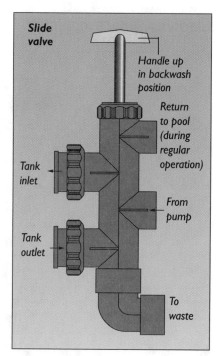

Slide valve
Handle up in backwash position
Return to pool (during regular operation)
Tank inlet
From pump
Tank outlet
To waste

line, and open the valve on the return line. If you have a multiport valve, turn it to rinse, so that water will flow through the filter bed in the normal direction and into the waste line, then turn the pump back on and run it for 15 to 20 seconds.

Shut the pump off again and turn the rotary valve to filter or lower the slide valve to the normal position for routing water through the filter and back into the pool. Turn the pump back on. Bleed the air from the filter by opening the valve at the top of the tank. Record the pressure and flow rate through the filter, so you'll know when it needs cleaning again.

Cleaning a diatomaceous earth filter

Turn off the heater and pump and clean the strainer basket. Bleed the air out of the filter to release pressure, then close the valves on the lines leading into and out of the filter. Adjust the valve to drain the water out of the filter and into the separation tank.

Carefully remove the elements from the filter one at a time and rinse them with a strong spray of water from a nozzle. To remove grease and oil, soak the elements in a commercially available filter cleaning solution or a solution of 1 cup trisodium phosphate (TSP) to 1 gallon of water for 4 to 8 hours (right). Then soak them in a solution of 1 part sodium bisulfate to 10 parts water for 4 to 8 hours. CAUTION: Always add acid to water, not water to acid. Finally, soak the elements in a solution of sodium bicarbonate (baking soda) and water for 2 to 4 hours to neutralize the acid, then rinse the elements with fresh water.

Replace the elements in the filter tank, aligning them carefully. Replace the lid and clamp assembly. Then fill the tank with fresh water, turn the pump back on, and add new diatomaceous earth.

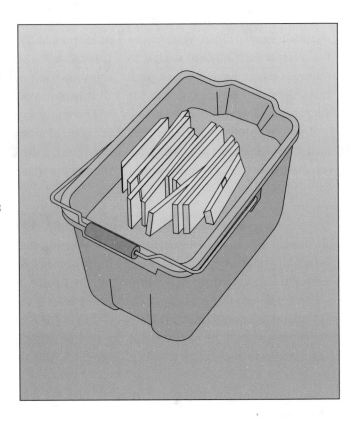

Cleaning a cartridge filter

If the filter is below water level, close the valve from the main drain and skimmer. Turn off the heater and pump and clean the strainer basket. Bleed the air out of the filter, then open the drain valve for the filter housing and allow the water to drain out. Open the housing and remove the cartridges, then rinse out the inside of the tank. Place the spare cartridges inside and close the tank, then close the drain, fill the tank, and restart the system.

To clean the dirty cartridges, first rinse them using a high-pressure nozzle on your garden hose. Direct the water stream at an angle to the cartridge to remove the dirt (left). Then soak the cartridges in a plastic container in a solution of 1 cup TSP to 1 gallon of water for 4 to 8 hours. Or use a filter-cleaning solution. Then soak them in a solution of 1 part sodium bisulfate to 10 parts water for 4 to 8 hours. CAUTION: Always add acid to water, not water to acid. Finally, soak cartridges in a solution of sodium bicarbonate (baking soda) and water for 2 to 4 hours, to neutralize the acid, then rinse with fresh water. Store the clean cartridges.

Seasonal Care

In cold climates, you'll need to prepare your pool or spa for the winter months and then get it ready in the spring for a new season. Even in more temperate regions, you may not use your pool during the winter, so it will require some special seasonal care.

Winterizing your pool: To empty or not to empty the pool? Many pool owners living in cold climates ask this question when preparing to winterize. The answer is almost always

not to empty the pool. Today's pools are carefully engineered to counterbalance the forces from the ground against the forces exerted by the water in the pool. Pools can be damaged or destroyed by external pressures acting on them when they're empty.

It's recommended that you do not empty your pool unless it's an above-ground model with a vinyl liner. If it is, follow the manufacturer's recommendations for winterizing.

Cold climate protection: There are steps you can take to protect your pool in areas where there is winter freeze. Generally, it's okay if the pool water freezes, as long as the pipes are drained and equipment is protected.

Blow water out of all lines with the reverse flow of a tank vacuum cleaner or with an air compressor. If there's a chance that any water remains, add a nontoxic antifreeze, such as propylene glycol, diluted

WINTER WEAR FOR POOLS AND SPAS

Covering a pool in winter is a good idea, and a safety cover is an especially good choice. Not only does it keep out debris and rain or snow, thus reducing your spring cleaning chores, it helps keep people and animals from falling into the pool.

If you choose a loose cover, a large floating ball under the cover will help prevent water from pooling on top. The cover should be at least 5 feet longer and wider than the pool to protect the coping and support the snow load, if any.

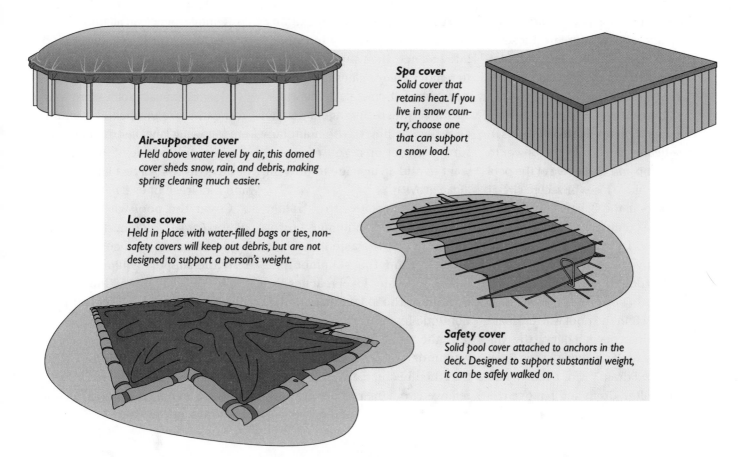

Air-supported cover
Held above water level by air, this domed cover sheds snow, rain, and debris, making spring cleaning much easier.

Loose cover
Held in place with water-filled bags or ties, non-safety covers will keep out debris, but are not designed to support a person's weight.

Spa cover
Solid cover that retains heat. If you live in snow country, choose one that can support a snow load.

Safety cover
Solid pool cover attached to anchors in the deck. Designed to support substantial weight, it can be safely walked on.

TIPS FOR A TROUBLE-FREE SPRING OPENING

A pool properly maintained during the winter months can be prepared for a new season of swimming with a minimum of effort.

• Pump, hose, or sweep away water, dirt, or debris from the cover and deck.

• Remove the cover and plugs from all openings.

• If the water was in good shape at the end of last season, you can keep the same water. Otherwise, drain and refill the pool.

• Raise the underwater lights from the bottom of the pool and install them in their niches.

• Turn on the electric power and start up the support system. Check for leaks and proper operation. If you find any problems, consult your owner's manual. Have the heater professionally serviced before you use it.

• Test and adjust the pH and total alkalinity. Superchlorinate and add cyanuric acid if required for your pool. See page 128 for more information about keeping the pool water clean. Run the pump 24 hours a day at the beginning of the season when it may be difficult to get the pool water balanced. You can reduce the pump operating time in one-hour increments once you've got the water in shape. Treat the water with an algaecide. After several hours of operation, test the chlorine level and adjust it as needed. If the chlorine level is high, do not use the pool until it drops to normal levels.

---

one part to two parts water. Don't use automotive antifreeze. Close off return lines, vacuum line, and skimmers with expandable rubber winterizing plugs.

Drain the water from the heater, filter, and pump. Turn off the gas to the heater and all electric power to the pump and to the rest of the pool area. Remove fuses or secure circuit breakers in the OFF position to prevent the pump from turning on accidentally. Disconnect, clean, and store any chemical feeders.

Thoroughly clean and vacuum the pool *(page 142)*. Any dirt or debris left in the pool will dissipate the chlorine needed during the winter months. If you have a sand filter, clean and drain it. For a D.E. or cartridge filter, drain and remove elements or cartridges.

Test the water and make any adjustments necessary to bring it into balance, then superchlorinate to remove chloramines. If you have a problem with metals in the water, add a sequestering agent to the water according to the manufacturer's directions. You may also want to add an algicide to prevent algae growth.

Clean and remove the strainer basket from the skimmer. Lower the water to the waste line. Close the valve on the skimmer line before the water level reaches the bottom of the skimmer opening. Continue lowering the water level until the return lines are exposed. Any underwater wet niche lights that then become exposed can be removed from their niches and lowered to the bottom of the pool.

Remove and clean all pool accessories, and store them indoors. If you have a jump board, remove it and store it flat.

Most chemicals don't store well. You can store unopened containers following label instructions, but it's best to dispose of open ones. Always dispose of test kit reagents and buy fresh ones each year.

Cover the pool with a winter cover *(page 153)*, and coat any exposed metal surfaces, particularly the support equipment, with grease or oil as protection against rust and corrosion. If the support equipment is not sheltered, loosely cover it with plastic sheeting. **Mild climate protection:** If your winters are mild, you need only to continue routine maintenance, but on a reduced schedule.

Run the filter for at least one hour out of four, so that the pool water is circulated through the system at least once a day. Clean the skimmer; check and adjust the pH and free chlorine once a week. Maintain the filter properly and vacuum whenever the pool looks dirty.

Covering your pool will keep it cleaner and minimize chlorine consumption. A safety cover is recommended. Superchlorinate and add an algicide before putting the cover in place. After superchlorination, the free chlorine level should return to normal. If not, add more chlorine. After you cover the pool, check the chlorine level occasionally and adjust it, if necessary.

Winter care for spas: If your climate lends itself to winter soaks, you can just continue regular maintenance and use the spa as usual. An insulated cover is especially important to avoid wasting time and energy reheating the water.

When the weather doesn't permit outdoor soaking, lower the heater thermostat but keep the circulation system running constantly. Insulating the pipes will help keep them from freezing.

During severe freezes, all support systems should be drained, even if they're insulated or sheltered. The spa should also be drained, unless it's a wood tub. Wood tubs cannot be left unfilled for more than two days at a time, and must be designed so that the plumbing can be drained while the tub remains full.

A Cold-Climate Ice Rink

In areas with at least two months of cold weather (average daily temperatures below freezing), you can turn your swimming pool into an ice rink.

Winterize the pipes and equipment as usual. Then lower the water to about 18 inches below the cop-ing. Lay a vinyl liner in the pool so that it floats on the water and extends up over the sides of the pool and out onto the deck about 2½ feet. Hold the liner in place with weighted water or sandbags around the perimeter of the liner, but make sure they don't pull it out of contact with the water.

Add four inches of water on top of the liner and let it freeze. Before you let anyone skate, make sure that there is at least 4 inches of ice. Check the ice depth daily.

If you have an in-ground pool and live in a cold climate, you might consider having your pool do double duty as an ice rink. The ice won't harm the pool, and the rink offers an easily supervised area for practice, lessons, or just a relaxing family skate.

Repairing
A POOL OR SPA

Most well-built and well-maintained pools and spas will provide years and years of enjoyment. But even a carefully maintained facility can show signs of wear and tear: decks can crack due to earth movements, the shell surface can change color, and the support system can break down. These small problems will turn into major repair jobs if the proper steps are not taken promptly. A few repairs—or a simple refurbishing project—may be all you need to restore the appearance of your pool or spa. This chapter describes some of the common problems you may encounter and explains the necessary repairs; you'll also find a discussion of possibilities for renewing the look of your pool or spa, such as adding accessories and decorative features.

Shell Problems

Deterioration of the shell is not only unsightly, but can also affect both water level and water quality. Repairs should be done as soon as possible to prevent complications.

You'll probably want to have a contractor do any major work for you. Try to find someone who specializes in repairs, and use the same criteria as you did in selecting a builder for a new pool *(page 37)*.

CRACKS

In-ground vessels, whether pools or spas, must withstand constantly changing pressures from movements in the surrounding soil. The walls may crack under the strain of these movements. Changes in water temperature, drainage problems, and structural flaws can also cause cracks.

Small cracks: Changes in water temperature can produce small cracks in concrete that usually can be repaired fairly easily, as outlined on page 158. Underwater patching materials are available, so it may not even be necessary to drain the pool or spa.

Large cracks: Although small surface cracks are fairly common and harmless, large cracks may indicate a serious problem that's usually hard to repair. Two conditions are of particular concern: cracks created by soil movement due to poor drainage; and cracks brought about by inadequate pool or spa wall construction. If you suspect either problem, you'll want to consult a soil engineer.

The only way to repair a badly constructed pool or spa is to undo what was originally done wrong. Review your warranty to see if the repairs are covered by the builder.

Cracks, whether large or small, in a fiberglass pool or spa may indicate a structural flaw in the shell. You should call in an expert as soon as possible.

SURFACE PROBLEMS

A host of annoying problems can mar your pool's or spa's surface— from algae growth to spalling to scaling. Sharp objects can tear a vinyl liner and even sunlight can take its toll. These problems are a nuisance, but only rarely do they present a serious problem.

Spalling plaster: Daily contact with chemicals and changing water temperatures slowly dissolve the plaster, causing it to flake and chip. This is called "spalling." Other causes of spalling include bond failure between the plaster surface and the structural layer underneath, improperly mixed plaster, and exposure to extremes of heat and cold.

Spalling detracts from the pool or spa's appearance and can produce rough surfaces that scrape bathers and are more likely to stain. Algae growth and scale deposits collecting on the weakened plaster contribute to more spalling. ➤

GELCOAT DETERIORATION

Though designed to be durable, the smooth gelcoat surface on a fiberglass pool or spa may eventually fade, chip, change color, or stain. As discussed on page 56, gelcoat deterioration detracts from the shell's appearance but rarely constitutes a serious problem.

Because of the likelihood of deterioration, gelcoat is no longer used as a surface coating on fiberglass spas. But if you have a fiberglass shell with a gelcoat surface, you may find that gelcoat deterioration is covered in its warranty.

If the damage is localized, more gelcoat is applied over the affected areas. If the damage is widespread, it may be necessary to drain the pool or spa and recoat the entire shell, or even replace the shell.

A coat of epoxy paint can improve the appearance of an older fiberglass shell. Be sure to follow the recommendations of the paint manufacturer; as always, preparing the surface properly before painting is essential if the paint is to adhere.

While spalling plaster itself isn't a structural danger, it can lead to more significant problems if the structural material underneath (such as concrete block or shotcrete) is exposed. Spalling should be repaired as soon as possible.

If spalling is slight, you may be able to sand and patch it with new plaster or an epoxy coating. Normal maintenance (brushing the walls) and water action will soon blend the spot into the surrounding plaster. Or hire a company to match the color. A coat of paint will freshen up a patched pool. Paint for plaster is usually either rubber base or solvent base. Repaint with the same type as is already on the pool, if possible. Otherwise, you'll have to sand the old paint off. Follow manufacturer's directions for painting.

Do not drain a pool or spa to work on it without a professional's assistance. A drained shell may crack or pop out of the ground. A hydrostatic relief valve *(page 93)* can reduce this risk.

Patching and painting, shown below and on the opposite page, is a time-consuming job, but it is something you can accomplish yourself. Obtain instructions and supplies from a pool service company or pool equipment supplier, and very carefully prepare the surface to be plastered.

If spalling is excessive, you may need to have a plasterer sandblast the old finish and replaster. It's an expensive job, but it will erase all evidence of the old problems. ➤

Patching a crack in concrete

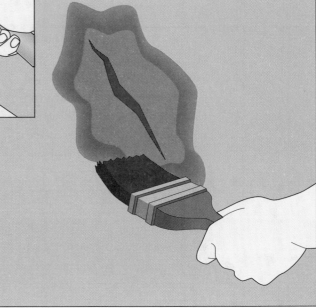

1 Cleaning up the crack
With a cold chisel and a hammer, remove loose material and enlarge the crack, smoothing the edges as much as possible. Tap the chisel lightly, being careful not to gouge too deeply into the concrete *(left)*.

2 Preparing to fill the crack
Dip a paintbrush in water and wet the crack and surrounding area along its entire length. If bits of concrete come loose, remove them.

3 Applying patching compound

Using a trowel or float, work patching compound into the crack until it is filled and the surface is even *(right)*. Portland cement or hydraulic patching mixture containing portland cement is suitable. Follow the instructions provided by the manufacturer.

Repeat this procedure for all remaining cracks.

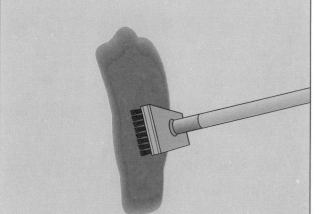

4 Etching the shell

While the patched cracks are still damp, etch the concrete of the entire shell with muriatic acid, mixing one part acid and two parts tap water in a nonmetallic bucket. (Always add acid to water, not water to acid.) Wearing rubber gloves, protective goggles, and rubber boots, apply the acid on all surfaces with a pool brush, as shown at left. Rinse the brush when finished.

5 Painting the shell

Using a paint roller, apply two or three coats of paint or plastic cement sealer on the entire inside surface of the shell. Solvent-base paints can also be sprayed on. Always follow the paint manufacturer's instructions carefully for best results.

A concrete pool or spa will probably need to be replastered about 7 to 10 years after it is built, and then every few years throughout its lifetime. (Replastering never lasts as long as the original plaster finish.) The surface will also need to be repainted every year or two.

Torn lining: Sharp objects can tear the lining of a vinyl pool, but such small tears can be repaired easily.

Two kinds of kits are available for fixing liners—patches and liquid sealers. Some vinyl companies even offer underwater patching kits, so you don't need to drain the pool to make repairs. The steps for applying a dry patch are shown below.

Making sound repairs to a tear longer than 2 or 3 inches can prove difficult. Try to repair it, but if that doesn't work, you'll need to replace the liner. Most liners are installed with special fittings that facilitate removing the old unit and installing a new one.

Like the original, a new liner must be manufactured to fit the existing pool size and shape exactly. Since the liner must be installed accurately to prevent buckling or stretching, you'll probably want to hire a professional to do the

Repairing a liner pool

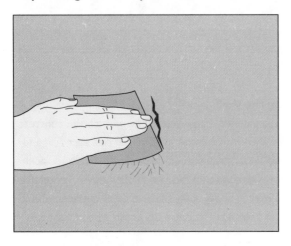

1 Preparing the liner
Roughen the area around the tear with sandpaper *(above)*.

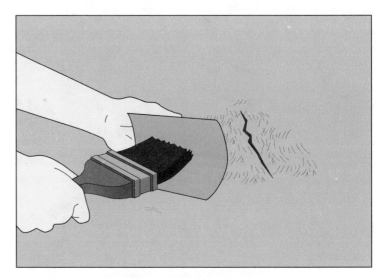

2 Preparing the patch
Cut a liner patch to extend about 6" on either side of the tear. Apply solvent cement to the liner and the patch with a paintbrush. Make sure the cement extends beyond the damaged area, while remaining within the edges of the patch.

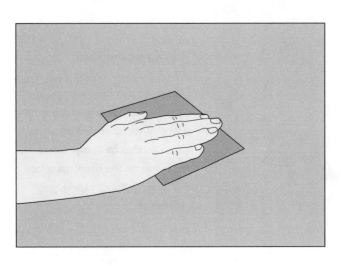

3 Applying the patch
Position the patch over the damaged area and smooth it in place *(left)*. If the damaged area is under water, apply pressure from the center of the patch toward the edges to squeeze out any water. If possible, use sandbags to weight the patch until the solvent dries.

work. If you want to replace the liner yourself, ask the manufacturer for instructions.

Discoloration: The most common shell problems—and the most easily repaired—are stains and color changes on pool walls. These stains may be the result of a number of things, including algae and excess metals in the water. Refer to the chapter beginning on page 128 if you suspect a water chemistry problem is your culprit. A list of other stain causers and possible solutions is given on page 137.

Sometimes, a plaster pool will become mottled, for reasons not fully understood. Though you may want to repaint or replaster the surface of a mottled pool or spa, you can choose to leave it as is. Sometimes, the mottled effect may even be pleasing, especially if yours is a naturalistic pool.

Vinyl-lined pools can also be discolored by overchlorination, by chemicals applied directly on the surface without proper dilution, or by stains from a wooden sidewall. The daily bombardment of ultraviolet light from the sun can also fade the liner. You can sometimes clean a stained liner or cover the stain with a patch; a faded liner is more likely to tear and probably will have to be replaced.

Stains on the bottom of a vinyl-lined pool that don't continue up the pool sides may indicate fungal growth in the sand below the pool. The stained liner should be replaced, perhaps with one that includes an antifungal additive in the material, and the sand below the pool should be treated with a 20:1 diluted solution of sodium hypochlorite to rid it of any fungus.

LEAKS

Pool walls or pipes that leak can prove very costly to pool owners. A leak is often insidious, going undetected until it has reached a serious level. Water leaking into the ground can cause major difficulties, either by undermining the pool or deck or by expanding the soil so it exerts enough pressure to crack the pool shell.

Leaks can also be expensive. Not only will you end up paying additional chemical, pumping, and heating costs to introduce new water into the system, depending on where you live, you'll also have to pay to replace the water itself. ➤

Bucket testing

If you suspect that your water level is dropping more than usual because of a slow leak, mark a line on the side of the pool at the waterline. Fill a bucket 3/4 full with water and mark the waterline on the inside of it. Leave the bucket inside the pool so they both have the same temperature, and don't add any water to either the pool or the bucket for 24 hours.

After this time, the water level in both the bucket and the pool will have gone down (right). Mark the new water level on both, and measure the distance between the marks on both the pool and the bucket. If water loss in the pool is due to evaporation only, the difference between the high and low marks will be the same for the bucket and the pool. If the difference between the marks on the pool is substantially greater, then the pool, or the circulation system, has a leak.

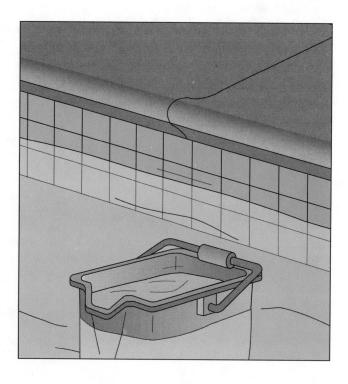

Evaporation will take a lot more water out of your pool than you might expect. However, if you feel your pool's losing water at a fairly high rate, a simple way to determine if it has a leak is to do a bucket test, as described on page 161. To reduce the amount of water your pool loses to evaporation, invest in a cover.

If you discover that you have a leak, the next step is finding it, which is often difficult. The leak could be anywhere—in the circulation system, in the pool wall, or around a light, skimmer, or wall fitting. You may be able to locate it yourself with a leak tester, a colored fluid added to the pool that, with sufficient suction, is drawn into the leak. Or you may decide to leave the job to a professional who has experience searching for leaks. Diving underwater may be required.

BULGES

If the walls of your vinyl-lined or fiberglass pool are bulging, it may indicate drainage or structural problems that need to be dealt with promptly. Whether the problem is one of drainage or structure, it's a major one that will likely require excavation and repair around the pool, or even replacement of side-wall panels in a vinyl-lined pool. Call in a pool professional.

MAJOR RENOVATIONS

If your pool shell has deteriorated to the point where it needs major repairs, you may want to consider building a new shell inside the old one. Treating the old pool as a big hole in the ground, your contractor builds a completely new pool in the hole; the new pool, of course, will be shallower and smaller than the original. Three new shell options are shown below.

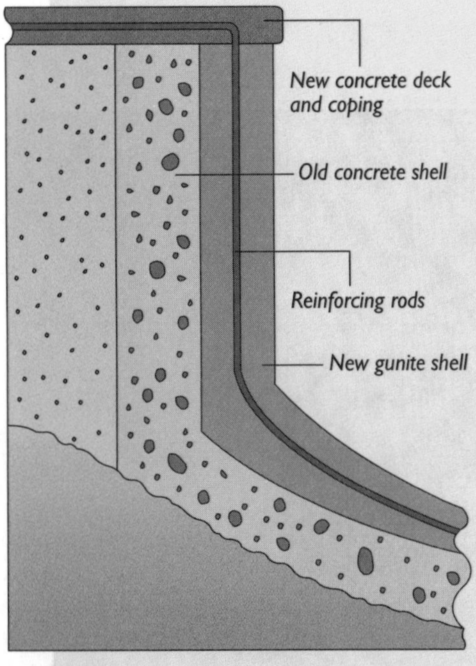

New gunite shell

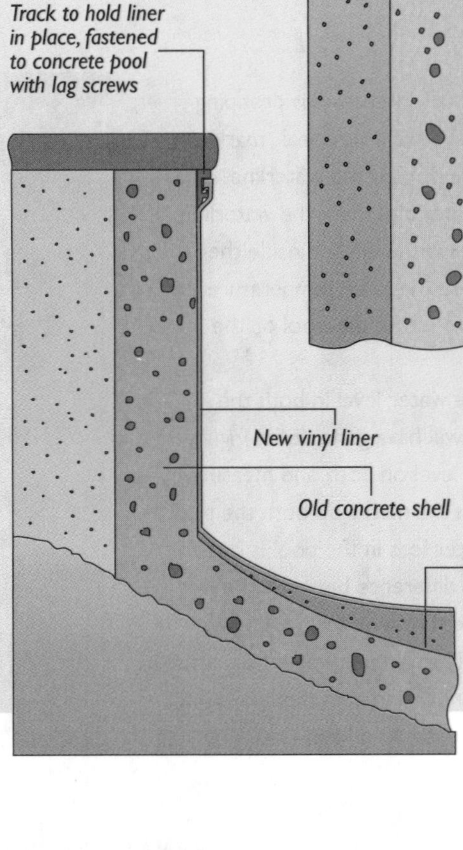

New vinyl liner

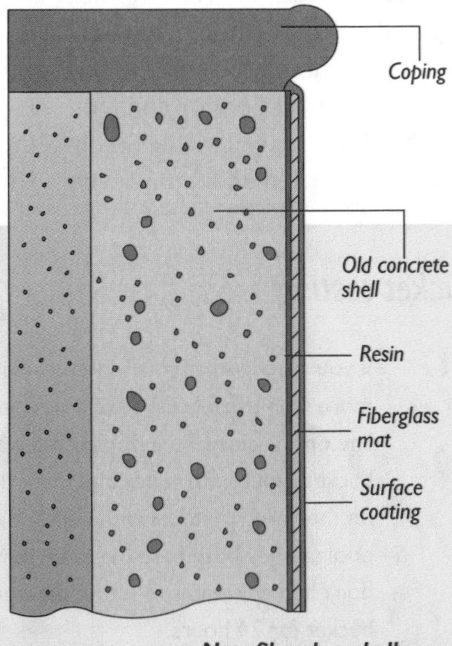

New fiberglass shell

162

Support System Problems

Over the years, you can almost certainly expect that some part of the mechanical support system—the pump, filter, heater, or pipes—will break down. This support equipment has a finite life and can be damaged by poor maintenance, water conditions, or the environment in which it's operating.

Even in the absence of any problems, you may want to consider upgrading or replacing a piece of equipment, such as changing to a filter that is easier to clean or installing a solar heating system or a more energy-efficient pump. For information on the different choices available, consult the chapter on pool and spa equipment. Any new equipment must meet the requirements of your pool or spa and be compatible with existing equipment.

Pump: The heart of the support system, the pump circulates water through the pipes, filter, and heater, enabling them to do their jobs. If the pump breaks down, your system will be inoperative.

Some of the most common pump problems, with some ideas for repairing them, are provided in the chart below. You'll also want to consult your owner's manual for the

PUMP AND MOTOR TROUBLE-SHOOTING CHART

PROBLEM	CAUSE	SOLUTION
Electrical problem	Bad timer or switch. Loose wire. Blown fuse or tripped circuit breaker.	For a blown fuse or tripped circuit breaker, remove the cause before restarting the motor. Otherwise, have a qualified electrician make repairs.
Humming	Internal motor switch set for wrong level of voltage.	Adjust switch to correct level of voltage (120 or 240 volts, depending on incoming voltage). Spin shaft. If it won't turn, some object is probably blocked inside.
	Something is jammed inside of impeller.	Remove jammed object and prime the pump if necessary before restarting it. If it does spin, capacitor may be worn out.
	Faulty or worn out capacitor.	Remove capacitor cover. Check for white residue or liquid discharge. Replace capacitor if necessary.
Noise	Loose connections between pump and motor.	Tighten connections.
	Worn motor bearings.	Replace bearings (refer to owner's manual for instructions).
	Cavitation; may be caused by excessive vacuum on suction side of pump; pump trying to discharge more water than is coming in.	Have system assessed by expert; pipe size may be wrong, flow may be too high, pump may be too large.
Overheating	No water passing through pump. Loss of prime.	Shut off pump immediately to avoid serious damage to pump and motor. Check that the strainer basket isn't clogged and that no valve has been closed by mistake. Reprime. If this doesn't work, and you can find nothing wrong, call a service technician.
Leaks around pump shaft	Seal around pump shaft worn.	Replace seal (refer to owner's manual for instructions).

pump. Though most pump repairs must be done by a professional, a pool or spa owner can make some of the basic repairs. If you think your pump is malfunctioning, turn it off; don't allow it to run dry or you can damage the motor.

Filter system: It's easy to spot a run-down filter system—the water is turbid and you may be able to see debris in it. Your filter may need nothing more than normal maintenance. Review the maintenance procedures for the filter beginning on page 149. Check that the baskets in the skimmer and the hair and lint strainer aren't clogged. Clean or replace your filter media or cartridge if necessary.

If the problems persist, the surface area of your filter may not be large enough. Perhaps more people are now using the pool or spa than you originally planned for when choosing the filter size. Or maybe there's been a change in the composition of your local water. Trees around the pool or spa may be shedding more leaves into it. If this is the case, covering the pool or spa between dips may help the filter do its job by reducing the amount of debris that falls in. Otherwise, you might have to increase the amount of chemicals you're using, run your filter longer, or replace the filter with a larger model or one of a different design.

Another possibility is that the pump is too powerful for the filter. If the pump pushes the water through the filter too quickly, not all the particles may be removed. With a sand filter, fast water flow encourages the water to form channels, bypassing the majority of the sand. For more on channeling, see page 150.

Consider, too, the water circulation system in your pool. Are there dead spots where leaves and debris are collecting? Are the outlets adequate to carry the water to be filtered? Inlets and outlets can be added to any type of pool. It's usually a major undertaking, requiring new openings to be made in the pool walls and new pipes connected to the circulation system. Call in a professional pool builder, preferably one with experience in repairing existing pools.

Heater: Is your heater undependable as a source of heat? Does your unit require more energy to heat the pool or spa than it once did? Most heater malfunctions result from mechanical problems, such as a breakdown of the thermostat, scale buildup in the heater lines blocking the water flow, or accumulated debris blocking air or water circulation through the heater.

A heater that's less efficient than it was in the past may have a problem with scale buildup. Water that's even slightly out of balance can allow scale to collect in the heater and block water flow. You may even see flakes of scale coming from the heater return line. If so, have a heater repair expert clean off the scale; if there's a large accumulation in an old heater, you may need to replace the unit. You can avoid scale buildup by keeping the water in proper balance. It's best to have the heater checked annually, and cleaned if necessary. This makes the cleaning job easier and may mean you can avoid the costly expense of having the heater replaced.

ENERGY-EFFICIENT EQUIPMENT

Ever-increasing energy costs are convincing many pool owners to replace units in their support systems with more energy-efficient ones. In some areas, solar heating your pool or spa is a real possibility. A solar-heating system can be used alone or in combination with a conventional one. See page 79 for more information. Another option to consider is the heat pump. Heat pumps are rapidly gaining in popularity and are up to four times as energy efficient as conventional heaters.

Problems around the Pool

In the same way that soil movement can crack a pool shell, it can also pop and crack tiles around the outside of the pool and damage decks and coping. Unless it creates a safety hazard for swimmers or sunbathers, damage to tiles and decks is not of serious concern, though it can detract from the appearance of your pool.

Tile problems: The tile trim that edges some pools is especially sensitive to earth movement—sometimes, it may only take 1/8 of an inch of soil movement around the pool to crack or pop tile. The problem is compounded when the deck or area surrounding the pool has been built improperly, such as an uneven bond beam or a deck expanding into the pool wall.

It may be possible to re-lay the tile with a better adhesive than was used originally. But if the cracking or popping problem is caused by faulty construction of the bond beam or deck, you'll have to dig up the area around the pool and rebuild it properly.

Deck and coping woes: Cracked paving and split expansion joints in the deck usually indicate substantial movement in the soil around your pool. But even a small movement can cause cracking, especially if your deck is constructed of several close-fitting materials expanding at different rates.

A cracked deck is not necessarily a harbinger of pool shell problems. If your pool has been solidly constructed, or if a drainage diversion underneath your deck is causing the cracking, the shell itself probably won't crack.

On the other hand, if your deck is expanding into the pool shell and putting pressure on it, you may want to have an engineering consultant advise you on how much pressure your pool can withstand.

Damaged coping, especially cracks and splitting at the joints between coping stones, usually indicates similar problems with earth movement. But your coping can also crack from its own expansion and contraction, if it was installed without being properly cured. Cracks in the coping or deck can be repaired as described below.

If yours is an exposed aggregate deck, it's unlikely you'll be able to match the patching material to the surrounding area. Chip out a square-shaped or other defined space around the crack; lay mortar, as described below, to slightly below

---

COVERING AN OLD DECK

If the deck is severely cracked, you can build a new deck over the old one. But there are cautions to this approach. First, the new deck should be pliable to allow for continued settling in the base underneath. Don't simply pour more concrete over a cracked concrete deck. Secondly, continued soil settling or surfacing tree roots can also cause your deck to move vertically. If you lay a new deck over an old one, the new deck too will be subjected to vertical pressures and damage.

One option is to lay bricks or flagstones in a bed of sand over the damaged deck, as shown at right. The old coping can be replaced with a brick set in mortar. Or you can cover the deck with rubber or a cementitious coating, or build a new deck of wood or tile on top of the old one.

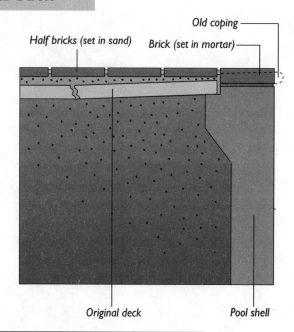

Half bricks (set in sand)

Old coping

Brick (set in mortar)

Original deck

Pool shell

the level of the surrounding deck. Using an aggregate that's similar in size and texture to the existing deck, sprinkle stone into the mortar, tamping down with a brick or other solid flat object. Brush the mortar until the stones project from the surface, and wash with a light spray of water. Cover the spot and allow the mortar to cure for three days; you can then uncover it and wash with a diluted muriatic acid solution.

Broken bricks or other paving stones in the deck or coping can be removed and replaced. Use a mortar rake or other tool to chip out the damaged stone, and replace it with one that's been cut to fit.

If your deck does move vertically, you can usually remove the affected slabs or paving stones and either build up the area underneath or cut away the growth causing the movement. But if your deck is concrete and is severely cracked by vertical movements, you may have to tear it up and start again.

Major deck construction can put pressure on your pool; contact a pool builder first for advice on how to avoid damaging the pool shell.

Expansion joints: Between the deck and the coping, and sometimes elsewhere in the deck, is a $1/4$- to $1/2$-inch gap filled with a backing rod and topped with sealant. This gap, called an expansion joint, allows the various materials to expand or contract with heat and cold without cracking; the sealant keeps the water out.

Eventually, the sealant will wear out and need to be replaced. Signs of wear include cracks in the sealant and gaps between the sealant and the edges of the concrete. To repair the joint, scrape out the old sealant using a chisel or screwdriver, then remove the backing rod, and clean the joint thoroughly with water and a brush. Once the joint is dry, add a new polyethylene foam backing rod and top it with a two-component polysulfide sealant, following the manufacturer's instructions.

Deck coatings: As your pool ages, the deck can be stained by calcium in splashed pool water, fade, or change color from ground-in dirt. Slippery spots can develop from the effects of weather.

Rather than replace the deck, you may choose to cover it with a deck coating or paint designed to produce an even, nonslip surface. Coatings come in a variety of colors (some match pool shell paints) and are available for most types of poolside pavings, though they're most often used on concrete decks.

Patching a crack in concrete

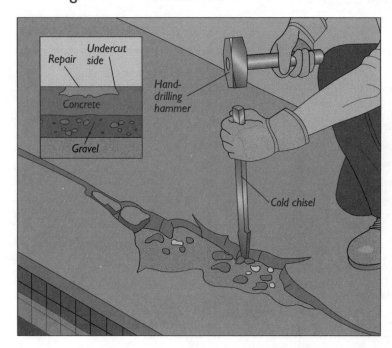

To repair hairline cracks in a concrete deck or coping, force a matching mortar, grout, or a latex patching compound into the crack and smooth it even with the concrete surface. Clean out larger cracks with a cold chisel and hand-drilling hammer *(left)*, undercutting the sides to hold the patching material. Fill the crack with a 1:2$1/4$ cement-sand and water mix with the consistency of soft mud, or a latex patching compound. Cover and cure for three days.

Spa Problems

In some ways, spas are not much different than pools: they're vessels that hold water, with the same type of support equipment and the same potential for breakdowns. But they do have features that make them more prone to certain types of problems.

In particular, spas are much more likely to leak than swimming pools, for a number of reasons. First, additional holes for hydrojets pass through the sides of the shell, creating more potential leak locations than the usual light fixture and skimmer openings. Second, spas are subjected to the stress of vibration when the jets are on, making the seals around the jets more likely to loosen and leak.

As with swimming pools, if you suspect the spa is leaking but you're not sure, conduct a bucket test, as described on page 161. If you know you have a leak, you can do a dye test to determine where it is. Or, you can hire a service technician to do the test and any necessary repairs.

To conduct a dye test, you'll need a small quantity of water-soluble dye. Red is a good choice because it's easily seen. With the spa filled and the jets off, step into the water and carefully make a circuit of the spa. Squirt dye close to each area that you suspect may be a source of leaks, such as any cracks, around light fixtures and jets, next to the drains, etc. If the dye just swirls around in front of one of these areas, you don't have a leak. If the dye is drawn in, you do have one, because it's being drawn through on water that's leaking out of the spa.

Leaks around fittings: If you find that a jet is leaking, the first thing to check is whether it's properly tightened. There are two kinds of jets, those that are tightened from the front (inside the spa) and those that are tightened from the back (outside the spa). If the jet is tightened from the back, you'll probably want to call in a professional, because accessing it will require excavation. If it's tightened from the front, you'll need a special jet wrench that fits into holes on the face of the jet to tighten it. Be careful not to apply so much pressure that you crack the shell.

A jet may be loose because the gasket that seals it against the shell has deteriorated. Removing the jet to replace the gasket is not recommended because it's very difficult

Fixing a leaking hydrojet

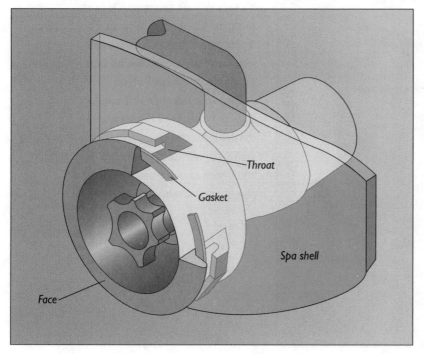

Drain the spa to below the level of the leaky jet. Loosen the jet and remove the old gasket. You'll probably need to cut it to slip it off the throat of the jet. Make a slit in a new gasket so you can slip it around the throat of the jet and slide it into place. Fill the slit with silicone sealant, then tighten the jet. Sealant will ooze out as you tighten. Smooth it around the edges of the jet to form a watertight seal.

to align the two pieces properly. However, you can slip a new gasket in place without fully removing the jet, as described on page 167.

Leaks in wood tubs: Wood tubs are somewhat more likely to leak than are other kinds of spas because they have many more pieces that fit together and therefore more joints through which water can leak.

A tub that leaks between the staves may need to have its bands tightened. The leak will probably not be along the whole length of a stave, but only for a short distance. Tighten the band closest to the leak.

If tightening the bands doesn't work, you'll have to plug the leak. One option is to use silicone caulk, but you may have to redo the job every few months, because the caulking material doesn't expand and contract the same way the wood does. Another option is to plug the hole with wool. This age-old method, using an organic material, makes a longer-lasting repair than silicone caulk because the wool expands and contracts more like the wood does. One drawback of wool is that it has more of a tendency to harbor bacteria; you'll have to be vigilant in sanitizing properly.

You can use wool intended for knitting, but make sure it's not a blend of wool and other fibers. Select strands of wool that are thicker than the hole to be plugged. Drain the tub to below the leak, then use a putty knife to push the wool into the gap; refill the tub. Water may leak out at the seam until the staves and wool have swollen. The leaking water will pull the wool more deeply into the gap, helping to seal it. If the tub is still leaking after a couple of days, drain it, and add more wool.

If the tub leaks at the croze, the joint between the floorboards and the staves, there may be pressure from a surrounding deck pushing the staves in at the top and out of alignment. If so, rectify the problem, then realign the staves and tighten the bands. Or it may be that the wood has begun to rot. If so, you can caulk the joint, as described below. If the wood is rotten in many places, it may be time to replace the tub.

Fixing leaks at the croze

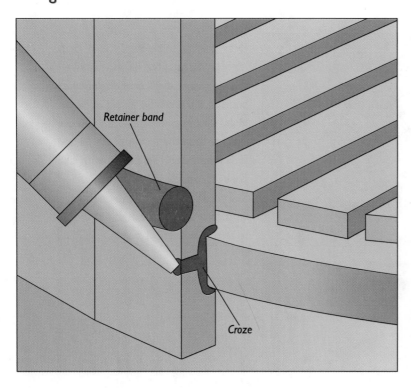

Retainer band

Croze

It's very difficult to repair a leak at the croze using wool because it's nearly impossible to get the wool into the joint. In this case, it's best to use silicone caulk instead.

Drain the tub, then drill a hole from the outside of the stave into the croze; fill the area that's rotten with silicone caulk. Plug the hole with more caulk or use a wooden plug. Refill the tub.

Remodeling

Does your pool's look need to be updated? Are there new accessories you want to add that weren't available when your pool was built? Do you need to remodel your pool to fit your changing lifestyle? If you answer yes to any of these, some simple pool and landscape refurbishments can make the difference.

Adding a spa: An easy way to introduce the warm-water advantages of a spa to your pool is to add a detached unit. If your lot isn't large enough for a separate unit or you prefer the look of an attached spa, you can add a custom unit at the edge of your pool. For a concrete pool, a spa can be connected to the pool wall; for a vinyl-lined or fiberglass pool, choose a prefab model.

In-shell features: Prefabricated steps can be added to the shallow end of a vinyl-lined or fiberglass pool, or an above-ground pool. You can also have steps custom-made for a concrete pool. Similarly, grab rails, ladders, and swim-out steps in the deep end can be easily installed.

To add lights to a vinyl-lined or fiberglass pool, you'll have to notch into the sides and possibly dig up the area around the pool for the wires. Such an installation is impossible on a concrete pool.

Another option is fiber-optic lighting. This technology allows you to locate the light source away from the pool. Fiber-optic cables carry the light to a lens or lenses in the pool where it is released. It can be added around the edge of any pool and can sometimes be retrofitted to an existing lighting system. For more on fiber-optic lighting, turn to page 87.

Face-lifting for a modern look: Perhaps you feel that your pool looks outdated, with worn or out-of-style materials and outmoded design details. In this case, consider giving the area around the pool a "face-lift" to bring it up to date. See the chapter on landscaping for ideas on the sort of improvements you can make, such as adding a raised planting bed, adding natural rock and lush plantings, building a structure for pool equipment and changing areas, or changing the pavement material around the pool.

If the pool itself looks outdated, with old coping, weathered tiles, or an uninteresting shape, consult a pool contractor and landscape architect. These days, many pool owners are choosing to have their existing deep, traditionally shaped pools made shallower. One way this is accomplished is by building a new shell inside the existing one.

Installing an enclosure

Enclosing your outdoor pool will extend the swim season in areas where nonsummer months are chilly or cold. You can either purchase a manufactured canopy or extend your house to include a pool room. The air-inflated canopy shown at right is the most economical enclosure. It anchors to the deck with fasteners and a blower supplies the slight pressure necessary to keep it inflated. Some canopies double as pool covers when they are deflated.

The World
OF HOME
SAUNAS

*Long a staple of Finnish homes, the sauna has become
increasingly popular in North America in recent years. We're
discovering what others have known for centuries—that
the dry-heat bath is one of life's most physically and mentally
refreshing experiences. If you've ever stretched out on a
bench in the heat of a 150-200° room long enough to perspire
freely from every pore in your body, and then enjoyed the
sensation of a cool dip in a pool, you've known the pleasure
of a Finnish sauna. In this chapter you'll find helpful
information on how to get the most out of the sauna
experience in your own home.*

The Sauna Experience

The sauna is an insulated wooden room heated to between 150° and 200°F that provides a restorative environment for the body. Its heat not only deep-cleanses the skin through induced perspiration, it stimulates circulation and reduces muscular tension as well.

Saunas are also known as dry-heat baths, partly because the humidity in the room is kept fairly low (usually below 30°), and partly to distinguish them from steam baths, which have significantly higher humidity.

"Going to sauna" involves a cycle, repeated once or twice, that begins with a shower, then a brief exposure to the sauna's intense heat, followed by cooling with a shower, a plunge into cool water, or—if you are a fit and hardy sauna enthusiast—a roll in the snow; and lastly, a period of quiet rest (page 172).

Health benefits: The combination of free perspiration, rapid cooling, and rest stimulates circulation to rid the body of impurities through the skin and liver, reduces muscular and nervous tension, and heightens mental awareness.

Some doctors prescribe it for patients with arthritis or rheumatism because the sauna's heat temporarily eases tension in the joints and muscles. It may also temporarily relieve symptoms of colds, sinus congestion, and other minor respiratory ailments or allergies; poor circulation; tension headache; and acne (heat softens the oil plugs that block skin pores).

What the sauna does not do, as some have claimed, is help you lose weight permanently (without dieting). While it's true you'll weigh less after a sauna, the loss is primarily the water lost through sweating.

The traditional ritual: Found everywhere in Finland, from modern urban high-rises to back-country farms, the sauna is regarded as a means of mental relaxation and quiet contemplation—not merely a source of physical renewal.

Traditionally, Saturday evening was reserved for the bath. After a good wood fire had heated the rocks in the stove and warmed the walls and benches, family and perhaps a few neighbors gathered in the soft heat of the sauna. Children would often sit on the lower benches, where it's cooler; adults preferring the hotter air higher up. When one of the bathers ladled water over the hot rocks, bursts of steam (loyly) added moisture to the air. Within 5 to 10 minutes most bathers would begin to perspire freely. Soon everyone would leave the sauna to cool off in the fresh air or in a nearby pond or stream, returning later to the friendly heat of the sauna. Then, taking vihtas (bundles of leafy birch twigs tied together) from their pegs, bathers would whisk themselves lightly from head to toe, stimulating circulation and filling the air with a delicate birch fragrance.

A brisk, scrubdown shower with soft brushes and perhaps another invigorating dip into cool water ended the bath itself; but it is also traditional to prolong the ritual with a period of rest and relaxation to cool down completely and to enjoy a light snack, called a saunapala.

Modern sauna: These days in Finland, some things have changed: Vihtas are rarely used, since leaves end up all over the sauna (a loofah or soft brush is used instead); families may take a sauna together, but otherwise men and women sauna separately; and electric sauna stoves make saunas possible in houses and apartments.

These changes are also reflected in sauna practices in the United States, where saunas have been multiplying in resorts, locker rooms, and executive offices since the 1960s.

TIPS FOR ENHANCING YOUR SAUNA ENJOYMENT

Every sauna enthusiast has a personal preference for temperature and level of humidity. Here are a few suggestions.

• While some experts say sauna temperatures can be as low as 150°, many feel this is too low for a real sauna experience. In a hotter sauna try several shorter stays, which are better for your health than one long one.

• If breathing seems difficult in the dry heat, increase humidity by splashing water on the sauna rocks. The sauna will seem hotter for a few seconds, but breathing will become easier.

How to Take a Sauna

(A) Shower briefly with warm water and soap, then dry off. (B) Enter the heated sauna and relax on one of the benches for 5 to 10 minutes; spill water over the stones for steam if desired. (C) Cool off with a shower or a swim. (D) Outside the sauna, rest for 10 to 20 minutes. (E) Go back into the sauna for 5 to 10 minutes; spill some more water over the rocks to increase humidity. Whisk yourself lightly with a loofah or soft brush. Turn off the sauna stove. (F) Have a good scrubdown shower. (G) Rest for at least 20 minutes to cool down completely. (H) Dress and have a light snack.

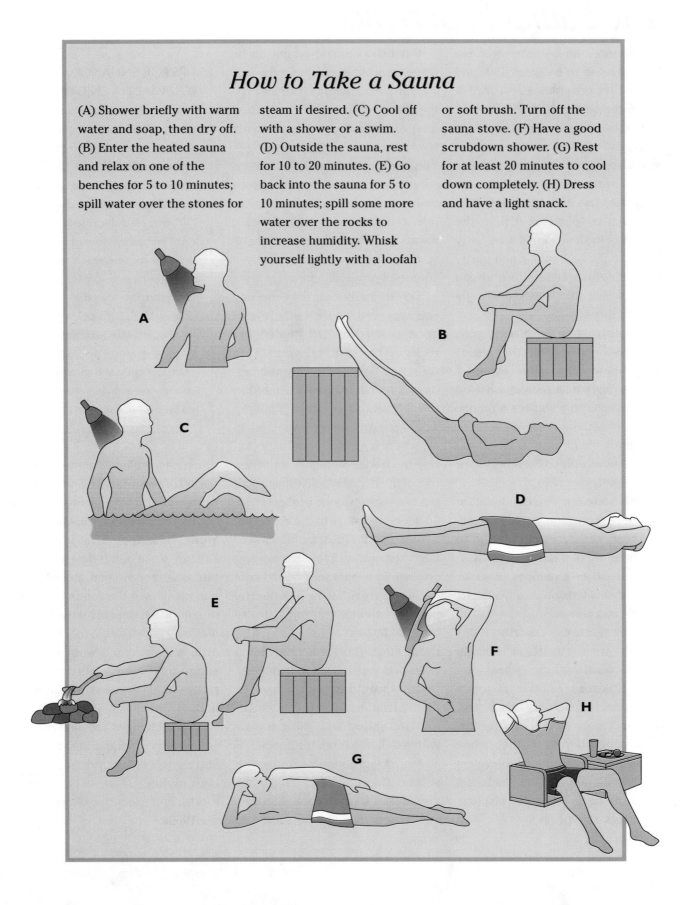

The Modern Sauna Complex

The Finnish word "sauna" technically refers to the room where the heat bath is taken, since for hundreds of years the entire sauna was simply a one-room cabin. With an architectural metamorphosis from cabin to complex, however, sauna has come to refer to the trio of rooms—shower, dressing/relaxation area, and stove room—as well as to the bathing process itself.

SIZE AND SHAPE

It's possible to have a sauna of any size or shape, but you should be aware of several rules of thumb that professional planners use in designing a sauna.

Size: The size of the sauna depends on 1) the number of people likely to be using the sauna at once (allow 67.5 cubic feet, about 2.5 cubic yards, of space for each bather); 2) the space available for the sauna, and perhaps accompanying bath and dressing room; 3) the arrangement of the benches (one wall

A ONE-ROOM CLIMATE

The sauna room is basically an insulated wooden box, usually rectangular, simply furnished with two or three tiers of wooden benches. It is warmed by a special stove designed to hold about 70 pounds of igneous or metamorphic rocks (page 177), which, when heated, generate a soft, continuous heat. Properly designed and built, the sauna will provide just the right climate for an enjoyable heat bath. It should be well insulated, neither too big nor too small, correctly vented (cross ventilation is important), and properly heated. Wood used for paneling and benches should stay pleasant to touch in a heated room, and benches should be wide enough for reclining bathers.

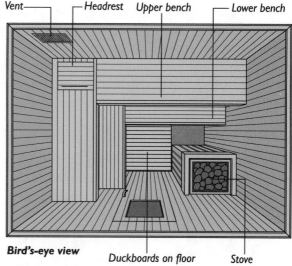

Vent — Headrest — Upper bench — Lower bench

Bird's-eye view Duckboards on floor Stove

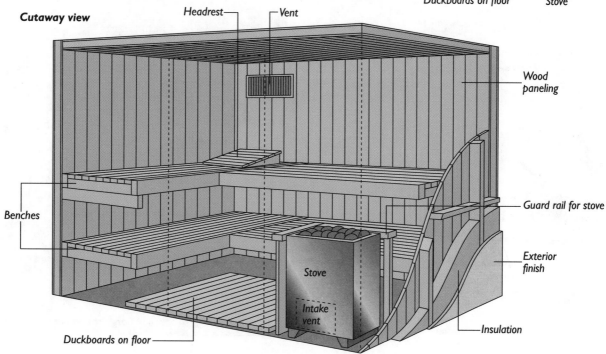

Cutaway view

Headrest — Vent

Wood paneling

Benches

Guard rail for stove

Exterior finish

Stove

Intake vent

Insulation

Duckboards on floor

should be long enough for you to lie down); 4) the size stove your budget can afford; and 5) your overall budget. Two popular family sauna sizes are 5 by 7 feet and 6 by 6 feet.

The sauna is the right height inside if all users can stand up straight without their heads touching the ceiling; 7 feet is common. This lower-than-average ceiling conserves energy by preventing heat from rising into unused space. For larger rooms, you'll generally require more powerful—and thus more expensive—stoves; extra lumber for framing, paneling, and benches; and additional insulation.

Shape: Rectangular and square saunas allow for maximum use of bench space—an important consideration in sauna design. Octagonal, round, even wedge-shaped saunas aren't unknown, but you cannot expect their bench arrangements to offer the same flexibility.

OTHER CONSIDERATIONS

Size and shape are only two factors that you need to examine when choosing your sauna. There are other important considerations.

Dressing room and shower: The dressing room, often the same size or larger than the sauna proper, is usually furnished with benches, a closet or pegs for clothing, a small linen closet for extra towels and accessories, and a place for jewelry, watches, and glasses.

If your dressing room is the only place you have to cool off (as is often the case with freestanding saunas), plan wide benches, perhaps cushioned, so you can stretch out comfortably to cool down.

Ideally, you should have a shower close to your sauna so that you don't have to traipse through your home. If there is no shower nearby, you may consider having a plumber install one.

CONTEMPORARY SAUNA PLANS

Whether it's linked to a bathroom or located outdoors, a modern sauna usually includes a dressing room and shower; some lead to open-air areas. Sauna doors should not have locks or latches, but should always open outward and have windows.

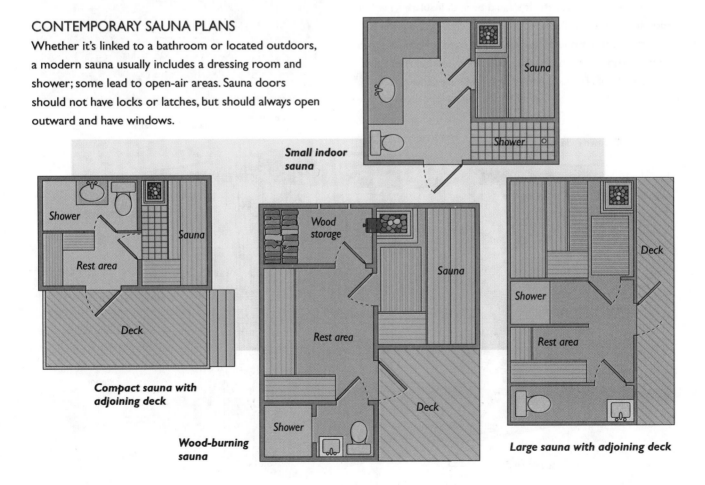

Small indoor sauna

Compact sauna with adjoining deck

Wood-burning sauna

Large sauna with adjoining deck

Locating your sauna: Outdoors may be a particularly good location for your sauna if you can install it near an existing swimming pool; this way, you're only a few steps away from a dip in cool water after you leave the sauna. You also may prefer an outdoor sauna if you can tuck it into an unused corner of the yard that's made private with trees and shrubs. Include outdoor furniture or benches in your plan so you can relax in the open air between sauna visits.

Your primary consideration in erecting an outdoor sauna is the cost of plumbing, electric wiring, or gas lines (if gas is your source

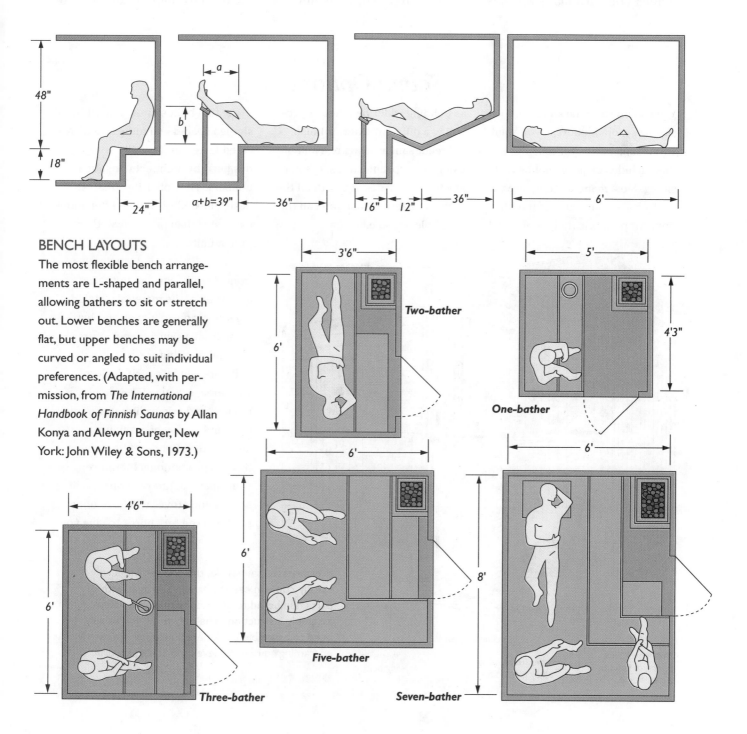

BENCH LAYOUTS

The most flexible bench arrangements are L-shaped and parallel, allowing bathers to sit or stretch out. Lower benches are generally flat, but upper benches may be curved or angled to suit individual preferences. (Adapted, with permission, from *The International Handbook of Finnish Saunas* by Allan Konya and Alewyn Burger, New York: John Wiley & Sons, 1973.)

Two-bather

One-bather

Three-bather

Five-bather

Seven-bather

of heat). When you do install an outdoor sauna, try to situate it on level ground. You'll need privacy screens or hedges if you intend to enter your pool in the buff.

Locating your sauna indoors provides you with many options for locating the unit, as well as the advantage of its convenience on winter days. If the sauna is adjacent to the master bath, you may also have the advantages of an existing dressing room, shower, and rest area. Or, consider converting part of your utility room, an extra storeroom, or a basement corner into a sauna. Other options include attic space, a spare bedroom, or part of a garage. In most cases, existing walls and floor can be used to simplify construction.

Sauna Options

You can buy a sauna kit for almost any size room indoors; if you want your sauna outdoors, consider a kit that includes exterior roofing and siding. Most manufacturers are willing to make some custom modifications for prefabricated rooms, such as building wider benches or providing a different exterior finish.

Precut saunas also are available; using your specifications, the manufacturer provides you with all the various materials that you can then assemble in place.

Custom-built saunas suit oddly shaped spaces and more sophisticated tastes, and usually are designed by architects or sauna builders. They offer the greatest design flexibility, but are often more expensive than prefabricated or precut units.

If you plan to build your sauna from scratch, you can purchase almost all of the materials, including stove, control panel, and hardware, from a sauna manufacturer or retail distributor.

Before you buy, visit dealers in your area, examine their display models, and ask for literature, price lists, and a copy of assembly instructions. But don't be dazzled by slick promotional literature; some manufacturers of fine quality saunas and stoves will have only photocopied brochures to give you.

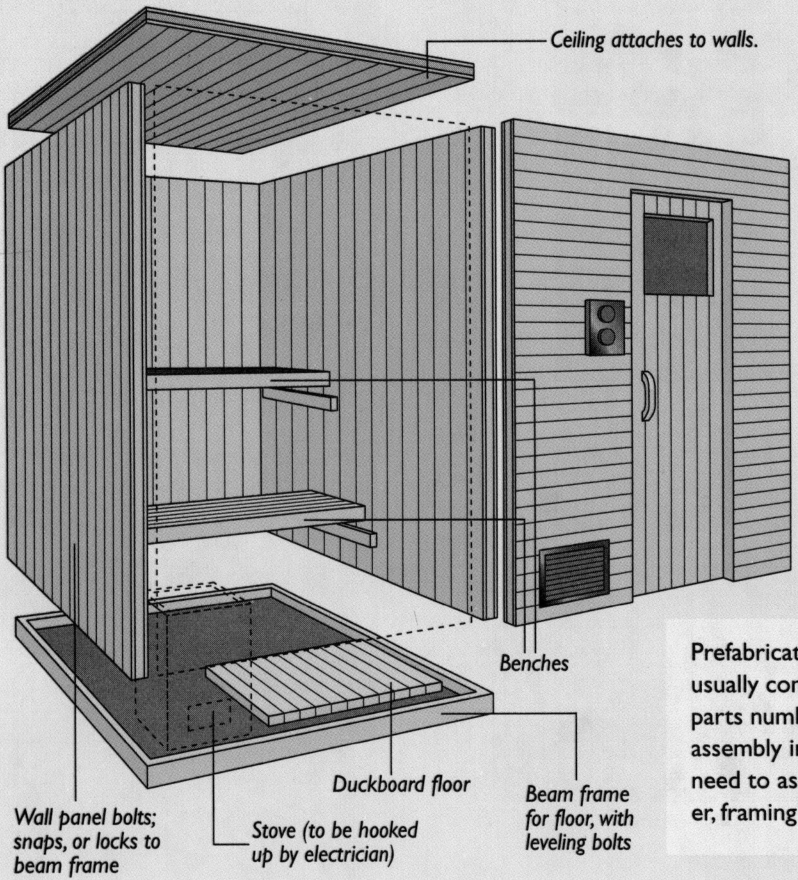

Ceiling attaches to walls.

Benches

Wall panel bolts; snaps, or locks to beam frame

Stove (to be hooked up by electrician)

Duckboard floor

Beam frame for floor, with leveling bolts

Prefabricated saunas like the one shown here usually come in easy-to-handle packages with parts numbered to coincide with step-by-step assembly instructions. The only tools you usually need to assemble the kit are a hammer, screwdriver, framing square and level, and perhaps a drill.

Sauna Stoves

A good stove, with the right rocks, is the heart of the sauna. If it's properly designed and the right size for the room, it will provide the soft, pleasant heat characteristic of the finest Finnish heat baths.

Sauna rocks: Important to the right balance of heat and humidity, sauna rocks distribute heat evenly throughout the sauna when they become hot enough. They maintain the proper temperature because they store heat well. And they are necessary for the burst of steam that results when a dipperful of water is splashed over them.

Rocks recommended for sauna use are fist-size pieces of igneous granite, formed by intense exposure to heat and pressure. Geologically old, they store heat efficiently and, unlike sedimentary rocks, which can crack, crumble, or even explode under the pressure of high heat, they are unaffected by temperature extremes.

Sauna stoves are almost always sold with a supply of rocks, often quarried in Finland. With regular use, the sauna rocks will "wear out," so you will have to purchase new ones from a sauna dealer. How

frequently you'll need to do this depends on use; for a home sauna, about every year or two is typical.

Selecting the stove: Wood stoves are considered by many enthusiasts to provide the ultimate experience in Finnish heat bathing. Traditional wood stoves were essentially a fire beneath a pile of rocks. Before the sauna could be used, it had to be "ripened": the rocks heated and the fire completely extinguished. In a modern wood-burning stove, the rocks are not in contact with the flames; the fire burns continuously while the

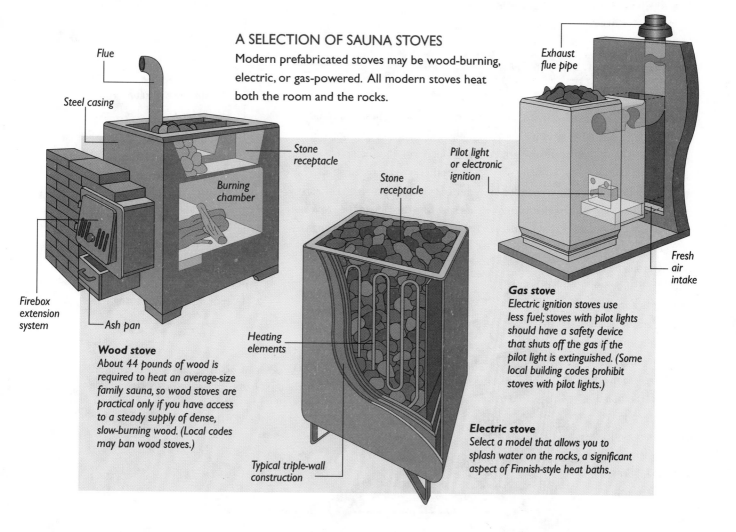

A SELECTION OF SAUNA STOVES

Modern prefabricated stoves may be wood-burning, electric, or gas-powered. All modern stoves heat both the room and the rocks.

Flue

Steel casing

Stone receptacle

Burning chamber

Firebox extension system

Ash pan

Wood stove
About 44 pounds of wood is required to heat an average-size family sauna, so wood stoves are practical only if you have access to a steady supply of dense, slow-burning wood. (Local codes may ban wood stoves.)

Stone receptacle

Heating elements

Typical triple-wall construction

Electric stove
Select a model that allows you to splash water on the rocks, a significant aspect of Finnish-style heat baths.

Exhaust flue pipe

Pilot light or electronic ignition

Fresh air intake

Gas stove
Electric ignition stoves use less fuel; stoves with pilot lights should have a safety device that shuts off the gas if the pilot light is extinguished. (Some local building codes prohibit stoves with pilot lights.)

sauna is in use, and the smoke goes out through the chimney (a carbon monoxide monitor is essential). Sized correctly, a wood stove takes about an hour to heat the sauna to the desired temperature. Wood stoves are prohibited by some local building codes and are not recommended for small saunas—they tend to make the room too hot before the rocks are hot enough.

Electric stoves are clean and efficient. They have a thermostat, either built into the stove or installed outside the sauna, that allows you to regulate temperature. The sauna rocks should come in direct contact with the heating elements; on some models, rocks sit in a slotted tray at the top of the stove and don't absorb adequate heat.

Because of their flues, gas stoves are more complicated but usually less expensive to operate than electric ones; they're also more fuel efficient. Some enthusiasts consider gas stoves best because they heat rocks faster and hotter than electric elements can. But many experts recommend against gas stoves because of the risk of leaks; always install a carbon monoxide monitor. In Finland, gas stoves are not legal for saunas.

SIZING THE STOVE

Electric stoves are measured by the number of kilowatts used to heat the elements. As a general rule of thumb, allow 1 kw for every 45 cubic feet of room space. To compute stove size, divide sauna volume (V = room length x width x height) by 45 to know how many kilowatts are needed in the stove. For example, a sauna that's 5 by 7 feet and 7 feet high has a volume of 245 cubic feet, so a 5.5 or 6 kw stove should provide adequate heat.

Gas stoves are sized according to the amount of heat, measured in British Thermal Units (Btu) the heater generates. Generally, you should allow 1,000 Btu for every 15 cubic feet of sauna volume. The 5- by 7- by 7-foot sauna mentioned above would require a 16,000-Btu heater.

No quick formula exists for determining the size of wood stove required, since so many variables are involved in heating a sauna with wood: the type of wood used, the design of the stove, etc. Follow manufacturer's specifications for sizing.

SAUNA ACCESSORIES

The simplest sauna usually is equipped with a thermometer, a bucket, and a long-handled ladle to throw water onto the hot rocks for bursts of steam during the bath. The ladle should be made of wood or metal, with a wooden handle at least 15 inches long. Timers that turn off the stove and clocks are recommended.

More elaborate saunas may have hygrometers to measure relative humidity, adjustable wooden headrests, cork bench covers, an automatic humidifier, and *vihtas* or scrub brushes. They may also have—to the distress of many traditionalists—telephone jacks, intercoms, and music.

Sauna thermometers are either bimetallic or liquid-filled and are made of metal, ceramic, brass, chrome, or wood. Hygrometers are sometimes combined with thermometers into a "hygrotherm" or "saunahygro." These devices should be installed at least 12 inches from the side of the stove and about 6 inches below the ceiling.

Wooden accessories add a traditional, aesthetic touch to the sauna experience. *Vihtas*, birch whisks, can be replaced by soft brushes or loofahs, which don't drop leaves.

Sauna Curing and Care

After your sauna is assembled or built, it's important to prepare or "cure" it before you indulge in your first heat bath. Curing a sauna is a fairly simple matter of removing construction debris and then allowing the stove to burn off any coatings used to protect it during shipping and installation.

First, sweep down the sauna ceiling, walls, and floor to eliminate wood shavings, chips, and sawdust. Then vacuum everything, including corners and benches.

Next, using a damp cloth and bucket of warm water, wipe down the ceiling, walls, benches, light fixtures, stove, railing, and floor.

Wash the sauna rocks to remove any sand and place them in the stove. Rocks should be loosely packed to allow for good air circulation, with larger ones on the bottom and smaller ones on top.

Now, prop the sauna door open and turn on the heater for about 30 minutes. (Don't worry if the stove begins to smoke—it's just burning off protective coatings.)

Finally, close the sauna door, bring the room temperature to about 195°F, and leave it there for five or six hours. Bring the sauna to the desired temperature (ideally, between 150° and 195°F), and the sauna is ready for use.

To care for your sauna, the most you usually need to do is scrub it down occasionally to remove perspiration stains and odors from the wood; a liquid household cleanser diluted in water does a good job. You might also want to use a disinfectant for the job.

After each bath, it's good to ventilate the room so wood surfaces dry. Prop any duckboards against the wall, and wash the water bucket after each use. Fill it with fresh water so the wood doesn't dry out.

In saunas that are heated by wood, it is especially important to keep the floor free of any debris and to remove ashes from the firebox regularly.

Sauna Safety

To help reduce the risk of accidents, you should make the physical environment of your sauna as safe as possible. Be aware that although taking a sauna is generally not harmful, some people should use caution. Keeping the following guidelines in mind will help keep your sauna experience enjoyable and trouble-free.

• The sauna stove should be surrounded by a wood railing or fence, to protect bathers.
• Look for a stove that's approved by the Underwriters Laboratories (UL) or the American Gas Association (AGA). And follow the manufacturer's recommendations for wall-to-stove clearance (usually 4 to 10 inches). Wood-burning stoves may be installed next to a brick or stone wall for additional fire protection.
• If you have high blood pressure, respiratory or heart disease, serious circulatory problems, or a chronic illness such as diabetes, epilepsy, or multiple sclerosis, check with your physician before using the sauna.
• Pregnant women should not use the sauna without checking with a physician.
• Avoid the sauna if you are taking antibiotics, tranquilizers or stimulants, or any other drug that might be affected by speeded-up metabolism.
• Stay out of the sauna if you're under the influence of alcohol or drugs—they impair judgment, and you can get a nasty burn if you lose your balance and come into contact with the sauna stove. (Deaths by dehydration have even been known to occur when individuals have passed out in the sauna.)
• While in the sauna, if you begin to feel dizzy, nauseated, or uncomfortably hot, or if your pulse is beating abnormally fast, leave immediately.
• Young children should not use the sauna unsupervised.

Safe RECREATION

For many, owning a pool or spa is a wonderful luxury, one of the great pleasures in life. It provides the ideal setting for family entertainment or private relaxation. But a pool or spa is also a great responsibility. You must provide a safe environment for family members and visitors, swimmers and nonswimmers alike. In part, this means making sure the water is clean (page 128), but it also means securing the area around the pool, encouraging your guests to act responsibly, and providing constant supervision to children. With a little imagination, and perhaps some sports equipment or water toys, you can transform your pool into a center for fun and games for all ages. But your ultimate enjoyment will be determined by the rules you adopt and the methods you use to ensure the safe use of your pool or spa.

Fun and Games

Many people buy pools with just one thing in mind: swimming. But pools, as well as spas, offer a wealth of additional recreation possibilities—from adapting favorite games to the water, to inventing games and exercises.

Coming up with creative ways to use your pool not only adds to your fun, but it also is a good way to channel in-the-pool activities in directions that are safe.

Water games: Pool games don't have to be complicated—the water itself is enough of an attraction to satisfy most people.

Always keep the ages of the players, and their swimming abilities, in mind. Though small children enjoy a balloon race across the width of the pool, older children and more talented swimmers may demand more vigorous games or sports, like tag or water polo.

Popular accessories for water games include sports goals and nets, such as those shown below, and floating toys and games, as shown on the next page. These in-the-pool floaters go in the water for fun and come out when the game's over. You can also find floating versions of more sedentary games, like checkers, for those who prefer cooling off with a quiet activity.

If you have a favorite sport, talk to your pool designer before you build the pool to see if your game can be incorporated into the plans. For example, the deck could be designed to include holes, with covers, for the poles of a volleyball net.

SPORTING GOODS

Enjoy the water version of your favorite sports with floating nets and goals. Stabilized by wide foam floaters, they're easily removed and stored when you want to swim. Deck-mounted versions, or ground-mounted versions for above-ground pools, are also available.

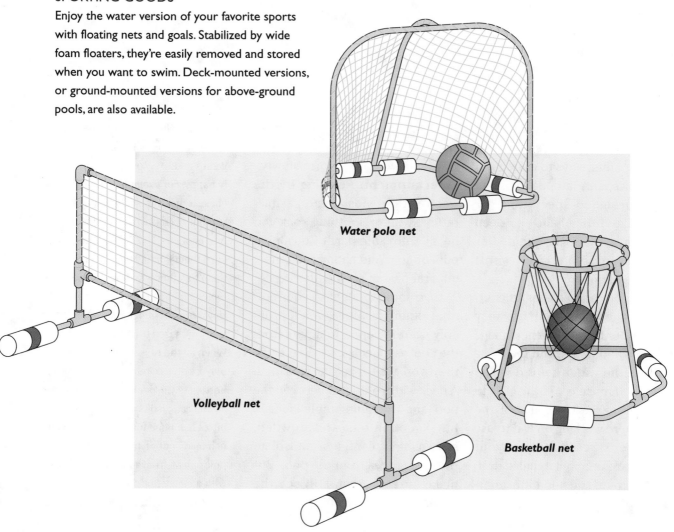

Water polo net

Volleyball net

Basketball net

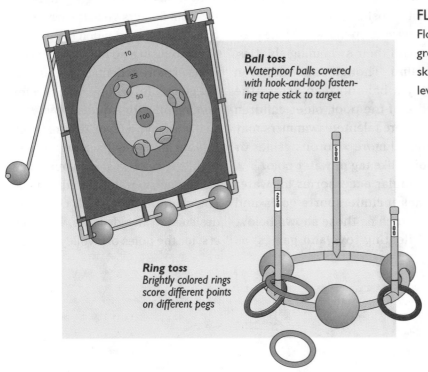

Ball toss
Waterproof balls covered with hook-and-loop fastening tape stick to target

Ring toss
Brightly colored rings score different points on different pegs

FLOATING FUN

Floating water games and toys provide a group activity suitable for young fry, less-skilled swimmers, or groups with varying levels of swimming abilities.

HOMEMADE GAMES

Playing water games can be a good way for young swimmers to develop confidence in the water. But take care to choose a game appropriate to the participants' skill level. For example, many games can be just as much fun played in the shallow end of the pool, where players can touch bottom if they need to.

Fun pool activities don't require fancy store-bought accessories. With a little imagination and clever use of household products, you can devise games and toys to keep the whole family happy. For example, rather than purchase a ring toss set, you might make one out of empty plastic soda bottles. Add enough water to the bottles to keep them floating upright and attach them together with hook-and-loop fastening tape. You can purchase plastic rings, or use rubber of an appropriate size purchased from a hardware store. When all the rings have been tossed, players dive to retrieve them from the bottom of the pool.

You can also turn the shallow end into a fish pond for youngsters, with fish made out of metal canning lids, and poles made from a long piece of dowel with a magnet on a string.

Exercise: Of course, swimming is a great way to get in shape, but there are other ways to exercise in a pool or spa. A lap pool or swim spa is designed specifically for exercise. But the shallow or deep end of any pool can be a center for aquatic exercise, and so can a spa, if it's deep enough.

There are advantages to exercising in the water—the buoyancy of the water helps prevent damage to bones and joints, and the resistance of the water helps develop well-toned muscles. The trick is to fully submerge the parts of the body you're working on and to use the water's resistance to your advantage. For a well-rounded exercise program, add aquatic exercises to lap swimming.

As in any conditioning program, check with your doctor before you start and work up to form slowly.
Entertainment: Relaxing by the water with friends after an exhilarating swim or soothing soak can be an enjoyable part of owning a pool or spa. And eating is often an integral part of such gatherings.

Give some thought to your outdoor dining facilities. You'll probably want to separate diners from the pool as much as possible, since they won't relish getting splashed. A deck width of 15 feet between the pool and the dining table is ideal, but if conditions are crowded, screens and plantings can isolate the dining area from the pool. But make sure you can still see the water to supervise children.

A Safe Environment

Accidental drownings in residential pools are unfortunately common, for both adults and children. Even the relatively small amount of water in a spa is enough to drown in. In fact, for children under four years of age, drowning is one of the major causes of death. Fortunately, you can take steps to prevent such a tragic accident from happening on your property.

The best prevention is constant adult supervision of children in and around the pool or spa. But physical barriers provide important additional protection, helping to keep unattended children and nonswimmers from the water. Three layers of protection—a fence, an alarm, and a cover—are best.

There may be specific regulations in your area that determine the safety measures required, such as the minimum height of the fence, the maximum size of any spaces in it, and whether or not the gate must have a self-closing mechanism. The guidelines given here are acceptable in many communities and are minimum safety recommendations, but check your local building code.

Some communities specify that a pool must be fenced on all four sides; others will allow just the yard to be fenced, with the house counting as the fourth side, provided certain safety devices are installed on the house. A properly covered spa may not need fencing.

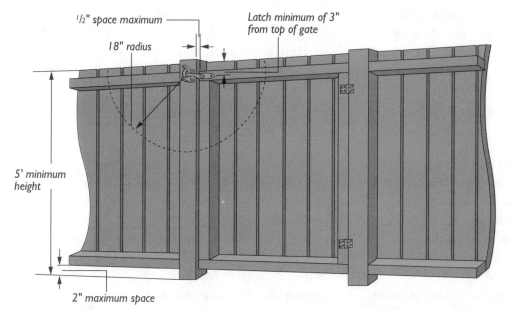

¹/₂" space maximum

18" radius

Latch minimum of 3" from top of gate

5' minimum height

2" maximum space

FENCE DIMENSIONS

For safety, a fence should be at least 5' high, with no more than 2" of space between the bottom of the fence and the ground. Spaces between members can be up to 4", but within an 18" radius around the latch, a maximum spacing of ¹/₂" is recommended, so people can't reach through to open the gate. The latch should be at least 3" down from the top of the fence.

SECURE GATES

Self-closing and self-latching mechanisms are recommended—and usually required—on gates. The most common type is a spring closer, which has a tightly coiled spring that returns the gate to the closed position, but other types are available. The gate should also have a latch like those at right, that closes automatically when the gate swings against it.

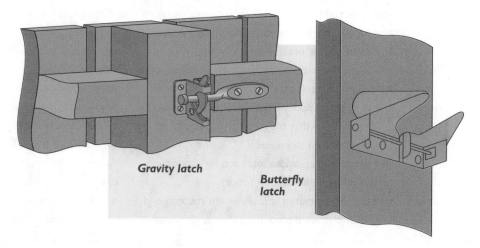

Gravity latch

Butterfly latch

Fences: When designing poolside fencing to protect children, keep in mind the following considerations:

• Toddlers and small children are usually safe behind a 4½-foot fence, but older children need one that's at least 5 or 6 feet high.

• Construct the fence out of an unclimbable material and choose a design with no toeholds. In a chain link fence, the holes should be no bigger than 1¾ inches.

• If there's a fence on all sides of the pool, it should not obstruct the view of the pool from the house.

• Garbage cans, lawn furniture, and any other objects that can be used to scale the fence should be out of reach. Also, locate the fence away from any trees that can be climbed.

• When the pool is not being used, keep gates into the pool area locked.

Inspect the fences around your pool or property often. Rainwater or burrowing animals can dig away the bases, creating holes large enough for a child to crawl through.

Alarms: Since they afford no protection when there's no one around to hear the buzzer, alarms alone are not commonly used for safety. But if you have small children, an alarm gives you some backup protection if a child manages to escape your attention and heads for the pool.

There are many alarm systems available, some that are installed at exit points from the house, such as on sliding glass doors, and others that are installed around the perimeter of the pool or in the pool itself. Alarm systems are only worthwhile if they're operating; consult the manufacturer's instructions and check the system periodically.

Covers: Consider installing a safety cover as one way to keep people out of the water. A safety cover is one that has a continuous connection between the pool and deck and is capable of supporting a 400-pound-per-square-foot load. For a spa, it may be all you need, though for a pool they're not usually acceptable as a substitute for fencing. Solar blankets and other similar covers are not meant as a safety measure.

ELECTRICAL SAFETY TIPS

Water and electricity don't mix. There are many precautions you can take, both in the design of the pool or spa area and in selecting appropriate appliances, to reduce the risk of electrical accidents. The following guidelines should help.

• All receptacles around the pool or spa should be protected with a ground-fault circuit interrupter (GFCI).

• No electrical receptacle should be installed within 10 feet of the water.

• Keep electrical appliances such as radios, tape players, and compact disc players well out of range of the pool or spa. They should be far enough away that they won't accidentally fall or be pulled into the water.

• Electrical appliances intended for indoor use should never be used outdoors.

• Battery-operated appliances are recommended. Or choose electrical appliances that have been approved for use near water. These appliances are designed with built-in safety features, such as double insulation, to prevent electric shock. Look for a third-party certification sticker, such as that of the Underwriters Laboratories, on the outside of the appliance.

• Uninsulated household extension cords should not be used on pool decks or near spas.

• Don't touch any electrical appliance while you're wet, especially if you're in contact with something metal, such as a pool ladder.

• If an electrical appliance does fall into the water, unplug it before retrieving it.

• Never use a regular telephone while in a pool or spa. Cellular or digital phones are okay.

• Always hire a qualified, and licensed, electrician to perform electrical repairs on pool or spa equipment. Never do these repairs yourself or entrust them to a pool service technician, unless the technician is a licensed electrician.

Water Safety

Normally, we think of a pool or spa as a place for relaxation and play, but it's also a potentially dangerous place. You can reduce the risk of fatal accidents, and increase your chances of a happy ending to an emergency, by following some basic guidelines. You'll want to consider who will be using the pool or spa and what rules you will need to adopt to guarantee fun and safety for everyone. The guidelines you set should include determining who can use the pool and when, what behavior is acceptable—and unacceptable—in and around the pool or spa, and what maintenance standards are necessary to keep the facilities safe.

The first rule for keeping children safe near water is to supervise them constantly. Physical barriers, as discussed on page 183, offer extra layers of protection, but there is no substitute for adult supervision.

Make sure that everyone using a pool has had water safety training and basic rescue methods. Make certain your children learn how to swim. Check with your local chapter of the American Red Cross, the National Swim School Association, the National Safety Council, your local parks and recreation department, or a community pool for information on classes. You should learn about helping a swimmer in difficulty, rescue breathing, first aid, family water safety, and survival floating, among other subjects.

Good signs can also help. Signs indicating the depth of the water and a contour depth chart that graphically represents the changing depth in the pool can help bathers judge which areas of the pool are a safe depth for them. Posting the instructions for rescue breathing and CPR will allow you to keep the procedure fresh in your memory. Post your pool rules and emergency phone numbers prominently.

Keep a first-aid kit and basic lifesaving equipment at hand. Important lifesaving aids are a ring buoy with rope attached and a rescue hook, both of which are illustrated below. The long, blunt-ended pole used for brushing the sides of the pool can be extended quickly to faltering swimmers.

You may think that the sample guidelines that follow on the next page are common sense, but don't assume that your neighbors or your children will follow them without

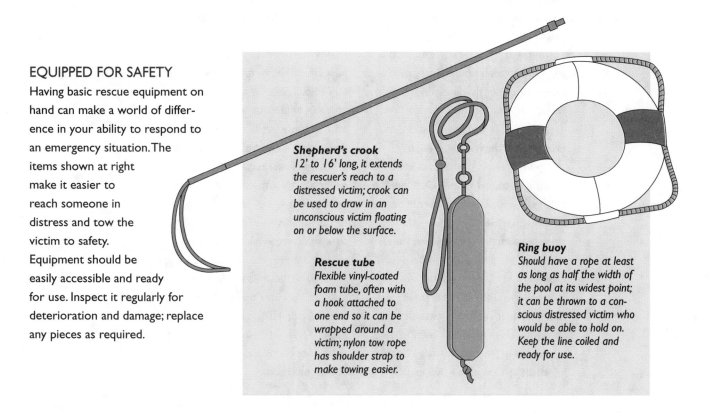

EQUIPPED FOR SAFETY

Having basic rescue equipment on hand can make a world of difference in your ability to respond to an emergency situation. The items shown at right make it easier to reach someone in distress and tow the victim to safety. Equipment should be easily accessible and ready for use. Inspect it regularly for deterioration and damage; replace any pieces as required.

Shepherd's crook
12' to 16' long, it extends the rescuer's reach to a distressed victim; crook can be used to draw in an unconscious victim floating on or below the surface.

Rescue tube
Flexible vinyl-coated foam tube, often with a hook attached to one end so it can be wrapped around a victim; nylon tow rope has shoulder strap to make towing easier.

Ring buoy
Should have a rope at least as long as half the width of the pool at its widest point; it can be thrown to a conscious distressed victim who would be able to hold on. Keep the line coiled and ready for use.

being reminded. Take the time to review these and other basic rules with the people using your pool.

Nonswimmers: Keep any adults or children who don't know how to swim a safe distance away from the edge of the pool. One swimming adult can supervise up to six nonswimming children in the shallow end of the pool at one time. Be sure any other nonswimming children are sufficiently away from the pool to be out of danger.

A floating life line installed across the pool before it begins to deepen will help prevent nonswimmers from going in over their heads. Even partially skilled swimmers should have constant one-to-one supervision, since they may overestimate their skills, or panic and forget how to handle themselves in the water.

No swimming alone: Never permit anyone in your pool, or near it for that matter, when no one else is around. A responsible adult who knows how to swim and has rescue skills should always be present whenever anyone is in the water. Even in a spa, children should always be supervised. Never leave them alone. Adults shouldn't swim alone either. People who are drown-

SAFE DIVING GUIDELINES

One of the major causes of injury in home pools is diving. Most pools are not deep enough to allow safe diving even from the pool deck, let alone from a board raised above the surface of the water. If being able to dive into your pool is important to you, have the pool constructed with safe diving in mind.

Just what constitutes a pool that's safe to dive into is a matter of some debate. The National Spa and Pool Institute has guidelines available but not all experts agree that these guidelines are stringent enough. The two major issues are how deep the pool is, and how far this depth extends from the end of the pool.

A pool that's deep enough in the deep end may slope up to the shallow end too quickly. In a significant number of diving injuries, divers hit their heads on the slope between the deep end and the shallow end of the pool. This is because unskilled divers tend to hit the water a long way from the end of the pool, sometimes as much as 17 feet from a diving board. It is recommended that no diving, whether from the deck or from a board raised up to 3 feet above the pool, be allowed unless the pool is a minimum of 9 feet deep for at least 25 feet from the end. Boards 3 feet or higher have greater depth requirements.

But even in a pool that's properly designed, there are safe and unsafe ways to dive. Some diving tips are given below. For more information, contact the National Swimming Pool Foundation.

• Plan your dive path before you start, since once you're in the water you won't have time. Shallow dives, in which you immediately aim for the surface, are the only safe kind in home pools. Deep dives, such as those familiar from competitive diving, take a long time to slow down and are safe only in specially designed pools.

• Extend your arms and hands above your head before diving. This will help you direct your dive and protect your head in case you come in contact with the pool bottom. Once in the water, steer up to the surface with your hands and arms, arching your back and holding your head up.

• Practice first. Diving safely is a skill that must be learned. Before you dive, practice using your hands and arms extended above your head.

Pool and Spa Safety

In addition to the issues discussed on these pages, here are some important considerations in providing a safe water environment. Contact your local branch of the Red Cross for a more complete list.

• Be sure nobody uses the pool or spa without the owner's knowledge and permission.
• Do not use the pool or spa if there is any damage to the drain grates. Replace the grates immediately. Do not allow anyone to sit on the grates or play on or near them. The suction in the system is enough to hold a person underwater and may even eviscerate the victim. Having more than one main drain reduces the risk.
• Use only unbreakable glasses and dishes for refreshments served near the pool or spa. Broken glass in the water or on the deck is nearly impossible to remove completely.
• Never serve alcoholic beverages around the pool or spa. Alcohol acts as a central nervous system depressant, slowing breathing and swallowing reflexes and reducing the amount of oxygen delivered to the brain and muscles; coordination and balance become poor and reaction time is slowed. Alcohol may also encourage some people to take risks or impair judgment in others. More than 50 percent of adult victims of water emergencies were drinking prior to their accident.

ing rarely call out for help or make enough noise to bring assistance. Don't leave the pool area for *any* reason when children are in the water. Add an outdoor telephone outlet or purchase a portable phone, which can also be useful in an emergency. **Handling guests:** You may want to allow neighbors and friends to use your pool by invitation only. Some pool owners set up certain hours for different age groups, reserving early evenings and weekends for adult relaxation. If neighbors arrive in their bathing suits with their own towels, it will curb dressing-room confusion and eliminate their tracking through the house to change.

Limit the number of people who can be in the pool area at one time. A swimmer in danger can easily go unnoticed amid the noise and confusion of an overcrowded pool; the presence of a lot of people can also lead to roughhousing and encourage some swimmers to show off and take dangerous chances.

Encourage rest periods of 10 to 15 minutes every hour to calm excited children and to settle the nerves of supervising adults.

Pool preparation: Before anyone enters the pool, be sure that all preparatory steps have been completed. The pool cover should be completely removed, since swimmers can be caught below the cover and drown. The water should not be cloudy, it should be in correct chemical balance, and all leaves, debris, and foreign objects should be removed. Proper water maintenance is important for safety. You need to be able to see the bottom of the pool clearly.

When not to swim: Thunderstorms can be deadly to swimmers—keep people away from the pool when there's a chance of lightning.

Do not allow nighttime swimming unless you have enough light in and around the pool so that a swimmer can be spotted easily. And don't swim at night if any of the pool lights are out of commission.

Behavior around the pool: Impress upon children that the pool area is only for swimming and supervised play and that they should never enter the pool area unless an adult who knows how to swim is present to watch them.

Do not permit any running, pushing, or horseplay around or in the pool. Organized, supervised poolside games are a good way to channel children's energy.

Diving and sliding: As explained on page 186, many pools are not safe for diving. If yours is, and you have a raised board, allow only one person to use it at a time. If you don't have a board, permit diving only into the deep end.

Water slides, similarly, are designed for one person at a time and always feet first in a seated position. Some of the most severe pool-related injuries occur from using slides. Always observe three rules on slides: stay seated, slide down in a feet-first position, and beware of hitting your feet on the pool bottom (leg fractures can result).

Whether sliding or diving, the right-of-way always belongs to the swimmer already in the water. If people are diving or sliding into the pool when others are swimming, keep the activities as separate as possible.

Signs of Drowning

In a water emergency, as in any emergency, speed of response is critical. If a person is unconscious and not breathing for more than four minutes, there's a good chance that irreparable brain damage will occur. The sooner you can respond in an emergency, the more likely the victim's chances of successful recovery, so it's important to be able to recognize the signs of distress and drowning and learn how to respond. Some signs to watch for are given below, but there's no substitute for emergency response training.

Distressed swimmers: These victims are conscious and aware that they're in a dangerous situation, but they may not be able to call out for help. They may be on or just below the surface of the water in a diagonal position and often make ineffectual swimming motions with their arms and legs.

These victims may progress to drowning if they're not assisted quickly. A shepherd's hook or ring buoy should be extended to a swimmer in distress.

Unconscious drowning victims: These victims will be either limp or rigid and sinking slowly toward the bottom of the pool. They won't be making any intentional motions but their bodies may be jerking or convulsing due to lack of oxygen to the brain.

Conscious drowning victims: These victims will be vertical or slightly diagonal in the water, their legs will be still, but they may be pushing and flailing against the water with their arms. Usually the head is back and face is looking up, with an open "O" mouth, eyes wide or tightly shut, and a surprised, disoriented look. They may be gasping for air or holding their breath. They are rarely able to call for help.

Victims drown either by taking water into their lungs or by suffocation from involuntary breath holding or spasms of the larynx.

A good course in water rescue techniques, basic rescue skills, or water safety sometimes included as part of an advanced swimming class will teach you how to recognize signs of distress, drowning, and other emergencies that could occur in and around a pool. You'll learn the best response to various situations— whether to reach out to the victim or go to them, how to safely get them to the side of the pool, and how to administer rescue breathing and/or CPR if necessary. Ideally, every person using the pool should be familiar with these techniques.

Further Resources

Whether you're already enjoying a home pool or spa, or are considering the addition of one for the first time, you'll likely find the following list helpful. Some of the many organizations and associations that provide information or services related to recreational water use are shown. All of them welcome public queries and many will provide literature and other material.

These organizations and associations can answer your questions on a wide range of topics, from making your pool environment safer, to starting a home water fitness program, to teaching your children—or yourself—to swim.

Some organizations provide construction guidelines, so whether you're building your pool or spa yourself or having a contractor do it, you can be sure it's done right.

We've also included *(below, right)* a few magazines that may be of interest to recreational swimmers and enthusiastic pool or spa owners.

ORGANIZATIONS AND ASSOCIATIONS

American Homeowners Foundation
6776 Little Falls
Arlington, VA 22213

Aquatic Exercise Association
P.O. Box 1609
Nokomis, FL 3427-1609

Aquatic Injuries Safety Foundation
1310 Ford Building
Detroit, MI 48226

Canadian Red Cross Society
5700 Cancrofs Court
Mississauga, Ont. L5R 3E9

Independent Pool & Spa Service Association, Inc.
17715 Chatsworth Street,
Suite 203
Granada Hills, CA 91344

Jewish Community Centers Association of North America
15 East 26th Street
New York, NY 10010

The National Association of Gas Chlorinators
30575 Trabuco Canyon
Road, Suite 105
Trabuco Canyon, CA
92678-1058

National Sanitation Foundation International
3475 Plymouth Road
Ann Arbor, MI 48105

National Spa & Pool Institute
2111 Eisenhower Avenue
Alexandria, VA 22314

National Swimming Pool Foundation
10803 Gulfdale, Suite 300
San Antonio, TX 78216

National Swim School Association
776 21st Avenue North
St. Petersburg, FL 33704

United States Diving
Pan Am Plaza
201 S. Capitol Avenue,
Suite 430
Indianapolis, IN 46225

United States Swimming
One Olympic Plaza
Colorado Springs, CO 80909

United States Water Fitness Association, Inc.
P.O. Box 3279
Boynton Beach, FL 33424

YMCA of the USA
110 N. Wacker Drive
Chicago, IL 60606

YWCA of the USA
726 Broadway
New York, NY 10003

PUBLICATIONS

Aqua
1846 Hoffman Street
Madison, WI 53704

Aquatics International
Leisure Publications
3923 West 6th Street
Los Angeles, CA
90020

Fitness Swimmer
Rodale Press
33 E. Minor Street
Emmaus, PA 18098

Spa and Sauna
1846 Hoffman Street
Madison, WI
53704-2586

Index

Acknowledgments

The editors wish to thank the following:
Applied Biochemicists, Alpharetta, GA
Aquatic Consulting Services, San Diego, CA
Aquatic Pools, Mission Hills, CA
Blue Devil Industries, San Diego, CA
Blue-White Industries, Westminster, CA
California Redwood Association, Novato, CA
Cover Pools, Inc., Salt Lake City, UT
Downes Swimming Pool Co., Inc. Wheeling, IL
Endless Pools, Inc., Aston, PA
E-Z Vac, Sunrise, FL
Finn-Am Trade L.L.C., Cherry Hill, NJ
GLB Pool & Spa, Milwaukee, WI
Hayward Pool Products Canada, Oakville, Ont.
Hayward Pool Products, Inc., Elizabeth, NJ
L.A. Spas, Anaheim, CA
Leisure Time Pools & Spas, Oklahoma City, OK

Link Automation, Inc., St. Paul, MN
Louisville Gym & Swim Supply Co., Louisville, KY
Markurban, Tustin, CA
Montreal Botanical Garden/Jardin botanique de Montréal, Montreal, Que.
Modern Pool & Spa Inc., Columbus, OH
Mutual Pools & Staff Pty Ltd., Campsie, NSW, Australia
National Association of Gas Chlorinators, Trabuco Canyon, CA
National Spa and Pool Institute, Alexandria, VA
National Swimming Pool Foundation, San Antonio, TX
Paco Pools & Spas, Baldwin, NY
Plastimayd Corporation, Clackamas, OR
Polaris Pool Systems, Inc., San Marcos, CA
Pulliam Pools, Fort Worth, TX

Purity Pool, Whitmore, CA
Sentry Pool, Inc., Moline, IL
Sta-Rite, Waterford, WI
Swim Chem, Sacramento, CA
Taylor Technologies, Inc., Sparks, MD
Zifco, Rancho Dominquez, CA

Contributing Illustrators: Gilles Beauchemin, Michel Blais, Jacques Perrault, La Bande Créative

The following people also assisted in the preparation of this book:
Lorraine Doré, Eric Beaulieu, Pascale Hueber, Ned Meredith, Valery Pigeon-Dumas, Matthieu Raymond-Beaubien

Picture Credits

4   Courtesy: Pulliam Pools (homeowner: Mrs. Terri Ward)
6   Jack McDowell
7   Tim Street-Porter
8,9   Phillip H. Ennis
8   (lower) Jean-Claude Hurni
9   (lower) Stephen Marley
10   Jean-Claude Hurni
11   (upper) Tim Street-Porter
11   (lower) Courtesy: Mutual Pools and Staff Pty Ltd.
12   (upper) Jean-Claude Hurni
12   (lower) Jack McDowell
13   Tim Street-Porter
14,15 Phillip H. Ennis
15   (upper, right) Stephen Marley
15   (lower) Jack McDowell
16   Phillip H. Ennis
17   (upper) Jean-Claude Hurni
17   (lower) Jean-Claude Hurni
18   Tom Wyatt
19   Courtesy: Paco Pools & Spas Ltd.
20   Jean-Claude Hurni
21   Jean-Claude Hurni
22   Courtesy: Paco Pools & Spas Ltd.
24   Jack McDowell
26   Stephen Marley
28   Bill Rothschild
34   Tim Street-Porter
36   Stephen Marley

38,39 Courtesy: California Redwood Association
40   Courtesy: Paco Pools & Spas Ltd.
41   Stephen Marley
44   Jean-Claude Hurni
45   Stephen Marley
48   Courtesy: Modern Pool & Spa, Inc. Designed & built by Frank L. Wall
49   Courtesy: National Spa and Pool Institute
50   Jean-Claude Hurni
51   Jack McDowell
52   Jean-Claude Hurni
53   Jean-Claude Hurni
55   Courtesy: Paco Pools & Spas Ltd.
58   Courtesy: California Redwood Association
60   Stephen Marley
62   Tom Wyatt
66   Jean-Claude Hurni
71   (both) Jean-Claude Hurni
73   Courtesy: Downes Swimming Pool Co., Inc.
80   Stephen Marley
82   Stephen Marley
83   Jean-Claude Hurni
85   Courtesy: Louisville Gym & Swim Supply Co./Pam Spaulding
88   Don Vandervort
89   Bill Rothschild

91   Jean-Claude Hurni
94   Jean-Claude Hurni
95   Jean-Claude Hurni
96   Jean-Claude Hurni
101   Jack McDowell
103   Jean-Claude Hurni
104   Courtesy: Modern Pool & Spa, Inc. Designed & built by Frank L. Wall
105   Richard Mendelkorn
107   Jean-Claude Hurni
110   Gerald French/Masterfile
114   (both) Jean-Claude Hurni
115   (upper) Courtesy: Pulliam Pools (homeowner: Mrs. Terri Ward)
115   (lower) Courtesy: Aquatic Pools
116   Bill Rothschild
117   (upper) Tim Street-Porter
117   (lower) Jean-Claude Hurni
118   Jean-Claude Hurni
119   Jean-Claude Hurni
120   Jean-Claude Hurni
123   Jean-Claude Hurni
124   Jean-Claude Hurni
126   Tom Wyatt
128   Courtesy: National Spa and Pool Institute
140   Courtesy: Cover Pools, Inc.
156   Don Vandervort
170   Stephen Marley
180   Jean-Claude Hurni